Reading Faulkner
LIGHT IN AUGUST

READING FAULKNER SERIES

Noel Polk, *Series Editor*

Reading Faulkner

L I G H T   I N
A U G U S T

Glossary and Commentary by

H U G H   M .   R U P P E R S B U R G

*With the editorial collaboration of the late
James Hinkle of San Diego State University and
Robert McCoy, Kent State University*

University Press of Mississippi   Jackson

Library of Congress Cataloging-in-Publication Data

Ruppersburg, Hugh M.
    Reading Faulkner : Light in August : glossary and commentary / by
Hugh Ruppersburg ; with the editorial collaboration of James Hinkle
and Robert McCoy.
        p.   cm. — (Reading Faulkner series)
    Includes bibliographical references and index.
    ISBN 0-87805-731-5. — ISBN 0-87805-732-3 (pbk.)
    1. Faulkner, William, 1897–1962. Light in August.   2. Faulkner,
William, 1897–1962—Dictionaries.   I. Hinkle, James.   II. McCoy,
Robert.   III. Faulkner, William, 1897–1962. Light in August.
IV. Title.   V. Series.
PS3511.A86L577   1994
813'.52—dc20   94-17077
                                                                  CIP

British Library Cataloging-in-Publication data available

CONTENTS

PREFACE

This volume is the first of a series of glossaries of Faulkner's novels which is the brainchild of the late James Hinkle, who established its principles, selected the authors, worked long hours with each of us in various stages of planning and preparation, and then died before seeing any of the volumes in print. The series derives from Jim's hardcore commitment to the principle that readers must understand each word in Faulkner's difficult novels at its most basic, literal, level before hoping to understand the works' "larger" issues. In pursuit of this principle, Jim, a non-Southerner, spent years of his scholarly life reading about the South and things Southern, in order to learn all he could about sharecropping, about hame strings, about mule fact and lore, about the Civil War, about blockade running, duelling, slavery and Reconstruction, Indian culture and history. When he had learned all he could from published sources, he betook himself to county and city archives to find what he could there. He was intrigued by Faulkner's names, for example, and over the years compiled a fascinating and invaluable commentary on their etymologies, their cultural and historical backgrounds, and, not least, their pronunciations: Jim is the only person I know of who listened to all of the tapes of Faulkner's readings and interviews at the University of Virginia, in order to hear how Faulkner himself pronounced the names and words he wrote. In short, for Jim, there was no detail too fine, no fact or supposition too arcane to be of interest or potential significance for readers of Faulkner: he took great pleasure in opening up the atoms of Faulkner's world, and in exploring the cosmos he found there.

It was my great fortune and pleasure to be Jim's friend and colleague for slightly more than a decade. In the late seventies, I managed to tell him something he didn't know; he smiled and we were friends for life. Our friendship involved an ongoing competition to discover and pass on something the other didn't know. I was mostly on the losing end of this competition, though of course ultimately the winner because of what I learned from him. It was extremely agreeable to me to supply him with some arcana or other because of the sheer delight he took in learning something—anything, no matter how large or small.

On numerous occasions before and after the inception of this series, we spent hours with each other and with other Faulkner scholars reading the novels aloud, pausing to parse out a difficult passage, to look up a word we didn't understand, to discuss historical and mythological allusions, to work through the visual details of a scene to make sure we understood exactly what was happening, to complete Faulkner's interruptions, to fill in his gaps, and to be certain that we paid as much attention to the unfamiliar passages as we did to the better-known ones, not to let a single word escape our scrutiny; we also paused quite frequently just to savor what we had just read. These readings were a significant part of my education in Faulkner, and I'm forever grateful to Jim for his friendship and his guidance.

This series, Reading Faulkner, grows out of these experiences in reading Faulkner aloud, the effort to understand every nuance of meaning contained in the words. The volumes in the series will try to provide, for new readers and for old hands, a handy guide not just to the novel's allusions, chronologies, Southernisms, and difficult words, but also to its more difficult passages.

Jim's death in December 1990 was a great loss to Faulkner studies; it was especially grievous to those of us embarked with him on this series. Absent his guidance, the University Press of Mississippi asked me to assume editorship of the series; I am happy to continue the work he started. The volumes in the series will not be what they would have been had Jim lived, but they all will bear his stamp and his spirit, and they all will try to be worthy of his high standards. And they will all be lovingly dedicated to his memory.

Noel Polk

INTRODUCTION

When Faulkner began *Light in August*, his seventh novel, in
1931, he had come into his maturity as a writer. Not only had
he finished *Mosquitoes* and *Soldiers' Pay*, his two apprentice novels, but also *Flags in the Dust* (in 1927), *The Sound and the Fury*
(1929), *As I Lay Dying* (1930), and *Sanctuary* (1931)—the last
three ranking among his greatest works. He had also completed
several of his best stories, including "Red Leaves," "A Rose for
Emily," "That Evening Sun," and "Dry September," which appeared in his 1931 collection *These Thirteen*. No longer was he
an artist casting about for a suitable mode of expression. He had
found a setting and a style particularly suited to his vision and
had learned to use them in a way that earned him an estimable
place in American writing.

   Light in August reflects the artistry not only of an established
writer but of a novelist in transition. Moving away from the
structural innovations of *The Sound and the Fury* and *As I Lay
Dying*, abandoning the richly gothic neo-decadence of *Sanctuary*,
Faulkner reflects in this 1932 novel a deepening interest in place
and the specific North Mississippi setting of Yoknapatawpha
County. Always apparent in his short fiction, this interest was
not especially prominent in the novels that followed *Flags in the
Dust*. Returning to a more traditional form of plotting in *Light
in August*, one demanding less reconstructive effort from the
reader, Faulkner placed greater emphasis on the substance of
narrative itself, and on characters who inhabit a recognizable
context of geography, history, and time. While we are ever
aware of structure in *The Sound and the Fury*, of an abstract but
undeniably present evil in *Sanctuary*, we are most conscious of
people, place, and event in *Light in August*.

We also encounter a work less concerned than its predecessors with stylistic virtuosity than with the content and meaning of an ambiguously related series of events. Although those events are told in chronologically disordered sequence, their essential coherence nonetheless comes clear. Joe Christmas, Gail Hightower, and Joanna Burden inhabit a world of mules, churches, country stores, railroad depots, and barns. It is a world of the external, and its details and features are always in evidence.

Perhaps because of his confidence as a writer, his increased emphasis on narrative, Faulkner felt little need to inflate *Light in August* with gratuitous literary and mythological allusions (as he had done in his earliest work). In the eighteenth chapter, when Byron Bunch believes he has lost Lena Grove and contemplates for a moment the possibility of suicide, Faulkner lends magnitude and resonance to the scene by alluding to the famous soliloquy from Shakespeare's *Hamlet*, in which the Prince of Denmark considers the same possibility. Allusions also contribute to characterization: the very name of Bobbie Allen, Joe Christmas's first love, in its reference to the Anglo-American folk ballad of love cruelly ended, metaphorically (and ironically) signifies the nature of their affair. The myths, literary works, and religious documents that occasionally resound in his text reflect not only the traditions of his own regional and national inheritance, but the cultural environment of the world in which his characters live, breathe, and struggle.

The explication of the world and the text of *Light in August* is the primary goal of this volume. In preparing these annotations I have attempted to explain, identify, and comment on any aspect or detail of the novel that a reader might conceivably find unfamiliar or difficult. The words, phrases, and passages that drew my attention tended to fall into several distinct categories. I frequently concerned myself with the features that constitute the external world of Jefferson and Yoknapatawpha County: colloquialisms, dialects (black and white), folk customs and sayings, farm implements, Bible verses, geographic and demo-

graphic details. Understanding the technical aspects of the Jefferson saw mill, and of the kind of work that Byron Bunch, Joe
Christmas, and Joe Brown did there, is important to an overall
appreciation of what life in rural north Mississippi was like
during the Depression. I also considered the mythic patterns
into which many of the novel's events fit. By identifying Faulkner's allusions to the Bible and to Greek myth, I did not intend
to predetermine the reader's understanding of the text, but
instead hoped to provide various kinds of information that
would make reaching conclusion about the novel's characters
and events easier.

Another dimension of explanation lies in the annotations that
explain, and sometimes unravel, the intricate density of Faulkner's prose. This is not so much a matter of interpretation,
where different readings may and must coexist peacefully, as it
is the task of analyzing Faulkner's manipulations of language,
his syntactical convolutions. My explications of difficult phrases
and sentences intend once again to open up the possibilities for
meaning in the novel rather than to close them down. A final
dimension is that of observation. These annotations often speculate on the inter-relationships of various images and metaphors.
They note repetitions, echoes, contradictions, and various bits
of narrative evidence that drive the novel towards its conclusion. They seek at times to suggest how the structural frame-
work of the novel contributes to its meaning and effect.

These annotations are keyed by page and line number to the
Library of America text of *Light in August* edited by Joseph Blotner and Noel Polk (*William Faulkner Novels: 1930–1935*. Library
of America, 1985). This is the most reliable text of the novel,
the one that, given the nature of the Library of America collection, is most likely to endure for a significant period of time and
is certain to outlast paperback editions of the novel currently in
print. Running heads will locate passages in this text and in the
Vintage International paperback text (New York, 1990).

Faulkner's greatness as a writer lies in the pertinence of the
themes, emotions, conflicts, and events in *Light in August* to a

wide range of human experience. Mature readers do not need these annotations to recognize that pertinence. They may find, however, that the explanations which follow illuminate the density and detail in the very real world that Faulkner evoked in this novel, that they provide additional testimony to the narrative achievement of a most accomplished American novelist.

I wish to thank Brad Cahoon and Sheri Joseph, my principal research assistants, as well as Ann Burroughs, Laurens Dorsey, Darren Felty, David Peterson, Dana Phillips, Catherine Rogers, and Martina Weiss, who also assisted with the research. I am grateful to Coburn Freer and the University of Georgia English Department for research time, summer grants, supplies, and graduate assistants in support of this project. I deeply appreciate the role that Noel Polk has played in this project. He assumed the editorship of the annotation series following Jim Hinkle's death and provided much needed advice, support, and criticism. James Hinkle and Robert McCoy made many useful contributions to these annotations. Jim Hinkle believed deeply in the value of the Faulkner Annotation Project, and this volume bears his mark in many ways. For witting and unwitting contributions I thank as well John Algeo, Sheila Bailey, André Bleikasten, Panthea Broughton, Calvin Brown, Ernest Bufkin, James Colvert, Robert Cooperman, Charles C. Doyle, Rosemary Franklin, Walter Gordon, William J. Kretzschmar, Warren Leamon, Hubert McAlexander, Thomas McHaney, Pearl McHaney, James B. Meriwether, Marion Montgomery, Deanna Palmer, Frances Teague, John Vance, and Karl Zender. I dedicate these annotations to my sons Michael, Charles, and Max, who provided the most important kind of support and motivation, and to my wife Patricia, for ten years' sufferance. I thank her most of all.

Hugh M. Ruppersburg

Reading Faulkner
LIGHT IN AUGUST

Light in August

GLOSSARY AND COMMENTARY

The present-time action of the novel occurs in August, 1932. Asked about the title, Faulkner explained:

> Oh that was—in August in Mississippi there's a few days somewhere about the middle of the month when suddenly there's a foretaste of fall, it's cool, there's a lambence, a luminous quality to the light, as though it came not from just today but from back in the old classic times. It might have fauns and satyrs and the gods and—from Greece, from Olympus in it somewhere. It lasts just for a day or two, then it's gone, but every year in August that occurs in my country, and that's all the title meant, it was just to me a pleasant evocative title because it reminded me of that time, of a luminosity older than our Christian civilization.°*

Faulkner also reportedly purveyed the notion that the title came from a folk-saying ("Heavy in June, light in August") about a woman or cow who had just given birth and was, thus, "light" in August.° Faulkner's wife Estelle recalled sitting one summer afternoon with her husband on the side porch of their home. When she asked him, "Does it ever seem to you that the light in August is different from any other time of the year?" he exclaimed, "That's it!," rose from his chair and disappeared into the house, returning a moment later. "What he had done was to go to his worktable and draw four pen strokes through the title 'Dark House.' Above and slightly to the left he printed '*Light in August*'."°

---

*The symbol ° indicates that a source is identified in the notes section following the chronology. Each source is keyed to the page and line number of the note it documents.

Faulkner's working title for the novel had been "Dark House," borrowed from the seventh poem of Tennyson's *In Memoriam*:

> Dark house, by which once more I stand
>   Here in the long unlovely street,
>   Doors, where my heart was used to beat
> So quickly, waiting for a hand.°

By the end of November 1931, however, he had chosen the present title.

CHAPTER I

401:2 **Lena** For a full discussion of Lena Grove's name, see entry 411:37. In 1934 Faulkner wrote: "I began *Light in August* knowing no more about it than a young woman, pregnant, walking along a strange country road."° Two decades later he added: "that story began with Lena Grove, the idea of the young girl with nothing, pregnant, determined to find her sweetheart."°

401:2 **Lena thinks** The narrator of this novel functions as an uninvolved spectator, a storyteller and overseer to the action, a central authority uniting various strands of plot and character. At points the narrator seems omniscient. More often, he seems limited to what the characters know, and the narrator often speculates about what they *might* have thought or done. The narrator relates the novel from three different perspectives: an external viewpoint which conveys the words and actions of characters, an internal viewpoint which explains what characters are consciously thinking, and an internal translating viewpoint which explains what characters are feeling and thinking, often presented in words the characters themselves would not use. Typically, words that characters speak are printed in the usual double quotation marks and punctuated normally. Their conscious thoughts are enclosed in single quotation marks and again are punctuated normally. The narrator's translation of their unconscious moods and thoughts are printed in italics, not introduced with a colon or other punctuation, and not concluded with a period, an indication of Faulkner's conception of the human unconscious as unarticulated and unordered.

401:2 **thinks** Verb tense in this novel signifies the time at which events occur relative to the narrative present-time, August 1932. Present-tense verbs signify the present-time of the narrative. In this chapter, they also signify state of mind. Lena is unbothered by the past and unworried about the future. She embodies the Faulknerian (and Bergsonian) concept of time's fluidity; Faulkner once explained: "time is a fluid condition which has no existence except in the momentary avatars of individual people. There is no such thing as *was*—only *is*."°

401:2 **I have come from Alabama** a statement Lena makes often in the first and twenty-first chapters. It is the first line of the well known Stephen Foster song "O Susannah!," whose first stanza begins:

> I have come from Alabama
> With a banjo on my knee
> And I'm bound for Louisiana
> My true love for to see.

The fourth line obviously refers to the object of Lena's journey, her "true love" and the father of her soon-to-be-born child—a connection that enhances the song's significance for her. But there may be a Faulknerian joke here: the lover in the song is a man going to see a woman who we may assume will be glad to see him. Lena is on her way to see a man who will not be happy to see her at all. Moreover, before too long she will have on her knee not a banjo but a baby.

401:3 **a fur piece** a far piece: a long distance

401:9 **six or eight times a year she went to town on Saturday** Saturday is the customary day for country folks to go to town. That Lena's family went to town this often, and that she owned shoes and a mail-order dress, suggests that her family was relatively well off compared to her brother's more impoverished family.

401:11 **shoes wrapped in a piece of paper** to protect them from dirt

401:24 **bugswirled** surrounded by swarming bugs, a Faulknerian usage

401:27 **Take care of paw** As the youngest girl in the family, Lena must care for her father after her mother's death. In the South such duty was customary and often meant the daughter would not marry until her father died.

401:28 **McKinley** Though Faulkner may have intended to link Lena's brother to President William McKinley (1845–1901), more likely he meant to suggest his Scotch-Irish ancestry.

401:31 **grove** As Lena's last name, 'grove' is associated with Diana of the sacred grove of Nemi: see entry 411:37. Frequently in this and other Faulkner novels 'groves' occur near houses (Joanna Burden's: 486, 565), churches (401, 748, 749), and burial places (401, 585). There is even a grove near the school house where Joe Christmas attacks McEachern. Joanna Burden speaks of the power that the 'cedar grove' and the graves of her ancestors hold over her (585). Clearly, 'groves' hold symbolic power in Faulkner's imagination, and they seem especially related to the power of the dead and the past over the living. Not coincidentally, Christmas, Burch, and Bunch engage in work at the saw mill that has the effect of destroying trees and the groves in which they occur.

401:32 **pine headstone** indicating the humble background of the person whose grave it marks

401:34 **The wagon was borrowed** McKinley Grove was not a wealthy man

401:37 **mill** saw mill

402:3 **Then some of the machinery and most of the men . . . would be loaded onto freight cars and moved away** Once the mill strips away the timber, it departs, leaving behind unusable machinery and unemployed men.

402:7 **bought on the installment plan** paid for with borrowed money. The mill owners do not have to earn enough money to buy the machinery with cash, only enough to make the first payment—another aspect of the waste that the mill embodies.

402:9 **gutted boilers**   rusted out boilers. Boilers held water that, brought to a boil by wood or coal heat, provided the steam that powered the mill.

402:11 **stumppocked**   littered with stumps that scar the land, like smallpox

402:12 **unplowed, untilled**   The land the mill leaves behind is unfit for farming. Thus the mill is especially destructive to a predominantly agricultural economy.

402:12 **gutting slowly into red and choked ravines**   eroding into ravines of red mud that are soon either overgrown with vegetation or clogged with sand and silt

402:13 **the long quiet rains of autumn and the galloping fury of vernal equinoxes**   The vernal equinox marks the first day of spring, on or about March 21. In Southern coastal states, spring weather includes rapidly moving storm systems, heavy rains, high winds, and occasional tornadoes. This passage suggests seasonal cycles and the passage of time.

402:16 **Postoffice Department annals**   the annually updated list of towns and villages to which the post office delivers mail. A village unlisted in the post office annals is no village at all.

402:17 **hookwormridden**   Hookworm disease was a serious problem for the rural American South during the early part of this century, when doctors treated nearly a half million cases. It is caused by a small nematode that enters the human body through the soles of the feet. Symptoms include coughing, fever, itchy skin, constipation alternating with diarrhea, stunted growth, secondary anemia, and an appetite for such unusual substances as clay. People contracted the disease by walking barefoot in warm, moist environments where worm-infected animal and human fecal matter has been deposited.°

402:17 **heirs at large**   those who come to possess the remains of the mill and the hamlet it once supported—whites and blacks poor enough to need to salvage scrap lumber for cooking and heat, likely to go barefoot in warm weather and, thus, often 'hookwormridden.'

402:19 **winter grates** frameworks of thin bars or heavy wire that hold the fire in a fireplace or cook stove

402:21 **mixed train** a train of both passenger and freight cars°

402:23 **by ordinary** usually

402:25 **like a forgotten bead from a broken string** Faulkner may have borrowed the metaphor from Henry Bergson's *Creative Evolution*, which suggests that the human intellect understands time to be a series of "distinct and, so to speak, *solid* colors, set side by side like the beads of a necklace; it must perforce then suppose a thread, also itself solid to hold the beads together."° Faulkner knew this book and admitted Bergson's influence on his work.°

402:30 **lying in** the time just before, during, and after childbirth

402:32 **I reckon that's why I got one so quick myself** Lena feels that being around children made her more likely to conceive.

402:34 **leanto room** a small room, usually built as an inexpensive addition on to the back or side of an existing house. Its roof adjoins the wall of the house at a sloping (hence, leaning) angle.

402:38 **eight years** Thus, Lena is about twenty-one years old in the narrative's present time.

403:7 **bleak heritage of his bloodpride** McKinley's heritage conditions him to respond to Lena's pregnancy with outrage and shame; 'bloodpride' suggests that the only possession his hard life and heritage have left him is pride, which Lena's condition affronts.

403:10 **sawdust Casanovas** Casanova de Seingault, Giovanni Jacopo (1725–1798), Italian adventurer and lover whose name has come to denote an impetuous, overbearing young romancer; a 'sawdust Casanova' works in a saw or lumber mill and is thus an irresponsible small-town seducer.

403:15 **Lucas Burches** Lucas Burch, the father of Lena's

unborn child. The name has possible mythological connotations linked to Lucas's brief association with Lena Grove. One reader finds a ribald pun in Lucas's surname: "Lena is pregnant by Lucas; i.e. Burch [the phonetic equivalent of birch, which can mean rod] has planted himself in a Grove."° Another reader notes the possible influence of Frazer's *The Golden Bough*, observing that "the first name of Lucas Burch is almost exactly the Latin for 'a wood, grove, or thicket of trees sacred to a deity.'"° See entry 411:37.

403:18 **It was a little difficult, this time** because of her expanding girth

403:23 **palm leaf fan** "a fan made of a dried and trimmed palm leaf, with the stem for a handle and some sort of binding to keep the edges from fraying. These fans were bought in stores, since there are no palms in Faulkner's country."° Such fans were occasionally given away in churches and funeral homes.

403:29 **she removed the shoes and carried them in her hand** Lena removes the shoes to protect them from the dust and because she likes the feel of the road on her bare feet. That she doesn't own a pair of shoes is an indication of her brother's poverty.

403:30 **Behind her the four weeks, the evocation of *far*** The introductory phrase merely suggests that Lena has put her journey of the last four weeks out of her mind—it does not trouble her, and she focuses on the present moment only. The italicized 'far' intensifies the distance she has traveled, which she measures not in the number of miles she has walked but in the succession of people who have helped her along the way.

403:31 **a peaceful corridor** The corridor image, important throughout the novel, is associated specifically with time and the individual's limited control over fate. Here it suggests that Lena measures the distance she has walked in units of time (weeks) rather than of distance (miles).

403:33 *Lucas Burch? I dont know . . . It will take you that far*

The italics mark the anonymous voices of people who have greeted Lena and offered help along her way.

403:35 **Pocahontas** a fictional town. There is a Pocahontas, Tennessee, as well as a Pocahontas, Mississippi, north of Jackson. We can assume that Lena approaches Jefferson from the southeast because she stops at Varner's store, which Faulkner's novel *The Hamlet* (1940) locates to the southeast of Jefferson.

403:37 **backrolling now behind her** literally, being passed and left behind by her. Lena appears to remain still, with the road rolling past beneath her feet and back behind her.

404:1 **a succession of creakwheeled and limpeared avatars** Derived from Sanskrit, 'avatar' originally denoted an incarnation of the Hindu god Vishnu and later came to mean any incarnation of a god or person. In Faulkner's usage, an 'avatar' is a person or thing that assumes the particular characteristics of the person or thing it replaces. The characteristics of the avatar become more important than the identity of the person or thing assuming them. Lena does not remember the individual wagons that stopped to give her rides. She knows only that in front of each of them was a team of mules pulling 'identical and anonymous and deliberate wagons.'

404:1 **like something moving forever and without progress across an urn** the first of several allusions to John Keats's "Ode on a Grecian Urn." Although the speaker in the poem delights in the beauty of the scenes on the urn, he recognizes they are a "Cold Pastoral" lacking the vitality of mortal life. Faulkner is hardly unaware of the poet's reservations about the urn, but he alludes to it primarily to imbue Lena with archetypal timelessness. The image of the youth pursuing his love, his "still unravish'd bride of quietness," will later apply to Lena Grove and Byron Bunch. The urn will also become an important expression of Joe Christmas's revulsion from female sexuality (538).

404:11 **Neither did she look back** Versions of this statement appear at least fifteen times in the novel. Faulkner carefully and repeatedly emphasizes what characters do with their eyes, when they are alone and with other people. But this particular instance of "not looking back" is an important reflection of character: of strength and resolute endurance.

404:12   **the shoes unlaced about her ankles**   Lena probably leaves the shoes untied because they don't fit well (they belonged to her brother).

404:21   **pinewiney**   suggesting the heavy fragrance of pine trees

404:25   **So much so is this that**   the illusion of the wagon's motionlessness is so strong that

404:27   **the road itself . . . like already measured thread being rewound onto a spool**   In conjunction with the urn image (404), the unwinding or unrolling road is an important motif in the first chapter. The notion that it is being 'rewound' implies that the fate and destination towards which the road will carry Lena has already been determined. Faulkner probably borrowed the image from Henri Bergson's *Introduction to Metaphysics*: "this inner life may be compared to the unrolling of a coil, . . . to a continual rolling up, like that of a thread on a ball, for our past follows us, it swells incessantly with the present that it picks up on its way; and consciousness means memory."°

404:34   **That far within my hearing before my seeing**   That is, I hear the wagon long before actually seeing it. Lena again exchanges measures of distance ('far') with measures of time (seconds, minutes).

404:40   **thinking goes idle and swift and smooth**   Wholly unperturbed and unconcerned, Lena knows that the approaching wagon will provide the kindness she needs—a ride.

405:2   **Springvale**   a town in or near the route Lena has followed. There is no "Springvale in any of these three states [Alabama, Mississippi, Tennessee], but there is a Springdale, Mississippi, ten miles south of Oxford, and a 'Spring V.' (presumably 'Springville' . . .) about 25 miles southeast of Oxford."°

405:8 **And so there will be two within his seeing before his remembering** When Lucas hears the wagon, he will imagine only the one driver. But when he sees me, whom he doesn't expect to see, he will see two, the driver and his passenger, before he remembers who I am. Perhaps also Lena is thinking of the baby soon to be born, part of the "two" that will confront Burch.

405:11 **While Armstid and Winterbottom were squatting** Here the verb tense shifts from the present tense of Lena to the past tense of Winterbottom and Armstid. See entry 401:2.

405:26 **a shapeless garment of faded blue** In paintings and icons the Virgin Mary is often shown wearing a blue cape. Blue conventionally symbolizes her heavenly nature, spiritual love, and constancy.° Six times in the first chapter Faulkner notes the blue color of Lena's garment.

405:29 **'She's hitting that lick like she's been at it for a right smart while and had a right smart piece to go yet** Lena is walking at the steady pace ('hitting that lick') she would use if she had been walking a long time ('a right smart while') and that she expects to continue walking for a good while to come.

405:33 **I would have heard about it** that is, from my wife

405:36 **augmenting afternoon** advancing afternoon

406:4 **in order to say it** to make his offer for the cultivator

406:5 **cultivator** an implement drawn by mule for breaking up the soil and destroying weeds°

406:6 **At last Armstid looked at the sun** to tell the time of day. He has spent enough time at small talk and is ready to make his offer so he can get back home in time to feed his stock and have supper.

406:12 **Sho** sure. A skeptical acknowledgment: I heard what you said, but I can't exactly say that I believe it.

406:14 **That is, he put them into motion, since only a negro can tell when a mule is asleep or awake** The implication is that mules can walk while they're asleep. A common folk belief held that African Americans intuitively knew whether mules were asleep because they spent so much time working the fields with them.

406:17   **I'd sho buy that cultivator at that figure.... I reckon the fellow that owns it aint got a span of mules to sell for about five dollars, has he?**   Winterbottom ironically suggests that the price he has asked for the cultivator is a good one, and that nothing comes cheap. Since an average span of mules was worth around a hundred dollars in 1932, Winterbottom means that any man foolish enough to sell a cultivator at the price Armstid mentioned is probably also foolish enough to sell a span of mules for five dollars.

406:18   **I be dog**   polite euphemism for "I'll be damned"

406:20   **span of mules**   a team of two mules

406:31   **the wagon crawls terrifically towards her**   The wagon moves at a rate so steady and slow as to inspire terror.

406:33   **dreamlike and punctuate**   The hooves of the mules move in a slow rhythm "punctuated" by the jingling harness and the bobbing mule ears; 'punctuate' is participial. Faulkner drops the 'd' to heighten the stylized language and to control the rhythm.

406:34   **the limber bobbing of jackrabbit ears**   A mule's ears are long and pointed like a jackrabbit's. He can flex them at will, and they bob in response to the motion of his head as he walks along.

406:36   **sunbonnet of faded blue, weathered now by other than formal soap and water**   A 'sunbonnet' is "a brimless hat, fastened under the chin by a ribbon" with "a flap to protect the back of the neck, worn by women as a protection against the sun."° Lena's bonnet has been more weathered by use and exposure during her walk than it has been by washing.

407:2   **She wears no stockings**   evidence of her country upbringing. In the urban South in 1932, "good" girls would not appear in public without stockings, but Lena, from Doane's Mill, has no idea that her attire might be improper. She also cannot afford stockings. Most people who see her walking along the road would recognize her rural character and not blame her for the missing stockings.

407:6 **bleacheyed** eyes pale blue in color

407:9 **pieceways** a short distance

407:16 **Armstid has never once looked full at her** He has never stared at her and has kept his eyes averted, for he would consider it rude to stare. He sneaks a glance now and then.

407:26 **Jefferson** county seat and largest town of Faulkner's fictional Yoknapatawpha County, the scene of most of the present-time action of this novel

407:27 **planing mill** A planing mill processes logs already roughly shaped and cut into lengths at sawmills, and seasoned in a dry kiln or green yard. It planes off the coarse grain to produce smooth-surfaced boards.° Calvin Brown suggests that the model for the novel's planing mill "operated for some years in the 1920s and 1930s by the railroad about a mile or so [south of downtown] Oxford. Thus the courthouse, the Burden house, and the mill formed a triangle and the route from the cabin to the mill was entirely different from the route between the cabin and town."°

407:39 **I reckon womenfolks are likely to be good without being very kind** Armstid believes that women will treat someone like Lena Grove well, giving her what she needs, but not extending any kindness. They will do their Christian duty, but no more.

408:2 **Men, now, might** Men might be both kind and good.

408:7 **How folks can look at a strange young gal walking the road in your shape and know that her husband has left her** It is out of character and a violation of country etiquette for Armstid to speak this sentence aloud. But the punctuation and Lena's response indicate that he does speak it.

408:10 **ungreased and outraged wood** The wagon's 'outraged wood' creaks and groans because it is ungreased and is weathered by long and hard use.

408:14 **the distance perhaps roadcarved and definite** The distance between Lena and her quarry Lucas is perhaps determined by the number of miles she will travel before reaching him. That is, there is no question that she will find him; she is too determined—it is only a matter of time.

408:17 **was a hand for** frequently took part in, enjoyed

408:18 **Get up, mules** words meant to start the mules walking or, in this case, make them walk faster

408:24 **The lane turns from the road, quieter even than the road.** Because the lane is narrower and less traveled, it is more isolated, 'quieter.'

408:32 **Varner's store** Will Varner's country store, not far from the Armstid house and on the road to Jefferson. In *The Hamlet*, it is located in Frenchman's Bend, some twelve miles from Jefferson; its front porch is a gathering place for men of the community.

408:38 **where womenfolks—where a woman can . . . if you** Armstid urges Lena to stay at his house so that his wife can help her if she begins to labor.

409:1 **There will be somebody going, on a Saturday** Saturday in the country is the usual day for going to town, so it is reasonable for Armstid to expect someone to be headed there.

409:6 **crossslanted** Late-afternoon shadows of trees and bushes along the way fall diagonally across the road.

409:6 **I reckon I got a few days left** a few more days before she has the child. Lena also means, by implication, that she has a few more days to find and marry Lucas Burch, thus to make the child legitimate and herself an honest woman.

409:14 **'I wouldn't be beholden.' she says, 'I wouldn't trouble'** A conventional, polite expression by which Lena offers to decline a favor that she clearly means to accept. She doesn't want to be in Armstid's debt (which she couldn't repay), and she doesn't want to inconvenience him. At the same time she offers to decline the favor, she also expresses gratitude for it: "I don't want to be placed in your debt, but I accept your favor and am grateful and obliged to you for it."

409:23 **You just let one of them get married or get into trouble without being married . . . That's why they dip snuff and want to vote** Armstid portrays women as ruthlessly moralistic and power-hungry. Women lose solidarity with the rest of their sex, he suggests, if they become pregnant out of wedlock, or if they marry. Then they spend their time trying to be like men in order to gain masculine power and influence. Such theorizing seems harmless and absurd, but it also reflects a distrust of women and their motives which other characters, especially Joe Christmas, share. American women were granted the right to vote in 1920, twelve years before the time of the novel.

410:2 **Step by step with her he enters the kitchen** i.e., imaginatively

410:7 **takes the team out** unhitches the mules from the wagon and takes them out of their harnesses

410:9 **gray woman** Though 'gray' may mean her undistinctive, colorless appearance, it also suggests her disposition: quiet, observant, unsympathetic to her husband or the woman he has brought home with him.

410:25 **Samson's** Samson's store

410:31 **split floursack** "When not bought in barrels, flour was bought in cloth sacks of from 20 to 50 lbs. These sacks, like some feed sacks, were often deliberately made with attractive patterns so that they could be used eventually for towels or even dresses."°

411:9 **clashes the metal eyes** the burners of the stove, on which Mrs. Armstid rests pots of cooking food. She angrily clashes the burners in reaction to Lena's pregnancy.

411:15 **beholden kindness** See entry 409:14.

411:20 **Her voice is quite grave now, quite quiet. She sits quite still, her hands motionless upon her lap** Lena's behavior suggests that she knows Mrs. Armstid is about to ask about the father of her unborn child. She is preparing herself for the uncomfortable tale she will have to tell: that she is pregnant, unmarried, and trying to catch up in time to the man whom she expects (hopes) will marry her.

411:31 **suddenly naked** suddenly dropping all pretense and polite deception

411:34 **savage screw of gray hair** Her hair is tightly bound in a knot at the base of her skull.

411:37 **Lena Grove** Lena's given name is a diminutive form either of Helena (Helen) or Magdelena (Magdelene). *Lena* thus combines the beauty and sexual allure of Helen of Troy with the connotation of Magdalene the redeemed prostitute. The surname Grove is also significant. Lena shares certain basic similarities with the mythical Diana of the Wood, whose temple stood in the sacred grove of Nemi, to the south of Rome.° Diana and the Grove at Nemi were a principal subject of Sir James Frazer in *The Golden Bough*, with which Faulkner was familiar.° Frazer's description of Diana is significant: "Diana, like Artemis, was a goddess of fertility in general, and of childbirth in particular. . . . the worship of Diana in her sacred grove at Nemi was of great importance and immemorial antiquity; . . . she was revered as the goddess of woodlands and of wild creatures, probably also of domestic cattle and of the fruits of the earth; . . . she was believed to bless men and women with offspring and to aid mothers in childbed." Lena's character also incorporates elements of the Virgin Mary (see entry 405:26), and the child to which she gives birth may be taken as a Christ-figure.°

412:13 **The night you told him about that chap** 'chap' = baby. Mrs. Armstid implies that Lucas suddenly discovered he had to leave when Lena told him she was pregnant.

412:27 **The foreman was down on Lucas . . . because it would just worry me** down on = didn't like. Lena appears to be paraphrasing, or even repeating word for word, Lucas's explanation of why he had to leave town.

413:3 **jollifying** having a good time

413:6 **interfering with his work unbeknownst to him** 'unbeknownst' = unknown. Lucas couldn't know that his laughing and joking would be so in demand, interfering with his work and preventing him from calling for Lena as he'd promised. Such "interference" is probably why the sawmill foreman was 'down on' him to begin with (412).

413:12 **Mrs Armstid does not answer** Lena has just asked whether Mrs. Armstid agrees that for a young man marriage lasts such a long time. The older woman's silence, on the surface, indicates either her lack of interest or her unwillingness to answer the question. Yet Lena's naive comments must remind her of her own marriage as a young woman, and of what she has experienced and learned in the years since. Perhaps she is thinking that passion and romance didn't last very long in her case. Perhaps she is thinking that Lena has no idea how a child can affect a marriage. Perhaps she remains silent simply because she does not know how to explain to Lena the truth about marriage as she has experienced it.

413:18 **mouthword** message by word of mouth. Since she probably can't read, and Lucas can hardly write (as we learn later), she expected him to send her a message via some traveler when he was ready for her.

413:34 **to up and not wait any longer** to get up and leave, not to wait any longer

414:9 **and impersonal contempt** Mrs. Armstid feels contempt not so much for Lena as for her naïveté and the situation she has gotten herself into, the man who helped her get into it, and her violation of a whole range of communal and moral values.

414:30 **your eggmoney** money that Mrs. Armstid has earned from the sale of eggs, which is hers to do with as she pleases

414:33 **sweated over them and nursed them** 'them' = chickens, eggs, and chicks

414:36 **dispute them hens** disagree that the hens are yours

414:36 **lessen** unless

414:36 **it's the possums and the snakes** Possums and snakes eat chicken eggs and occasionally small chickens; possums eat full grown chickens as well. Either, according to Armstid, might dispute Mrs. Armstid's ownership of the chickens. He is trying to keep the conversation humorous.

414:37 **That rooster bank, neither** No one will dispute your right to the money in that rooster bank either.

415:7 **take her away from here** Mrs. Armstid's willingness to give Lena her eggmoney does not lessen her disapproval for this unmarried pregnant girl, whom she wants out of her house.

415:14 **Mrs Armstid was not there** Her absence suggests that she does not want to have to hear Lena thank her for breakfast, that she does not want to argue with the girl about the eggmoney, that she remains angry with Henry for bringing this pregnant, unwed girl home.

415:38 **hopened** hoped

416:4 **heelgnawed porch** The floorboards have been worn down by the heels of the men who have walked, stood, and squatted there.

416:7 **Miz Burch** In Southern dialect, 'Miz' is how 'Mrs,' the term of address for a married woman, is pronounced. Armstid thus presents Lena to the men at Varner's store as a married woman.

416:9 **she will take it kind to ride with them** She will appreciate the favor of allowing her to ride with them.

416:14 **he watched his tongue seek words, thinking quiet and swift, thought fleeing *A man. All men. . . .*** Armstid understands his feelings in a fragmentary way, but he must struggle to express that understanding. Only after the italicized passage ends does he find suitable language. Even then, he has difficulty explaining what he feels.

416:21 **I wouldn't set too much store by** I wouldn't put too much faith in; I wouldn't believe.

417:2 **Jody Varner** son of Will Varner and manager of the store. An important character in *The Hamlet*, he appears also in *The Mansion* and *The Town*.

417:3 **that fellow in Jefferson at the planing mill is named Bunch and not Burch** Byron Bunch, a major character in

the novel, soon to become entangled with Lena. Armstid lets
Lena tell her entire story about Burch before telling her this.

417:7   **the Lord will see that what is right will get done**   a
common religious theme. See, for example, Psalms 119:
137, "Righteous art thou, O Lord, and right are thy judg-
ments," or the last line of the Lord's prayer, "Thy will be
done," Matthew 6:10, perhaps the source of Lena's opti-
mism. This statement foreshadows later events, for Lena
does have a family of sorts when her child is born, and Byron
Bunch is part of it.

417:9   **It required only one or two questions**   Driving away,
Armstid imagines that Lena would begin telling her story
'not even waiting for [the men] to ask' (416).

417:25   **young buck**   a young man, wild and sexually irresponsible

417:25   **that's throwed over what he was bred to do and them
that depended on him doing it**   Varner observes that the
man Lena is pursuing isn't the first to abandon a pregnant
woman.

417:34   **coattails perhaps already boardflat with running**   a
cartoon image of Burch's coattails stretched out flat behind
him as he runs at full speed away from Lena

418:1   **Even if it has got a brother in it that objects to his
sister's nightprowling**   Jody Varner guesses that Lena left
home in search of her errant lover partly because she has a
brother who objects to her 'nightprowling,' her sneaking out
at night to be with men.

418:4   *She has no mother because fatherblood hates with love
and pride, but motherblood with hate loves and cohabits*
Varner believes that Lena would be with her mother if she
had one. A mother would hate the fact of Lena's pregnancy
but would still love her daughter: she would 'cohabit' with
the sin. A father would condemn the sin and the daughter
with it.

418:10   **and even sardines if she likes**   Sardines, sold in small
flat tins, were considered a delicacy by rural Americans at

the time of this novel—about the only delicacy inexpensive enough for many of them to be acquainted with.

418:13 **I et polite** 'et' = past tense of *to eat*. Archaic rather than incorrect, it survives in a number of dialects in the Southern United States and elsewhere.

418:15 **strange bread** 'strange' because it was cooked by a stranger's hands, and because she is eating it in a strange place

418:20 **the approaching crisis** of labor and childbirth

418:21 **she is waging a mild battle with that providential caution of the old earth of and with and by which she lives.** She is trying to decide whether to spend Mrs. Armstid's egg-money on the sardines. She has been raised to be careful with what little money she has, but here she decides to splurge: 'I'm a-going to do it.'

418:24 **ranked battery of maneyes** Everyone stares at her as she enters the store.

418:27 **box of sardines** a tin of sardines

418:32 **shoeblacking** shoe polish

418:33 **noway** anyway

419:8 **From Varner's store to Jefferson it is twelve miles** Lena wonders whether she will arrive in Jefferson in time for dinner. She is trying to decide whether to eat the cheese and crackers she bought at Varner's store. She is probably sufficiently familiar with the slow pace of mules to know that she won't arrive in time, that she might as well go ahead and eat. In a mule-drawn wagon a twelve-mile ride will take at least four or five hours.

419:9 **dinner time** lunch time, around noon. Dinner was the noon meal for most Southerners in 1931.

419:11 **mought** might

419:15 **a right smart** fairly often

420:15 **Then she stops . . . the spasm passes** Since Lena will not go into labor for another ten days, according to the novel's chronology, she probably is not feeling an actual labor contraction, though she may think so since this will be her first baby. Her thought that 'It's twins at least' suggests that the unborn child has kicked her.

420:31 **she sees two columns of smoke: the one the heavy density of burning coal above a tall stack, the other a tall yellow column standing apparently from among a clump of trees some distance beyond the town** Ironically, Lena sees at the same moment both the black smoke from the planing mill where Joe Christmas and Byron Bunch work and the yellow smoke from the burning house where Joanna Burden has just been killed, near which Christmas lived, near where Lena herself will bear her child and find Lucas Burch. This panoramic view encompasses not only the whole of Jefferson but the totality of what is to happen in the novel.

420:38 **My, my. A body does get around.** This exclamation at the end of the first chapter anticipates the novel's concluding lines.

CHAPTER II

421:1 **Byron Bunch knows this** The point of view changes here from the objective focus on Lena Grove in the first chapter to a more penetrating, analytical focus on another important character, Byron Bunch. Such clues as this first sentence frequently orient the reader of *Light in August* to a particular narrative perspective. They allow the reader to judge the reliability of the information in each episode by making clear its source. The novel relies on Bunch's perspective more frequently than on any other character's. His growing attachment to Lena Grove compels us to regard skeptically at least some of what he says, especially about his own motives.

Byron's first name, Mario D'Avanzo suggests, "alludes to Shakespeare's voice of love and good sense and natural feeling, the Biron of *Love's Labor's Lost*. Biron becomes a model of the ideal lover through which Faulkner achieves a dimension of richly allusive art, irony, and high comedy that is, I believe, Shakespearean in its vision of what constitutes happiness in life." Noting its associations with a more recent figure, the poet Lord Byron, Carl Ficken argues for the satiric nature of Byron Bunch's first name: his story "has about it the quality of an idealized romance . . . he keeps trying with the earnestness of a genuine Don Juan, and has, in fact, won his lady's heart." Martin Bidney adds, "if there was one salient trait which left its stamp upon the entire being of the historical Lord Byron, it was a consuming passion for intense and varied experience. But Byron Bunch has spent most of his life in a determined flight from life—and . . . seems bent upon confirming the impression that he is wholly out of contact with reality." The name Bunch "is to be understood in terms of his role as a member of society, over against some of the other isolated individuals in the story."°

421:3   **planer shed**   where most of the work of a planing mill occurs, and which contains the important machinery

421:7   **serge**   the cloth of Christmas's trousers. Usually made of woolen worsted, serge is a twilled fabric with a smooth clear face and a diagonal rib on the front and back. It often develops a shine where it becomes worn. Christmas is wearing trousers which, though now soiled, were a relatively expensive item when first purchased. At some time in his past he apparently made enough money to dress well.

421:8   **stiffbrim straw hat**   Such a hat is conspicuously sporty, thus inappropriate for a worker in a planing mill.

421:11   **in his professional rags**   The word 'professional' suggests that Christmas dresses with the intention of looking like a tramp, a man without roots.

421:26   **planer**   a steam- or electrically powered machine which shapes and smoothes lumber at the planing mill. Faulkner evidently alludes to it in the 'whirring and grating belts and shafts.'

422:1   **scoop**   a shovel with deeply curved blade designed for such a task as shoveling sawdust

422:13   **move that sawdust**   from where it accumulates as it comes out of the mill to where it can be used to fuel the boiler's fires that power the mill

422:19   **Christmas**   In the sixteenth chapter (683), Doc Hines explains the origin of this name. Along with the first name 'Joe,' the last name 'Christmas' provides primary evidence of the symbolic role of Joe Christmas ("J.C." = **J**esus **C**hrist) as a Christ figure. See entry 683:29. At the University of Virginia, Faulkner said he did not intend any Christ symbolism in the novel, but then commented: the "Christ story is one of the best stories that man has invented, assuming that he did invent that story, and of course it will recur. Everyone that has had the story of Christ and the Passion as a part of his Christian background will in time draw from that. There was no deliberate intent to repeat it. That the people to me come first. The symbolism comes second."°

422:22 **foreigner** to the mill workers, any person with racial or cultural characteristics or mannerisms not immediately recognizable to citizens of Jefferson

422:23 **Did you ever hear of a white man named Christmas?** The foreman takes Christmas's unusual last name as evidence that he is not white

422:27 **a man's name, which is supposed to be the sound for who he is, can be somehow an augur of what he will do** At the University of Virginia, Faulkner used similar words to answer a question about character names in the novel: "that is out of the tradition of the pre-Elizabethans, who named their characters according to what they looked like or what they did. . . . Of course, it seems to me that those people named themselves, but I can see where that came from, it came from the—my memory of the old miracle plays, the morality plays in early English literature. Chaucer."°

423:3 **Sunday clothes** dress-up clothes, synonymous with "city clothes" (see 422). The foreman does not consider such clothing appropriate for work at a saw mill.

e423:15 **With the exception of Byron, they had brought no lunch with them today** Like most of the other people in Jefferson, the sawmill men work half a day on Saturday, spending the afternoon socializing or shopping in town. Byron works by choice at stacking staves of wood, perhaps heeding Isaac Watt's warning that "Satan finds some mischief still / For idle hands to do."

423:19 **the pump house where they usually ate** The pump house pumps water from a nearby river or stream into the mill where it is used to process lumber and to fill the boiler which produces the steam that powers the mill. Perhaps the men usually eat in the pump house because it provides a ready source of water which they consume with their meals, or because the water makes it cooler than other parts of the mill.

423:26 **His face was gaunt, the flesh a level dead parchment color**   Parchment varies in color from grayish yellow to ivory. Christmas's skin is slightly different in color from that of the other men, who notice the difference but cannot explain it. He is, simply, a 'foreigner' as a result.

423:37 **the action as reflex as the thought**   Both the impulse to be kind and the act of kindness itself were instinctive.

424:3 **Keep your muck**   Christmas has no intention of accepting Byron's offer or of acknowledging the generosity that provokes it. Throughout the novel he refuses numerous offers of food, which he regards as attempts to weaken him through kindness.

424:8 **Simms**   superintendent at the planing mill

424:23 **This is not what Byron knows now. This is just what he knew then, what he heard and watched as it came to his knowledge**   This passage establishes Byron as a central viewpoint in the narrative. It shows that the events narrated in this first section of the chapter occurred in the recent past, and that some of the facts about Christmas are being withheld for later revelation. A similar passage (432) narrows the time of the chapter's narration to the six months between the day Christmas and Brown quit the sawmill and the day of Joanna Burden's death. The chapter's second section (beginning 432) clearly indicates that the exact time of narration is the day of Lena Grove's arrival in town. Joanna is already dead, her house aflame, but the community has yet to learn of her murder. By introducing Christmas through withheld, gradually revealed knowledge, Faulkner allows the reader to learn about him in more or less the same way Byron and the rest of the town did.

424:26 **the veil, the screen, of his negro's job at the mill**   Shoveling sawdust is simple manual labor requiring no spe-

cial skill or intelligence. It is assigned to workers whom the
foreman will not entrust with more demanding responsibility. It is thus a 'negro's job.' It is a 'veil, a screen' because it
allows Christmas a certain anonymity, an advantage for a
man who bootlegs whiskey.

424:32 **colonial plantation house** a large house, constructed
of hand-processed wood and consisting of a stairway and hall
in the center, imposing entrance ways, large main doors, por-
ticos, and columns—the Southern mansion of antebellum
tradition. It is ironic that Joanna and her family—opponents
of the institution of slavery that made the plantation house
possible and which it symbolizes—lived in such a structure.

424:33 **a middleaged spinster named Burden** Joanna Burden. Her last name, a shortened form of the original 'Burrington,' is an apt emblem of her family history. Their
burden has been the burden of American history, of slavery
and of white guilt for slavery, guilt the Burdens have devoted themselves to expiating. Along with their abolitionism
is racism, for they look down upon as inferior the people
they want to serve (see especially 581, 585–86). Joanna recounts her family history to Christmas in the eleventh chapter, 576–87. She is named after her father's Spanish first
wife, Juana.

425:6 **like a mule does in front of an automobile in the
road** He is 'backlooking,' as if he is expecting something to
come up on him from behind.

425:14 **Simms is safe from hiring anything at all when he
put that fellow on. He never even hired a whole pair of
pants** In these and other comparisons (which liken him to
a mule, a car, a horse, and a locust) the men suggest that
Brown is something less than human. Mooney implies that
Brown is not man enough to fill his britches.

425:16 **one of these cars running along the street with a ra-
dio in it . . . when you look at it close you see that there aint
even anybody in it** Byron's way of suggesting that Brown

may talk non-stop but that inside him there is no brain (no driver). The first radio-equipped cars appeared in 1929.°

425:25 **always got a sore hoof when hitching-up time comes** never available for work when the need arises

425:26 **the mares like him** Women like him.

425:31 **a tone and manner that was the essence of the man himself, that carried within itself its own confounding and mendacity** The way Brown acts and talks provides ample evidence of his foolishness and lying, refuting any pretense he might make to the contrary.

425:35 **There was no reason why his name should not have been Brown** See entry 422:27. The name Brown connotes an anonymity peculiarly suited to the man who bears it.

426:20 **crap game** game in which players roll or "shoot" dice and bet on the outcome

426:21 **I would have thought that maybe shooting dice would be the one thing he could do** Since learning how to shoot dice requires idle time, Brown ought to be an expert.

426:39 **higharmed and erratic motion** inexpert and inefficient shoveling

427:35 **fall to again** begin to work again

427:37 **in its flagging arc** Its arc diminishes as Brown tires and shovels with ebbing vigor.

428:5 **serge-and-white** serge pants and white shirt; see entry 421:7

428:27 **Memphis** large city in southwestern Tennessee, almost always associated in Faulkner's work with gangsters, illicit whiskey, and prostitution—the last being the reason why 'the young men even went to Memphis now and then.'

429:3 **He arrived late, but that was not it. He hadn't shaved, either; but that was not it** 'it' = his uncharacteristic silence, which makes clear that something unusual has happened

429:12 **apprentice fireman** sarcastic epithet for sawdust shoveler. Brown and Christmas are 'firemen' because they shovel sawdust to fuel the fire in the boiler.

429:13 **spading into the sawdust pile as though it were eggs** He's not working very hard, barely shoveling at all, as if he's afraid of breaking eggs.

429:19 **I wasn't surprised at that** Mooney knows that Brown would be eager to drive the car, that symbol of wealth and leisure, even if to do so he had to serve as Christmas's chauffeur.

429:22 **I dont reckon Simms will have any trouble finding a man to fill his shoes in these times** One of the few topical references in the novel. The speaker refers to the severe economic conditions of the Depression which during the present-time of the novel had reached their worst level.

429:26 **he was doing pretty well** In hiring Brown, Simms had found a man who could do nothing at least as well as Christmas.

429:35 **I dont** I don't wonder: I know exactly how he got that car.

429:37 **"Well," Byron said, "if I could get rich enough out here to buy a new automobile . . . They looked at Byron. "Brown is what you might call a public servant** Byron's co-workers realize that he does not know that Christmas and Brown have made their money by bootlegging whiskey. The sarcastic reference to Brown as a 'public servant' reveals he has been bringing the whiskey to sell in town, rather than obliging customers to walk out to the Burden house.

430:8 **out of his shirt front** Brown hides the liquor in half-pint bottles inside his shirt. When he makes a sale, he steps into an alley, unbuttons his shirt, and removes the merchandise.

430:9 **six bits** two bits = a quarter; six bits = seventy-five cents

430:16 **He aint going to walk around in public with his pants down** Unlike Brown, Christmas will try to avoid drawing attention to himself.

430:18 **He aint going to need to** Brown's association with Christmas makes clear his involvement in bootlegging.

430:20 **And Mooney was right** in his prediction that Brown would either 'quit at noon or work on until six oclock' (429)

430:28 **Cold muck out of a dirty lard bucket** Muck is garbage, slop. A 'lard bucket' is "a gallon bucket with a bent-wire bail for carrying. Lard was regularly sold in such buckets, and the empty ones were used for lunch-pails and various other such uses."°

430:31 **maybe some folks work like the niggers work where they come from** 'some folks' = Brown and Christmas; 'they' = 'some folks.' Mooney is telling Brown, "Maybe where you come from the white folks work like the niggers work," by which he means they don't work much at all.

430:32 **a nigger wouldn't last till the noon whistle, working on this job like some white folks work on it** Laziness that would be tolerated in a white man would not be tolerated in a black man.

431:4 **clutching the shovel as though it were a riding whip** Brown holds the shovel by the shaft, not the handle. A riding whip is either a buggy-whip, about five feet long, used in controlling the horse or team pulling a carriage or buggy, or possibly a crop, or short whip, used by a rider to control a mount.°

431:11 **On the idea that he's a bigger fool than even I think he is** The whole point of this conversation is Mooney's contention that Brown is trying to convince himself to quit the mill job and go to work with Christmas as a bootlegger. Mooney considers Brown a fool for his big mouth and lack of common sense. Brown considers himself a fool for working at the mill for such low wages, but he also suspects that as a bootlegger he might get himself into serious trouble. Mooney knows that Brown's fear of proving himself a worse fool than he already is will not prevent him from quitting the sawmill and going to work with Christmas.

431:13 **His address from now on will be the barbershop** where Brown can meet potential customers

431:17 **draw his time** collect his hourly wages

431:20   **as Christmas had done on that day three years ago, as if somehow the very attitudes of the master's dead life motivated . . . the willing muscles of the disciple**   'three years' agrees with this chapter's first sentence and is one more bit of evidence establishing Christmas's age at his death. Chapter X (565:20) says that he was thirty-three when he arrived in Jefferson; three years later, in the novel's present time, he would be thirty-six.

The 'master's dead life': a difficult phrase, perhaps meaning "the absent master's life" or the "life of the master whose absence from the sawmill makes him seem dead to the workers still there," though the latter possibility is unlikely. In any case the phrase is satirical. The words 'master' and 'disciple' give ironic twists to the Christ motif, especially since on 431 the 'master' is described as 'sullen and quiet and fatal as a snake.' The reference to Brown as a 'disciple' becomes especially ironic later when he seeks to betray Christmas for the thousand dollar reward.

431:26   **Lay into it**   lean into it, work harder

431:29   **Then Brown's teeth didn't show**   They showed when he was laughing, but when he realizes that Mooney is taking offense at being called a 'slaving bastard,' he stops smiling, and his teeth no longer show.

432:1   **The half of it, that is. Do you want me to come up there and whisper the other half in your ear?**   The 'half of it' Mooney suggests Brown has told 'God's truth' about was when Brown called himself a bastard. The other half, which Mooney offers to whisper to Brown, we can assume is something obscene.

432:7   **not making a very good job at being dissolute and enviable and idle**   He's not fooling anyone—he's really hard at work trying to sell whiskey.

432:16   **bootlegging**   The illegal sale and/or distribution of whiskey. Because Christmas and Brown do not manufacture whiskey themselves, they are not moonshiners, the distillers of illegal whiskey.

432:21 **she is still a stranger, a foreigner** They continue to regard her as an outsider. See entry 422:22.

432:22 **Reconstruction** the years between 1865 and 1877 when the Federal government established provisional or military governments in the defeated Confederate states. Former Confederates who refused to sign a loyalty oath to the Union were denied the right to vote. They were thus angered when Federal authorities enforced the right of ex-slaves to vote.

432:25 **sixty years since her grandfather and her brother were killed on the square by an exslaveowner** killed by Col. Sartoris, the chief war hero of Yoknapatawpha County, and a major character in *The Unvanquished* (1938). Joanna Burden discusses the killing in Chapter XI and Bayard Sartoris relates it in the "Skirmish at Sartoris" chapter of *The Unvanquished*. See entry 582:4.

432:28 **it still lingers about her and about the place** 'it' = 'talk of queer relations with negroes' (432) and the memory of her grandfather's and brother's murders

432:32 **it is there: the descendants of both in their relationship to one another's ghosts** Their memory of the hostile relations between their ancestors causes them to continue to feel hostility towards one another.

432:37 **If there had been love once, man or woman would have said that Byron Bunch had forgotten her. Or she (meaning love) him, more like** We can read these lines literally: If Byron Bunch had ever loved a woman before, any man or woman who knows him would say that he had forgotten her, or more likely that she had forgotten him (because he is such a dull and meek fellow). Or we can read them more abstractly: even if Byron had ever believed in love, it plays no part in his life now. He may have forgotten about the possibility of love (never having encountered it) but more likely love has forgotten him (or has not given him the opportunity to discover it). By spending so much time at the mill, Byron has left himself little chance to encounter love.

433:11   **The other workmen . . . believe that he does it for the overtime which he receives.**   Throughout this novel characters, townspeople, and even the narrative itself gossip and speculate about why people behave as they do. Faulkner implies repeatedly that their failure to understand one another is a major cause of estrangement and isolation: it is certainly so for Christmas and Hightower, and the narrative suggests that this may be the case with Byron too.

433:20   **Hightower**   Name of one of the novel's main characters who does not appear until the next chapter. See entry 440:33.

433:21   **Twenty-five years ago**   The novel refers five times to the 'twenty-five' years since Hightower's disgrace: 433, 441 (twice), 697, 698. This repetition emphasizes the length of the ex-minister's self-imposed isolation. It also links him to the isolation of the Hines couple, and perhaps also to Christmas. Chapter XV reveals that, although the Hineses have lived in Mottstown for thirty years, for 'twentyfive years the couple had had no visible means of support' (652) and 'for twentyfive years now the couple had lived in the slack backwater of their lonely isolation' (652). The event which apparently began their isolation was Doc Hines's attempted kidnapping of Christmas from the orphanage (see chapter V); for Hightower the crucial event was his wife's death and the loss of his church. Both periods of isolation began at roughly the same time. In both cases, the isolation ends because of Joe Christmas, though Byron Bunch and Lena Grove affect Hightower's short-lived emergence to a degree.

433:25   **Mrs Beard**   She appears in *Flags in the Dust* (96–97, 216–17) as "a woman in a soiled apron, with straggling, damp grayish hair and an air of spent but indomitable capability" (96).

434:8   **fifty-year-old outcast who has been denied by his church**   See entry 447:36.

434:12   **physical inviolability**   virginity, sexual purity

434:13   **Two miles away the house is still burning, the yellow**

smoke standing straight as a monument on the horizon
See 420. The yellow smoke, with its connotations of evil
and defilement, suggests the yellow fog in the opening lines
of T. S. Eliot's "The Love Song of J. Alfred Prufrock." Rising from the symbolic ruins of their corrupted love, the
smoke also suggests the relationship of Joanna and Christmas, which occurred in and around the house, and which
leads to both their deaths.

434:22 **My pappy says he can remember how fifty years ago**
. . . Fifty-six years earlier, two members of the Burden family
were killed by an 'ex-slaveholder and Confederate soldier'
over what Joanna Burden later describes as a 'question of
Negro voting.' See her account beginning on 582.

434:32 **Watt Kennedy** sheriff of Jefferson

434:34 **From the way the square looks . . . he wont have
much trouble finding anybody he wants out there to arrest**
The town square, normally full of shoppers and loiterers on
Saturday afternoon, is empty because everyone has gone to
watch the fire, and the speaker is thus observing that anyone
the sheriff might want to arrest will likely be out there watching the house burn.

435:2 **tow sack** a Southern term for a burlap bag, a gunnysack

435:3 **burdens of staves** bundles of wooden sticks or narrow
strips of wood

435:7 **her mouth already shaped upon a name** the name of
Lucas Burch

435:25 **Miz Burch** Mrs. Burch. Byron asks Lena whether
she is married to the man she is looking for. He is also asking, discreetly, whether she is married at all.

435:38 **dark complected** skin dark in complexion. Lucas has
such skin; Byron does not.

436:6 **a right smart of** a good number of

436:14 **suspicious of the now** Uncertain of what is happening at the present moment, not sure that Byron is telling the
truth, Lena is suspicious because the 'now' has not turned
out to be what she so confidently expected.

436:18   **set**   dialect form of sit

436:18   **hard streets**   'hard' because they're paved, and Lena is not accustomed to them

436:25   **You'll set easier**   The sack will make the stack of planks a softer place to sit, thus she can "sit easier," more comfortably.

436:33   **Saturday evenings**   Saturday afternoons. The rural South divides the day into three parts: morning, evening, and night.

437:5   **Byron in his turn gets the picture of a young woman betrayed and deserted and not even aware that she has been deserted**   Compare this view of Lena with 417: 'The squatting men . . . think as Armstid thought and as Varner thinks: that she is thinking of a scoundrel who deserted her in trouble and who they believe that she will never see again.' Though Byron is aware that Lena has been made pregnant by another man, he does not fully admit the physical reality of that fact until later.

437:17   **judgment**   divine judgment, punishment justified by the fact that she is a Yankee, and by the activities of her family during Reconstruction

437:25   **Now he does not look at her, looking a little aside**   Byron begins to suspect that Joe Brown may in fact be Lucas Burch, whom Lena is looking for. He looks 'a little aside' to avoid looking directly at Lena because he does not want her to see that he suspects he knows where Brown is—Byron is falling in love with her already.

437:39   **splint chairs**   "a chair with seat and back woven of long thin flat strips of wood, usually split white oak"°

438:2   **when you think of a fellow named Joe Brown, you think of a big-mouthed fellow that's always laughing and talking loud**   Byron may be referring to the American film comedian Joe E. Brown, known for his big and loud mouth. He had made only a few films by the time of the novel's publication, but perhaps Faulkner had seen one of them. Maybe Lucas Burch, impressed by Brown's success at getting laughs, deliberately chose the name for an alias.

438:7 **drew time on his mouth** earned money for talking

438:27 **a fellow is bound to get into mischief soon as he quits working** For a possible source to Byron's wisdom, see entry 423:15. That he takes this wisdom to heart is evident in his work habits on Saturday afternoons. See, for instance, 439 for more evidence of his innocence, his fear of involvement in the real world. However, Byron himself has paused from work, and during that pause he falls in love with Lena and dooms himself to more mischief than he could imagine.

439:18 **white scar** This detail confirms that 'Joe Brown' is Lena's man, Lucas Burch. Byron has obviously suspected this for a while now. He probably keeps talking to avoid acknowledging Brown's true identity.

439:21 **could have bitten his tongue in two** in regret over having talked too much and given away to Lena the fact that her lover is in Jefferson

CHAPTER III

440:5 **crepe myrtle and syringa and althea** 'crepe myrtle': a
small East Indian tree that flourishes in Mississippi. It blooms
from June until September. Joan Serafin notes the mythological association of this plant with "the love-Flower, once
thought sacred to both Venus and Dionysus." She suggests
that its presence in Hightower's yard is significant because he
"has long failed in love."° But in two other instances (*The
Town*, where Charles Mallison calls it "the myrtle of grief,"
337; and in *Sartoris*, 26, which describes it as the "roses of
death"), it symbolizes love and grief, and that meaning is
likely here as well. Robert E. Bell notes the association of
crepe myrtle with a number of mythological figures, especially Venus: "*Venus murcia* (*murtea* or *murtia*) was a surname
of Venus at Rome. . . . This surname . . . was believed to
indicate the fondness of the goddess for the myrtle tree, and
in ancient times there is said to have been a myrtle grove in
front of her chapel at the foot of the Aventine."°

'Syringa' or mockorange: a flowering ornamental shrub.

'Althea': a small summer-blooming tree prominent in the
South.

440:9 **the sign, which he calls his monument** He probably
does so ironically, regarding the sign as a 'monument' to his
past and to what he suffers for it.

440:20 **delinquent girls** unwed pregnant women

440:21 **he lost his church, he lost the Church** When he lost
his pulpit in the church, he lost his faith both in God and in
the church as a social and religious institution.

440:23 **the bereavement and the shame** that he felt over his wife's death and the loss of his church and the circumstances leading to both

440:32 **The letters glittered with an effect as of Christmas** Since the novel's main character is named Christmas, that word's presence in this sentence and on the sign itself is significant. Christmas dies in Hightower's kitchen. The sign prefigures events shortly to come in Hightower's life.

440:33 **Gail Hightower, D.D.** 'D.D.' = Doctor of Divinity, an honorary title for seminary graduates rather than a degree earned in a graduate school. The name 'Hightower' suggests several possible meanings and sources. Isolated in a small house on a side street of Jefferson, immersed in Tennyson and memories of his grandfather's glorious death, the ex-minister in effect inhabits a "high tower," cut off from the world. His first name, "Gail," may suggest sexual ambivalence, or by ironic contrast may suggest both his lack of sexual passion (gales of passion) and his compensatory obsession with family history. According to Joseph Blotner, a man named "G. Hightower had been president of Mississippi A&M for years before he had gone on to head a farmers' group."°

Another possible source for Hightower's name occurs in *Psalms* 18:2: "The Lord is my rock, and my fortress, and my deliverer; my God, my strength, in whom I will trust; my buckler, and the horn of my salvation, and my *high tower*" (my emphasis).°

Hightower had his beginnings in a series of short stories not published until 1979 in the *Uncollected Stories*: "The Big Shot" (c. 1926), "A Dull Tale" (1930), and "A Rose of Lebanon," also titled "A Return" (1930). In those stories, Gavin Blount's fixation on the past and his dead father, killed in the Civil War, controls his life. Blount, like Hightower, is an ineffectual dreamer who inhabits the real world only with difficulty. In her study of the composition of *Light in August*, Regina Fadiman observes, "As far as extant records show, the story of the novel begins with the three holograph pages,

now at the University of Texas, about Gail Hightower. . . .
In less than two and one-half pages and in a completely
straightforward manner, an omniscient narrator describes
Hightower in his study, the painted sign outside his window,
and the Negro nurse and children who peer at the sign. . . .
All the facts familiar from the novel about Hightower's childhood, his house, sign, and garden are reported on the first
page of this early version."°

441:6 **a negro nursemaid with her white charges would loi-
ter there and spell them aloud** A 'nursemaid' is a baby sit-
ter to small children ('white charges'); to 'spell them aloud'
means to sound out phonetically, to read with difficulty.

441:13 **"Oh yes," the friend would say. "Hightower . . .**
This account of Hightower is given to a 'stranger' by 'an acquaintance in the town.' It varies significantly from what the
novel later reveals as true. For instance, Hightower's wife
does not die in 'a house or something'; she jumps or falls
from a hotel window. The speaker also professes ignorance
about why Hightower remained in Jefferson after his disgrace, although the novel later makes clear his reasons. Such
discrepancies reflect the community's passing back and forth
of information.

441:15 **Presbyterian church** Faulkner's interest in different
forms of Puritanism (religious and secular) makes logical his
frequent use here of the Presbyterian church, especially
since the novel explores questions of sin and predestination
central to the Calvinist (i.e., Presbyterian) tradition. Compared with the Methodist and Baptist churches, the Mississippi Presbyterian church was small during the 1930s. In
1926, 365 Mississippi Presbyterian churches listed a membership of 28,096; by 1936 the number of churches had
declined to 272 and the membership to 22,493. By contrast, there were 486,864 Baptists in Mississippi in 1936 and
191,686 Methodists.°

441:37 **So the sign . . . is even less to him than it is to the
town** To the town the sign represents the whole story of

Hightower's life in Jefferson. Since he takes the sign for granted, 'is no longer conscious of it,' it means little to him at all.

442:9 **it would be night save for that faint light which day-granaried leaf and grass blade reluctant suspire, making still a little light on earth** 'daygranaried' = combination of 'day' and 'granary' (a storehouse for threshed grain). Faulkner fuses the words in a participle meaning "filled with light stored up during the day" and modifying 'leaf and grass blade.'

442:12 *Now, soon,* **he thinks;** *soon, now* Hightower anticipates the arrival in his imagination of the cavalry, which he waits for each evening around this time. See entry 453:23.

442:13 **There remains yet something of honor and pride, of life** This reverie of the charging cavalry, and the story surrounding it, is the only shred of honor and pride left in his life.

442:16 **When Byron Bunch first came to Jefferson** . . . The narrative assumes an authorial perspective here, and the account that follows of Hightower's disgrace necessarily rings with more credibility than the story told earlier from the viewpoint of community gossip (441).

442:22 **any other call** assignment to any other church

443:6 **General Grant's stores burning in Jefferson** In November of 1862, Union Brigadier General Ulysses S. Grant began moving his forces southward from Grand Junction, Tennessee, along the Mississippi Central Railroad towards Vicksburg, some 250 miles distant. By the middle of the month he had established a supplies and munitions depot in Holly Springs and moved twenty miles south to Oxford, where he headquartered for most of December. On December 20, General Earl ("Buck") Van Dorn led a Confederate cavalry of 3500 into Holly Springs, surprising the Federal forces there, burning the depot, and capturing 1500 Union soldiers. A humiliation for Grant, the raid made Van Dorn a hero to his fellow Mississippians. In *Light in August*, Faulkner changes the setting of the Van Dorn raid to Jefferson. Hightower's grandfather dies during this raid, the source of the 'galloping hooves' of the ex-minister's imagination. The burning of 'Grant's stores' thus means the destruction of his supplies and munitions depot, not of private retail businesses.° See 751.

443:11 **the Book** the Bible

443:20 **that is why women have to be strong and should not be held blameable for what they do with or for or because of men** Byron thinks because men subject them to such irrational, eccentric behavior that women should not be held responsible for what they do as a result of men. In the context of the paragraph, he is thinking that because she had Hightower as a husband, she should not be harshly blamed for her behavior.

443:25 **who at first the town thought just had nothing to say for herself** who the town thought too timid to speak up

444:4 **absolution** the forgiveness of sins by a priest or minister in a formal church ritual

444:4 **choirs of martial seraphim** a Miltonic phrase: choirs of angels ranked in military formation, ready for battle

444:9 **that frozen look** the look of one who has begun to suffer again; a look of anguish or desperation

444:10 **Hightower would meet them alone, in his shirt sleeves and without any collar, in a flurry** That Hightower has to greet his own visitors, that his wife does not greet them or make sure that he is prepared to meet them, suggests to the parishioners that she is not acting as a proper minister's wife.

444:21 **watching the door, maybe wondering if he knew what they believed that they already knew** They watch for the entry of Hightower's wife, or at least for a glimpse of her. In this wonderfully convoluted sentence Faulkner illustrates the basic nature of gossip. The women believe they know the truth about Hightower's private life—that his wife is mentally ill, or worse—and they wonder also whether he is aware of what they think they know.

444:26   **they would see her get on the early train**   Apparently this is a southbound train, and the townspeople do not discover the falsehood of Hightower's story until his wife is seen in Memphis. Hightower says that he is sending his wife off to see her relatives 'downstate,' but she switches to a northbound train in another station. See entry 444:29.

444:27   **gaunted**   grown emaciated

444:29   **And he would tell that she had gone to visit some of her people downstate somewhere**   "downstate" = in the southern part of the state. Does Hightower know where she has gone? He likely paid little attention to her nor ever thought to doubt what she told him about her trips. The words—'And he would tell'—suggest that the townspeople doubt whether Hightower has told the truth, or perhaps whether he is even aware that he has not told the truth. When they learn that his wife has been seen in Memphis, they *know* his story is false.

444:33   **But the next day Hightower was in the pulpit**   The 'but' suggests the town's amazement that he appears in church at all. The assumption is that if the woman told one person in Jefferson about seeing Hightower's wife in Memphis by Sunday morning everyone would have heard, including Hightower. He probably does not know he is being deceived, or that he is being talked about.

444:37   **sitting by herself at the rear of the church**   A proper minister's wife would sit in a more prominent location near the front of the church.

444:38   **She came every Sunday after that for a while**   apparently in reaction to being seen in Memphis. Whether she attends at Hightower's insistence, or by choice, we are not told.

445:6   **his religion and his grandfather . . . as though the seed which his grandfather had transmitted to him . . . had been killed**   Hightower so thoroughly confuses religion, his grandfather, and his own self-image that it is as if the 'seed' that his grandfather might have transmitted to him had also been killed in the cavalry raid, and that as a result nothing had grown from it since the grandfather's death, not even Hightower himself, who is so fixated on that moment that he is in effect dead to the world.

445:23 **thundering and allegorical period** A period is a rhetorically stylized, rhythmical sentence of at least several clauses. Such sentences occur frequently in sermons and political speeches.

445:28 **superintendent** probably the Superintendent of the Sunday School

445:31 **vestry room** church room for storing choir vestments and for meetings of the church elders

445:34 **made up** got together, collected

445:35 **an institution, a sanatorium** a "rest home" where the mentally or physically ill can relax and recover, where alcoholics can dry out

446:25 **that purpose regarding which all had the same conviction** They believe she goes to Memphis to meet a lover.

446:27 **good women dont forget things easily, good or bad, lest the taste and savor of forgiveness die from the palate of conscience** If the women forget or overlook Mrs. Hightower's misbehavior, then they'll lose their moral superiority to her.

446:29 **the town . . . believed that bad women can be fooled by badness . . . But that no good woman can be fooled by it** Bad women, the misogynous town believes, spend part of their time "being bad" and the rest of their time trying not to provoke suspicion. They do not have as much free time as good women to investigate and understand evil. Good women, this passage suggests, are never too busy to concern themselves with the sins of others. A good woman might mistake another person's goodness for evil, but she will never mistake evil for good. She has spent too much time pondering evil to commit such an error.

447:20 **her rightful name where she had written it herself on a piece of paper and then torn it up and thrown it into the waste basket** Perhaps, believing that the paper would be found after her death and bring scandal to her husband, she does this as revenge on him for the life he has led her.

447:36 **The ladies got up first and began to leave. Then the men got up too** They leave in outrage at the scandal Hightower has brought them. This event marks the beginning of the church's rejection, or 'denial,' of Hightower. The narrator in chapter II refers to the 'fifty-year old outcast who has been denied by his church' (434:8). The verb 'denied' suggests Peter's denial of Christ, but any similarity between Hightower and Christ is ironic.

447:39 **his head not bowed** not bowed in prayer, a sign of his defiance of the expectations of his church, and of his failure to grieve for his wife.

448:24 **It was not a funeral** Her burial is not a funeral because Hightower does not want it to be. He is still defying social expectations, though he may have decided against a formal church service because his wife died by suicide, or because he wanted to avoid the disgrace. The ceremony is more a scandal, a public occasion, than a proper funeral.

448:31 **Then even the members of the other churches knew that his own had asked him to resign, and that he refused** In his account of how the church pressures Hightower to resign the pulpit, Faulkner accurately portrays the hierarchy and government of the Presbyterian church. *Presbyterian* derives from *presbyter*, which means *elder*; hence, a "Presbyterian" church is one governed by elders. "Presbyterianism is a representative form of government in which the congregation elected ruling elders who, with the pastors, form the session, charged with maintaining the spiritual government of the church. The presbytery consists of all ministers within a district and representative ruling elders for each congregation. It is the focus of authority, having jurisdiction over ministers and churches in its district. The removal or installation of a minister is by mutual agreement of congregation, presbytery, and individual." The elders of Hightower's church might request his resignation, but they

could not fire him without the consent of the local presbytery, which Faulkner calls the 'church board' (449). According to Lefferts A. Loetscher, "no ecclesiastical power could
impose a pastor on an unwilling congregation. But a presbytery, after careful deliberation, did have the power to remove a pastor."° The board doubtless considered the re-
current subject of Hightower's sermons a deviation from
standard doctrine. However, he was obviously removed from
his pulpit because of the scandal of his wife's death.

449:11　**the loafers and such would gather**　Although the
wording suggests that Hightower preached to an empty
church more than once, Faulkner implies in 'the Sunday after that' that there was only one such occasion.

449:20　**he had gone to the elders and resigned his pulpit**　In
fact, since a Presbyterian minister belongs to the presbytery
rather than to the church in which he serves, Hightower
would probably have tendered his resignation to the presbytery rather than to the elders. By noting earlier (449) that
the church board has already considered his dismissal, however, Faulkner evinces uncertainty over the order in which
events might occur.

449:22　**the town was sorry with being glad**　Now that the
town has gotten what it desired, Hightower's resignation, it
can afford to feel sorry for him. Its sympathy is thus hypo-
critical.

450:14　**not a natural husband, a natural man, and that the
negro woman was the reason**　The gossip implies that Hightower could not satisfy his wife sexually, and that he had
sexual relations with the black woman, thus driving his wife
insane. Alternatively, it implies that his wife could not satisfy
him sexually because she refused to do the unnatural things
he asked of her, so he turned to a black woman instead.

450:21　**that single idle word**　not literally some specific word,
but any word suggesting suspicion or scandal

450:23　**carelessly masked men**　They are 'carelessly masked'
because they know no harm will come to them if they are
recognized. They are doing the community's will.

450:25   **the woman told** [that] **. . . her employer asked her to do something which she said was against God and nature** This is the gossip of townspeople, not the woman's testimony—whatever she might have said would have passed among many people before reaching Byron. She might have explained her resignation in this way to preserve her own honor and reputation, especially after the visit of the masked men the night before. Romans 1:26–7 defines sodomy and homosexuality as sins 'against nature.'°

450:28   **she was what is known as a high brown and it was known that there were two or three men in the town who would object to her doing whatever it was she considered contrary to God and nature** 'high brown' = racist description of a light-skinned black woman considered attractive to white men. Faulkner implies that the men objecting to her unnatural activities have had sex with her, that they object from jealousy rather than moral outrage.

450:38   **And that finished him** That was the last straw. Hightower used up his last chance when he hired a black man to cook for him, because it allowed the town to suspect him of homosexuality.

450:39   **not masked either** They're expressing the entire town's open indignation, acting on its behalf, so need no disguise.

451:3   **K. K. K.** Ku Klux Klan, a vigilante organization, founded shortly after the Civil War and resurrected early in the twentieth century, especially prominent in the Southern United States. Dedicated to the supremacy of white Anglo-Saxon Protestantism in America, responsible for numerous murders and other criminal acts from 1900 to 1960, the Klan typically employed terrorist tactics such as those used against Hightower.

451:7   **He refused to tell who had done it. The town knew that this was wrong** The pronoun 'this' refers to Hightower's refusal to identify his attackers; more generally 'this' refers to the general situation. The town does not care so much that the attackers go unidentified as it disapproves of the position Hightower has placed himself in, which it sees as creating the opportunity for citizens of the town to disgrace themselves by attacking him.

451:10 **they might kill him** The pronoun 'they' means the Klan, not the men giving him this advice, though some of them might belong to the Klan.

451:14 **the whole thing seemed to blow away, like an evil wind** an allusion to the proverbial evil wind that blows no good; Thomas Heywood, *Proverbs*: "An ill wind that bloweth no man to good, men say."° Cf. Shakespeare's *II Henry IV*: "Falstaff: What wind blew you hither, Pistol? / Pistol: Not the ill wind that blows no man to good" (V.iii.85–86).

451:17 **the entire affair had been a lot of people performing a play and that now and at last they had all played out the parts which had been allotted them** The figure of performers playing out their parts occurs frequently in Shakespearean plays: *As You Like It* [II.vii.139–42]: "All the world's a stage, / And all the men and women merely players"; *Macbeth* [V.v.19–26]: "Life's but a walking shadow, a poor player, / That struts and frets his hour upon the stage."

451:27 **poor mill family** a family trying to live on the poor wages paid by a sawmill or planing mill

451:32 **they dont even know that I know, or likely they'd take us both out and whip us again** What Byron alludes to here is explained in the next paragraph. He believes the townspeople still hold this 'one other thing' against Hightower, and that they would whip him for knowing about it, and Hightower for telling him.

451:34 **folks dont seem to forget much longer than they remember** People can remember what they have forgotten as quickly as they can forget, a backward way of saying that people never really forget, and a down-to-earth variant of the opening of chapter VI: 'Memory believes before knowing remembers. Believes longer than recollects, longer than knowing even wonders' (487).

451:35 **Because there is one other thing** Because there is something else about Hightower that the town holds against him, explained in the next paragraph

452:7 **instead of entering, the negro stood there for a time and then went on up the street towards town** A white man whose wife needed a doctor would not hesitate to go to any white house with a telephone and ask that a doctor be called. But blacks were conditioned not to disturb whites with their problems, so this man walks into town to find a doctor on his own rather than risk offending a white homeowner. The interesting question concerns why the black man felt free to approach Hightower, a white man. He probably feels that this exminister, an outcast among the whites, and victim of the same vigilantism that terrorized blacks, is probably the safest white citizen to approach.

452:23 **the doctor when arrived** the doctor, when he arrived

452:35 **when anything gets to be a habit, it also manages to get a right good distance away from truth and fact** Habits are sterile, fossilized responses to human situations. As a situation changes, so do 'truth' and 'fact,' or what people perceive these to be. Byron will soon put this pragmatism to work as he begins to try to justify to himself and to Hightower his schemes concerning Lena. Having fallen in love, he discovers that the traditional morality he has always believed in suddenly begins to lose its power.

452:40 **both master and servant of their believing** As a minister Hightower had been his congregation's spiritual master and the servant of their spiritual needs.

453:1 **outrage** to affront by contradicting, proving wrong

453:10 **Why do you spend your Saturday afternoons working at the mill while other men are taking their pleasure down town** Hightower poses this question to force Byron to answer his own question about why the former minister remains in Jefferson: answers to both questions concern deeply ingrained habits, beliefs, and traits of personality.

453:14 **But I now know why it is** why it is that Hightower has remained in Jefferson

453:20 **It's the dead ones that lay quiet in one place and don't try to hold** [a man], **that he cant escape from** Why does Byron believe this? It is tempting to speculate that events in his own past, about which the novel reveals virtually nothing, have taught it to him. At any rate, this is what Byron thinks as he muses over his quiet life, and also as he talks to Hightower. Note Hightower's question: 'is it any wonder that this world is peopled principally by the dead?' (758). Byron's statement expresses one of the novel's main themes, the hold of the past over such characters as Hightower, Christmas, and Joanna Burden.

453:23 **They have thundered past now . . .** 'They' = the phantom hooves of the fantasy Hightower was awaiting on 442. The juxtaposition of the end of his revery with the sentence on 453 about the dead who don't try to hold on to the living is ironic.

453:26 **bitten shadows of the unwinded maples** ragged, uneven shadows of maple trees as the light from the street lamp shines through them; 'unwinded' = motionless, unstirred by wind.

453:29 **the sonorous waves of massed voices from the church . . . swelling and falling in the quiet summer darkness like a harmonic tide** This image of communal worship emphasizes Hightower's estrangement from the town and the church.

453:30 **a sound at once austere and rich, abject and proud** The oxymoronic quality of this church music typifies this novel's attitude towards Protestantism in general. The music is 'rich' because it is an expression of communal faith; it is 'austere' in its limiting view of mortal humanity and its repressive morality (later evident in Simon McEachern and Joanna Burden). It is 'abject and proud' because it declares humankind's dependence on God and simultaneously expresses self-righteousness for that dependence, especially in comparison to those without faith.

453:37 **puny, unhorsed figure** unhorsed = not riding a
horse. Byron's mundane appearance at the gate contrasts
with the heroic images of Hightower's vision.

454:14 **Byron Bunch in town on Sunday** Hightower is surprised because Byron, a person of strict habit, has spent every Sunday for seven years 'leading the choir in a country
church' (433). His appearance in town on Sunday evening
bodes something out of the ordinary.

CHAPTER IV

455:1   They sit facing one another across the desk. The study is lighted now, by a greenshaded reading lamp sitting upon the desk   a common narrative frame in Faulkner's fiction: two characters facing one another across a desk or table, one talking and the other listening

455:11   And with the house burning too, right in my face   Byron thinks he should have seen in the fire an omen that he was not as safe as he had thought.

455:22   I never even suspicioned then that what I didnt know was not the worst of it   First he learns that Lena isn't married to Burch, that she's looking for him so he will marry her before the baby's birth, and then he learns that Burch has been somehow involved with Christmas in the murder and fire at the Burden house.

456:1   I asked a passing negro, but he didn't know   Virtually every citizen in Jefferson, black or white, knows about the fire. As later chapters reveal, many of the white citizens went out to watch the house burn. Black citizens probably took special notice of the burning house, inhabited as it was by the woman who had tried to serve them for so many years. The black man hides the truth from Hightower, probably for his own preservation, since it is soon (if not already) suspected that a black man set the fire.

456:5   color of flour sacking   grayish-white. Hightower's skin color and his loose, flabby obesity suggest possible ill health (later evidence hints at a heart condition). The skin pallor is not from lack of sunlight, for Hightower works in his garden and makes frequent walks to town.

456:9   That would be for me to do too. To tell on two days to

two folks something they aint going to want to hear   Apparently, Byron means that first he told Lena Grove that his name was not Lucas Burch—something she did not want to hear, because it meant that she had not found the man she was looking for. Now he must tell Hightower that Lena isn't married, and that Joanna Burden has been murdered. That Hightower hasn't heard about the murder is another indication of his isolation from the community.

456:37   **the half a pint**   the standard small size in which bootlegged whiskey was sold for immediate consumption. The point may be that Christmas sold discreetly to a few well established customers, and that Brown sells to anyone with a quarter. Brown's method would obviously attract more attention and increase their chance of getting caught.

457:10   **You ought to be careful about drinking so much of this here Jefferson hair tonic. It's gone to your head. First thing you know you'll have a hairlip**   The 'Jefferson hair tonic' is bootleg whiskey. Christmas is making a joke, thinking of sarcastic comments he has heard about rotgut liquor that can "grow hair on a billiard ball" and hair tonic that can either be rubbed on the head or consumed, however the user likes. This 'hair tonic,' Christmas says, is going to Brown's head, affecting his thinking, and soon likely to make hair grow on his lip. Since a "hare lip" is a split lip, Christmas is also promising that if Brown doesn't stop talking he'll get a hare lip from Christmas's fist.

457:28   **something latent, about to wake**   dawning awareness that the situation is more complicated than he has realized

457:29   **as if something inside the man were trying to warn or prepare him**   The pronoun 'him' refers to Hightower, who becomes unconsciously aware of what Byron is trying to tell him before his conscious mind realizes it.

457:33   **I had already told her before I knew it. And I could have bit my tongue in two**   Byron implies that Joe Brown is the man she is looking for. By 'told' he means that he had told Lena enough about Joe Brown for her to realize who he is.

457:40   *Dont even need to not listen*   Hightower does not have to try to ignore the organ music; he does so through habit, by instinct.

458:12   **the other. The rest of it. The worst of it.**   that she is not married, that the man she wants to marry was involved in the murder and fire at the Burden place. Hightower still does not realize that Lena is unwed.

458:17   **just because he was a little behind in getting back**   a little slow in getting back from replenishing his stock of moonshine

458:18   **had just stepped into a alley for a minute**   to make a sale, out of sight of the law

458:23   **I have been thinking how easy it would be if I could just turn back to yesterday**   Ironically, this is precisely Hightower's problem, that he lives in the past, and for better or worse Byron is in the process of learning to live in the present.

458:30   **Unless. . . . . . .**   unless there's more to it than you have told me so far

458:35   **He remembers only that Byron is still young and has led a life of celibacy and hard labor, and that by Byron's telling the woman whom he had never seen possesses some disturbing quality at least, even though Byron still believes it is only pity**   'by Byron's telling' = by Byron's account. A difficult sentence primarily because the verb 'remembers' is followed by two direct objects in the form of noun clauses, and because 'telling' functions as a noun synonymous with "account" or "testimony." Byron's monastic life of work, relative poverty, chastity, and obedience to God has insulated him from the temptations of the outside world, leaving him naive and vulnerable, unable to judge women such as Lena. Hightower senses that Lena has had a profound effect on Byron, that perhaps he has fallen in love with her, though at present Byron thinks what he feels is 'pity.'

459:5   **a quality of shrinking and foreboding**   a look suggesting fear and dread of what Byron is telling him

459:11 **he, who had not yet heard, without having to know that something had happened which made of the former dilemma of his innocence a matter for children** Byron senses without having been told yet that something terrible has happened at the Burden house, something so terrible that the fact of his having fallen in love, and thus out of innocence, becomes insignificant.

459:27 **Not responsibility for the evil to which he held himself** the evil of having fallen in love with another man's pregnant woman, for which he blames himself

459:33 **It was just to give himself and her time to be shocked and surprised** Byron rationalizes to himself, and to Hightower, why he did not tell Lena of Lucas Burch's possible involvement with the murdered woman. Byron believes that he wanted time to recover from the shock of discovering that he loves Lena and that Joe Brown is the man she intends to make her husband, and he wants Lena to have time to recover from the shock of discovering where her husband is— before they both have to confront an additional shock: news of the murder and fire in which Brown may have been involved. In fact Byron wants to save Lena Grove for himself, and he hopes (probably not consciously at this point) that circumstances surrounding the murder will remove his competition for Lena from the scene.

460:17 **a comfortable woman** a fat woman

460:18 **This here is Miz Burch . . . Then he believed that she had got his meaning** As Lena listens Byron tries very hard, with unintended comic effect, to make clear to Mrs. Beard that he does not want Lena to hear about the fire and the murder.

460:19 **His expression was almost a glare: importunate, urgent** By the urgent look on his face Byron is trying to tell Mrs. Beard something without having to say it aloud: he wants her to understand that he doesn't want this pregnant young woman to hear about the events at the Burden house.

460:26 **recapitulant, urgent, importunate** These adjectives describe the sound of Byron's voice, which has just 'ceased,' so that what they really describe is the effect of his voice, as if its sound hangs in the air when he stops talking. Faulkner uses 'recapitulant' in a special sense that blends "repeating" with "recapitulating": repeating what has already been said, but summing it up too with each repetition. A 'recapitulant' voice says the same thing over and over.

461:10   **taking out**   leaving (for the country church)

461:13   **I aint going tonight . . . the man who all his life has been selfconvicted of veracity whose lies find quickest credence**   Despite Mrs. Beard's suspicions and his own sheepishness, Byron does fool her. He lies successfully because of his upright reputation.

461:33   **that lie**   the lie he would tell Mrs. Beard to prevent Lena from having to eat supper with the other men of the boarding house, who would be talking about the Burden murder.

461:34   **that which he was trying to shield was its own protection**   Byron wants to prevent Lena from hearing about the Burden murder. Mrs. Beard is quick to recognize that such news is not what a pregnant woman (especially one she has figured out must be unmarried) needs to hear. Hence, her pregnancy, which Byron is trying to protect, becomes its own protection.

461:36   **I reckon a woman in her shape (*and having to find a husband named Burch at the same time* she thought with dry irony) aint got no business listening to any more of man's devilment**   Mrs. Beard implies a connection between the events at the Burden mansion and Lena's pregnancy: both are the result of the evil men can do, of which she probably believes Lena does not need further evidence. She suspects Lena is not married. There is a further possibility: that she is wondering whether Byron Bunch is responsible for Lena's pregnancy, that he has been going to see her every weekend instead of going to the country church, and that since now she is about to have a child he has brought her to town under

the pretense of looking for the husband who abandoned
her. Note her comment at 462:8.

462:21   **them two with the same like**   the same common interest: bootlegging

462:22   **dared the law**   broke the law and dared it to catch him

462:28   **I dont reckon about it at all**   I don't think about it at
all: I know exactly what he nearly told about him and Christmas hijacking a truck. Alternative reading: I just don't think
about such matters—I've got better things to do, this is none
of my business, and I don't want to get myself in trouble by
wondering about another man's affairs.

463:4   **Being a Yankee and all**   Being a Yankee, and all the
other unspecified, vaguely reprehensible qualities that Yankees possess. Attaching 'and all' to the end of a declarative
statement is a common Southern way of talking.

463:20   **not knowing that I knew that her and that fellow
wasn't married yet**   Byron's first open announcement of
what we can assume he has known nearly from his first meeting with Lena

463:37   **on his face now that expression of denial and flight**
Hightower's look—which was first 'grave and interested'
(456) and then assumed 'a quality of shrinking and foreboding' (459) and of 'shrinking and denial' (459) becomes now
one of 'denial and flight'—the desire to deny and run away
from what he fears he is about to hear.

464:4   **Christmas is part nigger**   See entry 423:26.

464:7   **a thistle bloom falling into silence without a sound**
A thistle bloom is a cluster of seeds surrounded by feathery
plumes so light the slightest breeze can waft them along. The
image suggests how deceptively unaffected and calm Hightower's voice seems when he repeats the news of Christmas's supposed mixed blood.

464:18   **Between his parallel and downturned palms and with
his lower body concealed by the desk, his attitude is that of
an eastern idol**   This sentence recalls two descriptions of
Marlow in Joseph Conrad's *Heart of Darkness*: "[Marlow] had

sunken cheeks, a yellow complexion, a straight back, an as-
cetic aspect, and, with his arms dropped, the palms of the
hands outwards, resembled an idol"; "[Marlow] began again,
lifting one arm from the elbow, the palm of the hand outwards, so that, with his legs folded before him, he had the
pose of a Buddha preaching in European clothes and without a lotus-flower."°

464:21 It was yesterday morning Byron Bunch is a good
storyteller. Many of the facts in the story he begins to tell
here he got from townspeople who attended the fire and
from the sheriff's deputies. There is much here, however,
that is his own elaboration.

464:21 a countryman later identified (469) as Hamp Waller

464:24 when he broke down the door Joanna kept her front
door locked, but left her kitchen door unlocked for Christmas and for black neighbors who might need her help. Significantly, though she wanted to help black people, she was
unwilling to admit them through her front door, which was
always locked, a sign of her removal from society. Blacks must
enter by her back door, traditionally reserved in Southern
plantation houses for servants and other menials. Whites, of
course, never call at all.

465:30 Her head had been cut pretty near off Faulkner
borrowed this detail from Nelse Patton's murder of Mattie
McMillan in September 1908, just outside Oxford. The no-
torious event surely made an impression on the young Faulkner; see entry 743:1 for details. Joseph Blotner notes that in
a later murder that Faulkner probably also heard about a
black man named Leonard Burt killed his wife and set the
house afire to hide the crime. Faulkner may have appropri-
ated this detail for use in Joanna's death.°

**466:9 she was laying on her side, facing one way, and her
head was turned clean around like she was looking behind
her** like Janus of Roman mythology, whose two faces "were
turned towards the past and the future, denoting both aware-

ness of history and foreknowledge."° The macabre position of Joanna's head seems grim vindication of Faulkner's belief in the importance of "not looking back." See entries 404:11 and 466:10.

466:10 **he said how if she could just have done that when she was alive, she might not have been doing it now** The countryman jokes that if Joanna had been looking behind her while she was alive, she would have seen her assailant approaching and could have avoided being murdered.

466:36 **then last night Brown showed up** Brown's desire to betray Christmas for the reward money suggests Judas Iscariot's betrayal of Christ for thirty pieces of silver (see, for example, Matthew 26:14–17, 47–50). Brown was earlier described as the 'disciple' of Christmas; see entry 431:20.

467:22 **joking Christmas about gray hair** teasing Christmas about the gray hair, and thus the age, of the woman he is sleeping with. Perhaps also a joke about the supposed sexual avidity of unmarried, middle-aged women.

467:23 **he would take it week about with him paying the house rent** Brown jokingly offers to sleep with Miss Burden on alternate weeks, as if sex is the rent she is charging for the cabin.

468:6 **[Christmas] looked at Brown. 'Cant you trust me?' and Brown said he said 'Yes.'** Christmas threatens to kill Brown if he talks about what he has discovered.

468:16 **Brown . . . had a kind of rat smell** Brown realizes that he is a suspect in the murder, that he smells as much like a rat to his listeners as he claims Christmas does.

468:29 **at the outside** at worst

468:33 **the big house** the plantation house, Joanna Burden's house

470:3 **his eyes going and going** looking excitedly from one person to another

470:12 **it was almost worse for a white man to admit what he would have to admit than to be accused of the murder**

itself To confess that he had shared a room with and even worked for a black man would be a terrible humiliation for Brown, 'almost worse' than being accused of killing a woman.

471:2 **he said to me "I made a mistake last night. Dont you make the same one" and I said "How do you mean a mistake?" and he said "You think a minute"** I made the mistake of talking too much to you last night. Don't you make the mistake of talking too much too. If you do, I'll make you sorry.

471:19 **and that's why you didn't tell what was going on out there until tonight** The pronoun 'that' refers to the whole of Brown's testimony to the possibility that Christmas is part-black, which Brown offered in response to the Sheriff's insistent questioning about the time of the fire and why Brown didn't report it (see 469).

471:28 **Buck** Buck Conner, marshal of Jefferson.

472:8 **That's what Brown says** 'That' = Brown's assertion that Christmas is a black man

472:10 **same as a honest man can be tortured into telling a lie** Byron, who has recently discovered the truth of this statement, is talking about himself. He has already lied in his failure to tell Lena what she wanted to know, and by offering her false assurances. His dilemma while walking with her from the mill to town hinges on his awareness that he cannot both tell the truth and shield her from the truth. He resolves this dilemma by lying.

472:13 **But they have not caught him yet. They have not caught him yet, Byron** Hightower asks for this assurance because he believes that as long as Christmas remains free there is a chance to avert the tragedy that he believes will inevitably follow his capture. The prospect of such a tragedy haunts him until the end of chapter XIX, as if he fears the lynching of Christmas might force him to relive his own persecution at the town's hands.

472:28 **I reckon he's safe enough** Brown's desire to get the reward money will keep him in town, along with his desire to see Christmas caught. If Christmas learns that Brown has told the truth about him, Brown's life will be in jeopardy. Brown wants Christmas in jail.

472:29 **I reckon she can find him now** she = Lena. All she need do is ask the sheriff.

472:40 **in hock for the time being** held in a pawn shop, retained as security, until redeemed for a set price. Held more or less on suspicion of involvement in the murder, Brown will remain in the sheriff's custody until the capture of Christmas provides a better suspect. The capture of Christmas will also allow Brown (so he believes) to redeem the reward money.

473:5 **I aint told her. Nor him. Because he might run again, reward or no reward. And maybe if he can catch Christmas and get that reward, he will marry her in time.** a good example of Byron's capacity for self-deception. He believes that he hasn't told Lena about Brown's possible involvement in the murder because he does not want to upset her. He wants Brown to help find Christmas and win the reward money, so that when he is told about her he will have no excuse to avoid marrying Lena. Byron's real reason for not telling either of them is his fear that Brown will try to leave town when he learns about Lena, and that she will then follow.

473:9 **Swolebellied** with a belly swollen by pregnancy

CHAPTER V

474:1 **It was after midnight** On a Friday morning. This chapter focuses exclusively on the perspective of Joe Christmas and his activities the day before Joanna Burden's murder. Chapter XII recounts the events which lead Christmas to commit the murder. In chapter IV, which occurs two days later on a Sunday night, Byron narrated events immediately following the murder.

474:29 **a voice level as whispering** a vicious monotone

475:19 **He stood in the darkness** Darkness is the medium in which Christmas is most at ease. Most of the fifth chapter occurs in darkness, and Christmas conducts his affairs with Bobbie Allen and Joanna Burden mainly in darkness. It is the daylight world he has trouble understanding. Darkness signifies his alienation from the conventional world and his spiritual isolation.

475:20 **Brown's breath alternately hot and cold on his fingers** Christmas feels the warmth of Brown's breath on his fingers when he exhales. When Brown inhales, that warmth is replaced by the normal coolness of the night air, so that his breath seems to alternate between 'hot and cold.'

475:21 *Something is going to happen to me* Christmas means that he feels both compelled to do something and as if something is about to happen to him. It is a tragic sense of impending disaster—the consequence of both who he is and what he is about to do. See also 486:11.

475:23 **he could reach . . . to his pillow beneath which lay his razor** This is the first evidence that the violence Christmas feels compelled to commit is murder. The razor is a straight razor, the stereotypical concealed weapon of the

Southern black male: a long narrow blade with a wooden
handle, some five inches in length.° When not in use, the
blade folds into the handle. Christmas's choice of the razor
as a murder weapon is significant. There are other weapons
available, but he intends to kill as a black man, with a black
man's weapon. Murder thus becomes his assertion of identity, committed against the white woman who urged him to
live as a black man.

475:25 **But he did not do it. Perhaps thinking had already
gone far enough and dark enough to tell him** *This is not the
right one* Christmas's thinking had gone 'far enough and
dark enough' (far enough for him to be at least partially
aware of the enormity of what he intended to do) for him to
realize that Brown was not the person he was driven to kill.
Though the meaning of this passage is clear enough, its fatalism suggests that Christmas is acting at least partially on
instinct, that forces stronger than his own will are driving
him towards his destiny.

476:8 *God perhaps and me not knowing that too* Christmas
suddenly suspects that these sounds and voices evoking the
totality of his life may be the sound of God's voice, or like it.

476:9 **fullborn and already dead** fully formed and already
meaningless in his mind

476:9 *God loves me too* perhaps a reference to a religious
motto under a picture showing a white and black baby together, popular among Southern African Americans during
the 1920s and 30s. In *Look Homeward, Angel*, Thomas Wolfe
alludes to such a picture with its "motto in flowered scroll-
work, framed in walnut: God loves them both."°

476:10 **like the faded and weathered letters on a last year's
billboard** difficult to read now, perhaps outdated and ir-
relevant. Echoing the description of Hightower's 'monument'
in chapter II (440–41), these words foreshadow Christmas's
fatal encounter with Hightower in chapter XIX.

476:20 **It's because** 'It' = his anger, his need to do something violent

476:29 **Overhead, the slow constellations wheeled** 'wheel'

= the nightly movement of the constellations in their revolution around the North Star

476:30   **the stars of which he had been aware for thirty years**
Other references to Christmas's age suggest that he is thirty-six when he dies, though a less literal interpretation of these references could have him die at the age of thirty-three. Faulkner does not mean here that Christmas has been alive for thirty years, only that he has been aware of the stars, the world around him, for that long, since about the time of his adoption by the McEacherns.

476:37   *If she is asleep too. If she is asleep*   If she is asleep as Brown was. Christmas seems to be basing what he will do next on what he will find at the house, specifically on whether Joanna Burden is awake or asleep. If she is asleep, he can avoid murdering her until the next night. He feels committed to act, but he welcomes the opportunity to procrastinate.

477:7   *Perhaps that is where outrage lies. Perhaps I believe that I have been tricked, fooled*   The first 'that' refers to both what precedes and what follows it: the two years since the height of Christmas's affair with Joanna Burden, and the lie he believes she told about her age that 'tricked, fooled' him. He is trying to understand the causes of his anger. A convention throughout this novel is the use of pronouns whose antecedents follow (rather than precede) them by several sentences. The effect is momentary reader confusion followed ultimately by clarification, hence deeper involvement in the narrative.

477:8   **she lied to me about her age**   She may not have lied. He chooses to believe she did, as if to relieve himself of blame for what he is about to do. See the Chronology.

477:9   *about what happens to women at a certain age*   menopause, for which Christmas holds her responsible, and which wholly befuddles him. As chapter XII suggests, he believes that her loss of sexual desire was a result of menopause. All aspects of female sexuality repulse him.

477:17 **he appeared to be watching his body, seeming to watch it turning slow and lascivious in a whispering of gutter filth like a drowned corpse in a thick still black pool of more than water** Christmas is remembering his affair with Joanna (we learn the details in Chapter XII). Since we have just been told that he believes she had tricked him, and he is 'cursing her with slow and calculated obscenity' (477), it seems clear that he blames her for immersing *him* in their two-year orgy. He sees himself as having been 'sucked down into a bottomless morass' (591); 'It was as though he had fallen into a sewer' (588). By 'gutter filth' Christmas means what Doc Hines will refer to as 'womanfilth' (494)—menstrual blood and anything else associated with female sexuality. The 'more than water' may be blood, that crucial element in his reaction against the sexuality of women.

477:24 **A woman had sewed them on** As chapter VII will reveal, this woman was his foster mother, Mrs. McEachern. Christmas moves by association from cursing Joanna to thinking about Mrs. McEachern, about women in general.

477:31 **he would cut off the buttons which she had just replaced** To avoid feeling indebted to her. To allow her to sew on lost buttons would give her a hold over him which he means to avoid. Chapters VI through IX explain the development of this attitude.

477:35 **The dark air breathed upon him . . . the cool mouth of darkness, the soft cool tongue** He imagines the night air caressing him as if it were his lover.

478:3 **The road ran before him** the first mention of what is later to be called the road that ran 'for fifteen years' (563), that led him to the Burden house, and that now can lead him away if he lets it. It is also the road of flight he will take after the murder of Joanna Burden.

478:9 **He watched his body grow white out of the darkness like a kodak print emerging from the liquid** Faulkner compares the illumination of Christmas's body to the gradual emergence of the image on a developing print in the emulsion of a photographer's darkroom; 'kodak print' = photograph. A number of interesting associations are at work here. First, the image of the developing photograph links Christmas to Hightower, who as chapter III reveals develops photographs (440). Second, his body emerges from the darkness as if he is being born, created out of nothing. He has just finished imagining his body 'turning slow and lascivious in a whispering of gutter filth like a drowned corpse in a thick still black pool of more than water' (477). In response to that imagined image he takes off his clothes and stands naked in the night air, as if cleansing the filth from himself, becoming a new self. Yet it is also a potentially self-destructive self, for by standing naked by the road and shouting at the car carrying the white woman, he is practically inviting death. Perhaps for a moment he entertains the notion of death, tries to force a white man to kill him, which would certainly purge the tension he feels.

478:13   **"White bastards," he shouted. "That's not the first of your bitches that ever saw . . . ."**   she's not the first white woman who ever saw a black man's penis

478:19   **he was free again**   free of the compulsion that drove him to shed his clothes and stand by the road, waiting to expose himself; free too, for the moment, of the need to stand besides Joanna Burden's house and consider killing her.

478:35   **half cotton blanket**   the other half is probably wool

479:1   **It's because they are not women. Even a mare horse is a kind of man**   Horses connote maleness to Christmas, whether they are stallions, geldings, or mares. He wants to sleep in a place untainted by female corruption.

479:7   **faintly ammoniac**   the acrid odor of stale horse urine

479:12   **It was the unexpected sleep**   that had refreshed him

479:14   **he descended the perpendicular ladder**   having slept in the stable loft

479:16   **onehanded swoops**   Holding his blanket in one hand, Christmas has only one free hand to climb down with. He thus must let go of one rung and grab hold of the next one as he descends.

479:19 **increasing east** brightening eastern sky

479:36 **cloth cap** a loose fitting cap with a hard narrow brim in front

479:37 **a magazine of that type whose covers bear either pictures of young women in underclothes or pictures of men shooting one another** pulp magazine of a sort popular during the 1920s and 30s. Representative titles are *Black Mask, All-Detective, The Shadow, Weird Tales, Horror Stories, Amazing, Astounding.* The 'young women in underclothes' suggests one of Henry Steeger's Spicy pulps: *Spicy Detective and Spicy Mystery*, for example. Steeger's magazines were the first to use such covers.°

481:1 **sunshot leaves** Only a few rays of sunlight penetrate the canopy of leaves covering the ditch; hence the 'sunshot' effect, scattered sunlight, like buckshot.

481:1 **Maybe I have already done it** done the as yet unknown thing that he feels driven to do

481:4 **like a corridor, an arras, into a still chiaroscuro** literally, down a hall, through a door, into a quiet room of dark and shadow. 'Corridor' appears seventeen times in the novel, fourteen times in this chapter.° Almost always it suggests the rigid, unbending course that events in the sixth chapter destine Christmas's life to follow. An image of determinism—whether imposed by Christmas himself or by external agents—'corridor' implies a pre-established sequence of events that cannot be changed.

'Arras' functions similarly. An 'arras' is a veil or tapestry curtain, such as the one behind which Polonius hides to overhear Hamlet's conversation with his mother in Act III of *Hamlet.* Christmas's arras scene comes in Chapter VI, when the dietitian discovers him in her closet.

'Chiaroscuro' is an artist's term for a scene drawn in shades of light and dark. The scene Christmas envisions will occur in Joanna Burden's darkened bedroom, at midnight.

481:6 **the yellow day contemplated him drowsily, like a prone and somnolent yellow cat** 'yellow day' = sun-lit day. This metaphor suggests the cat-like yellow fog of T. S. Eliot's

"The Love Song of J. Alfred Prufrock" ("The yellow fog that rubs its back upon the window-panes, / The yellow smoke that rubs its muzzle on the window-panes").°

481:36 the whiskey the illegal moonshine Christmas and Brown have been selling in Jefferson. Christmas destroys his hidden cache to put his affairs in order before he kills Joanna. He is also making sure that there is nothing left for Brown to sell.

482:4 that evening Friday evening

482:22 It was as if he had just paused there for Brown to look at him as a reminder of his warning in chapter IV that Brown had better not talk too much. See entry 471:2.

482:26 Freedman Town section of Jefferson inhabited by African Americans. The name comes from the term for freed slaves after the Civil War, "Freed Men." Calvin Brown observes that this was also the name of a black section in Faulkner's hometown of Oxford, and that it was also bordered on one edge by a railroad. Faulkner varies this name from town to town and story to story. On 659, a Mottstown citizen refers to the black section of his town as 'Niggertown.'°

482:31 He went on . . . from street lamp to street lamp The persona in T. S. Eliot's "Rhapsody on a Windy Night" measures his progress along a lonely street by the light of the street lamps under which he passes.

483:3 Then he found himself He became aware of where he was.

483:5 the summer smell . . . of invisible negroes Faulkner reflects the common belief of his region and time that African Americans have a distinctive odor. If there was an odor, it was likely the result of diet, living conditions, and heat.

483:7 murmuring talking laughing in a language not his Because he has lived most of his life as a white man, Christmas does not speak an African-American dialect. Thus the talk of African Americans is 'a language not his.' He is not part of the community that speaks it.

483:8 As from the bottom of a thick black pit he saw himself enclosed A metaphor suggesting that while Christmas chooses to identify himself as a black man, he feels suffocated by the identification, which he views as a form of hell. He is attracted to the idea of being black but repulsed by the reality. This and other scenes make clear his essential racism. See 598, where Christmas views the 'second phase' of his affair with Joanna Burden as 'the bottom of a pit.' See also 484, 643.

483:10 **as if the black life, the black breathing had compounded the substance of breath . . . and with the now ponderable night inseparable and one** as if black life and black breathing had become part of the air so that all elements become fluid and gradually cohere in the substance of night, a tangible thing capable of being examined and appraised. All that Christmas senses becomes part of the black nighttime ambiance.

483:19 **fecundmellow** For Christmas the basic qualities of black woman are sexual attraction, vitality, and the promise of a motherly embrace calm and protective as well as sexual.

483:22 **lightless hot wet primogenitive Female** the primal, archetypal womb that gave all people life

483:24 **narrow and rutted lane** There are two significant occurrences in the novel of a similar phrase: the approach that the young Christmas first takes to the McEachern house is 'up a frozen and rutted lane' (505) while Percy Grimm, during the final pursuit, runs down a 'rutted' lane (740). This is a variation of the corridor image; see entry 481:4.

483:26 **black hollow** Freedman Town, 'black' because black people live there, a 'hollow' because one must descend a hill to enter it and climb a hill to leave.

483:30 **the cold hard air of white people** as opposed to the hot and wet atmosphere of the black hollow

483:33 **low bright birds in stillwinged and tremulous suspension** Faulkner uses this strange image to suggest how Christmas perceives the lights of the square, as a cluster of birds frozen in mid-flight, close to the ground. The metaphor suggests Christmas's strained and oddly detached state of mind.

484:2   **the bare arms of the women glaring smooth and white**
women who are the restrained, cool, white counterparts to
the fecundmellow black women. The phrase suggests "The
Love Song of J. Alfred Prufrock":

> And I have known the arms already, known them all—
> Arms that are braceleted and white and bare
> (But in the lamplight, downed with light brown hair!)°

484:4   **That's all I wanted**   the American Dream: a house, a
spouse, a few friends, quiet evenings playing cards. Christmas is lying to himself. Domesticity repels him. Compare
with 481: 'All I wanted was peace'; see also 644.

484:6   **This street in turn began to slope. But it sloped safely**
The street began to descend again, but because it was not
descending into Freedman Town, it did so safely.

484:6   **His steady white shirt and pacing dark legs died among
long shadows bulging square and huge among the August
stars**   Having moved beyond the street lamps and other
lights of the town, the outline of Christmas's body fades
among the other night shadows.

484:19   **the other street, the one which had almost betrayed
him**   the street from the square to Freedman Town

484:25   **Augusttremulous lights**   'tremulous' because of the
summer heat and the distance through which Christmas
views them

484:26   **original quarry, abyss itself**   The Abyss or Void before the moment of creation, the quarry from which God
took primal matter to form the world. See 643. The language of the passage recalls Book II of Milton's *Paradise Lost*.

484:32   **his blood began again, talking and talking**   His passion, his anger, begins rising. There is some suggestion that
his blood is talking in sympathy with or rejection of (probably both) the Negro cabins he is approaching. On the one
hand he seems driven in the scene that follows by his own
belief that he has black blood. But the fight he tries to pick
with the black people he meets during his walk suggests the
compulsion of his "white" blood to assert dominance over

those he regards as inferior. The end of this chapter suggests his intense racial confusion.

484:36 **defunctive dust** This redundancy calls attention to
the dust itself, symbolic of death and mortality.

485:10 **cheap cloth and sweat** See entry 483:5.

485:16 **Jupe** diminutive for "Jupiter," a common name
among slaves and free blacks in the nineteenth century, and
more common in 1932 than now

485:18 **cap'm** captain, a friendly but deferential term of address once used by black men to white men. The black man
clearly does not want trouble with Christmas.

485:21 **the two heads, the light and the dark, seemed to hang
suspended in the darkness** The black man in this scene
stands not merely as a dark figure but as a shadow or reflection of the white man who regards him. After confronting
the black man, Christmas finds the unopened razor in his
hand, though 'It was not from fear.' He has encountered his
own dark shadow, his dark self. This döppelganger symbolizes the inner division which has plagued him throughout
his life.

485:26 **found that he had the razor in his hand** to defend
himself. The razor, with which he would have willingly killed
the black man, suggests metaphorically his suicidal tenden-
cies and at the same time signifies his willing identification
with the black race. See entry 475:23.

485:26 **It was not from fear** He wields the razor in anger at
the Negroes whom he hates yet who represent to him what
he has sometimes chosen to be.

485:27 **"Bitches!" he said, quite loud. "Sons of bitches!"**
Characteristically, Christmas insults the women first simply
for being women ('Bitches!'), then the men for being born of
women ('Sons of bitches!'). His anger is directed towards
women in general, and Joanna Burden in particular, but
since his misogyny is complexly bound up with his racism
(which is, to an extent, self-hatred), this encounter with black
women and men especially provokes him. See entry 478:13.

486:5 **grove** the grove of trees around the Burden house is

mentioned several times (486, 565, 585). The name Joanna
("Jana") is a form of "Diana," a fact associating Joanna with
the Grove at Nemi and the shrine to Diana discussed in Frazer's *The Golden Bough*. Frazer notes that shrines or sanctu-
aries dedicated to Diana were often located in groves and
that groves of trees were regarded throughout Europe as
holy places.° Juan Cirlot's characterization of Diana seems
more applicable to Joanna than to Lena Grove, who closely
parallels the Diana of Frazer's study. Cirlot observes: "her
characteristics vary with the phases of the moon: Diana,
Jana, Janus [Jana and Janus are feminine and masculine cog-
nates of Joanna]. This is why some mythological and em-
blematic designs show her as Hecate with three heads, a famous, triform symbol . . . . these threefold symbolic forms of
the underworld allude also to the perversion of the three
essential 'urges' of man: conservation, reproduction, and
spiritual evolution. If this is so, then Diana emphasizes the
terrible aspect of Woman's nature. Nevertheless, because of
her vows of virginity, she was endowed with a morally good
character as opposed to that of Venus."° In such a context,
Joe Christmas would serve symbolically the role of Diana's
male partner Virbius, who was, according to Frazer, "clearly
the mythical predecessor or archetype of the line of priests
who served Diana under the title of Kings of the Wood, and
who came, like him, one after the other, to a violent end."°
Cirlot's description of phases in the life of Diana (corre-
sponding to the three phases of Joanna's affair with Christmas), along with his discussion of her links to the underworld and the destructive aspects of the feminine, suggest
that Faulkner presents the mythical figure of Diana in two
diametrically opposed aspects: that of the fertility goddess
(Lena Grove) and the goddess of the underworld and destruction (Joanna Burden). See entries 401:31 and 411:37.

486:8 **the voices had not begun now either** the conflicting
voices of his mind and experience, those voices driving him
to violence against Joanna Burden. These are the same

voices he has heard earlier in the chapter: 'the voices of invisible negroes' (483), the 'voices talking laughing murmuring in a language not his' (483), the 'fecundmellow voices of negro women' (483), 'the rich murmur of womenvoices' (484).

486:9 **he heard the clock two miles away strike twelve** It is early Saturday morning as Christmas begins moving towards the Burden house.

CHAPTER VI

487:1 **Memory believes before knowing remembers. Believes longer than recollects, longer than knowing even wonders.** The events of one's life influence thought and action long before 'knowing' (the conscious mind) 'remembers' and comprehends them (even if one does not remember them at all). They influence human behavior longer than the mind consciously remembers them, longer than it can wonder why they happened and what they meant. These famous lines emphasize the importance of memory and the past on the present-day behavior and personality of the individual—a central theme of the novel. They introduce the six-chapter retrospective account of Joe Christmas's life at the orphanage, with the McEacherns, and at Joanna Burden's. About them François Pitavy observes: "memory is the intuition of a being who sees himself as the sum of his experiences—the significance of which is not apparent until an instant in the present recalls them into being; it is an assertion of the continuity of existence, an intimate adherence to a past become destiny even though it disappears into subconsciousness or oblivion." André Bleikasten agrees: "For Faulkner, memory is not just a mental function, but a man's whole relationship to his past, a relationship including his whole being, body, and mind." Noel Polk terms the induction to chapter VI "Faulkner's poetic rendering of Freud's description of the unconscious."°

487:3 **Knows remembers believes a corridor** Of this passage Karl Zender writes: "This phrase enacts in inverse order the process of mind described [in the first two sentences]. Joe's conscious mind 'knows' that he grew up in an orphanage because it 'remembers' his being there. But Joe's memory 'believes' far more than this fact. It 'believes' the weight of emotionality conveyed in the remainder of the passage, a weight that will never allow him to know or remember the orphanage neutrally." Noel Polk calls this phrase "a backward progression (into Joe's unconscious, which is what chapter VI and the [five] chapters following are: all of the childhood trauma that Joe has suppressed) from consciousness (knows/remembers) into unconsciousness (memory/believes)."° The phrase thus constitutes a bridge between the present time of the novel and Joe Christmas's conscious mind to the past, which resides in his memories, both conscious and unconscious.

487:3 **long garbled cold echoing building** Joe's memory of the building has been 'garbled'—obscured, confused—by the passage of time.

487:10 **in and out of remembering but in knowing constant** He may not always consciously remember these children, but their influence on his life, on his attitude towards life ('knowing'), is always apparent.

487:12 **yearly adjacenting chimneys** 'Adjacenting' = increasing in number. Each year, as more factories are built, more chimneys appear, and the city grows more cramped and industrialized.

487:14 **he was like a shadow ... sober and quiet as a shadow** The two occurrences of this word in one sentence, only two pages after the encounter at the end of chapter V between Christmas and the shadowy black man, is hardly coincidental. In the sixth chapter, the shadow self becomes the self of his past, which Christmas casts behind him in the present. Throughout the novel shadows are often associated with Christmas, either as aspects of his appearance and behavior, or as part of his immediate environment. Metaphorically, shadows suggest human mortality ('the shadow of autumn was upon her [Joanna]'—593), the past, and the uncertainty of Christmas's racial identity, a meaning Joanna invokes with her grandfather's words: 'You must struggle, rise. But in order to rise, you must raise the shadow with you. . . . The curse of the black race is God's curse. The curse of the white race is the black man who will be forever God's chosen because He once cursed Him' (585–86). See entry 484:36.

A related connotation concerns the shadow as what Juan Cirlot calls "the negative 'double' of the body, or the image of its evil and base side. Among primitive peoples, the notion that the shadow is the alter ego or soul is firmly established. . . . 'Shadow' is the term given by Jung to the primitive and instinctive side of the individual."° Hence, the 'black shadow' is the other self or other side of the white race. Applied to Christmas, the shadow assumes various meanings. He can be seen as the "negative double," for in much of his behavior he embodies base and evil aspects of humanity. The misanthropic Christmas is the shadow, the alter-ego, of the conventional, civilized white world. By his own refusal to conform to a standard behavior or racial identity, he serves as a cultural reflector, exposing white cultural biases and prejudices. See entry 485:21.

487:20   **the dietitian**   She does more than prescribe the daily food for the children of the orphanage. Her tryst with Charley and its aftermath—young Joe's adoption by McEachern— literally taint Christmas's appetite for the rest of his life, establishing his aversion both to food prepared by women and to sex—an aversion strengthened by such later characters as Bobbie Allen.

487:23   **parchmentcolored finger**   This compound adjective calls attention to Joe's ambiguous racial heritage.

487:31   **womangarments:**   lingerie a woman might hang in her closet, slips and petticoats, for instance. It also suggests simply the strange and alien atmosphere of the closet and the clothing hanging there, all later associated in Joe's mind with the abstract and offending presence of Woman.

487:35   **wooden forms**   forms = benches and tables

488:4 **On that first day . . . he had gone directly there, who had never heard of toothpaste either** Just as the dietitian was nothing to him yet, he does not know the name for toothpaste 'either,' only that he likes the taste of the 'sweet and sticky substance.'

488:9 **parochial doctor** the local doctor. Or the doctor employed by the church parish or the local government which operates the orphanage.

488:19 **too young yet to escape from the world of women for that brief respite before he escaped back into it to remain until the hour of his death** This statement describes the pattern of Joe Christmas's life to come: his escape from the dietitian and from Mrs. McEachern briefly frees him from the dominion of women until he falls under the influence of Joanna Burden, which he never escapes until his death. On the other hand the statement offers a generalization about the lives of men.

488:31 **He saw by feel alone . . . By taste and not seeing he contemplated** Because of the darkness, he cannot see with his eyes: he must compensate with his other senses. He 'saw' the cylinder of toothpaste by feeling its shape and size; he 'contemplated' it by imagining how it would taste.

489:15 **rife, pinkwomansmelling obscurity** the smell of the woman and her garments (some of her undergarments are pink, and she is twice characterized with that color—488, 489), of the pink toothpaste, perhaps even of the sex which he does not know he is overhearing, all merged into one odor associated with Woman. The image grows from the relatively inoffensive image of 'pinkwomansmelling' to the 'womanfilth' of 496.

489:27 **little nigger bastard** The dietitian's main defense against the possibility that the child will tell on her is her increasingly energetic assertion that he is part black.

490:6 **strike the balance and write it off** The child believes he "owes" the dietitian a debt for his transgression with the toothpaste. He makes himself available for the expected

punishment, wanting her to total the damages so he can pay
his debt.

490:13   **The young doctor was now, even less than the child,
merely an instrument of her disaster and not even that of
her salvation**   The doctor was even less a cause of her problem than the child, whose presence behind the curtain accounts for her situation. Before, if the doctor had married
her, he could have saved her ('been the instrument of her
salvation') from being twenty-seven years old and unmarried. But that is no longer an issue for her. If anyone can
save her, it is the child, and she does not know his intentions.

490:35   **the muscles of his backside were becoming flat and
rigid and tense as boards**   as he prepares himself for a
spanking.

491:17   **Some**   some toothpaste

491:23   **he seemed to see ranked tubes of toothpaste**   Compare with 538: 'he seemed to see a diminishing row of
suavely shaped urns in moonlight, blanched.' The parallel is
a striking one, especially since both scenes help to explain
Joe's revulsion against women. See entry 538:18.

492:1   **her natural female infallibility for the spontaneous
comprehension of evil**   Note Mr. Compson's observation in
The Sound and the Fury that women "*have an affinity for evil for
supplying whatever the evil lacks in itself for drawing it around
them instinctively . . . fertilising the mind for it until the evil has
served its purpose*" (110). Compare with the opinions of the
people of Jefferson concerning women and evil, 446.

492:7   **the janitor**   As chapters XV and XVI confirm, the janitor is Doc Hines, the grandfather of Joe Christmas. In this
chapter he remains unidentified, a man with a link to the
child, but whose background remains undisclosed, thus deepening the mystery of the boy's origins and racial heritage.

492:7   **There was no ratiocination in it**   There was no logic
or thought in her going to the janitor; the act was instinctive.

492:15   **She would have passed him without knowing him,
even though he was a man.**   Though he is a man and she is

desperate for a man, he is too old and unattractive for her. Now, however, she has a use for him.

493:13 **I've got to know . . . Tell me. Tell me, now.** The dietitian wants him to verify her suspicion that the child is partially black, so she can proceed with her plan to remove him from the orphanage before he tells on her.

493:14 **And Charley may—will—** Charley may be fired or may stop paying attention to me, or both.

493:16 **I know who set him there** i.e., God set him there

493:17 **a sign and a damnation for bitchery** proof of, punishment for, the sexual evil that produced the child, according to the janitor

493:21 **Aint I made evil to get up and walk God's world?** Hines apparently refers to his belief that by fathering the daughter who later became the mother of Joe, he is responsible for (he 'made') the evil that now walks the world.

493:22 **A walking pollution in God's own face** The child, the product of sin, is now sin incarnated in human form, and Hines expresses shock that this 'walking pollution' so far remains unpunished and is allowed to walk the world in front of God's eyes. Hines often seems to be quoting or at least alluding to biblical passages, but much of what he says is biblical only in tone.

493:23 **Out of the mouths of little children** the other children of the orphanage, whose insults, Hines believes, speak the truth about the boy's racial identity. These words come from the Bible: "Out of the mouths of babes and sucklings hast thou ordained strength" (Psalms 8:2); and "Have ye never read, Out of the mouths of babes and sucklings thou hast perfected praise" Matthew 21:16).

493:25 **name of his damnation** Because Hines believes that God has cursed Negroes and that the boy has Negro blood, the word 'Nigger' signifies to him the boy's damnation.

493:29 **the sign, wrote again in womansinning and bitchery** In some vaguely crazed sense, Hines believes that Christmas will play a part in God's plan for the Last Judgment. Perhaps he believes the boy is the Anti-Christ, or an agent of the devil whom the Lord has assigned him the responsibility to watch over and oppose. He takes the dietitian's discovery of the boy in her closet as the Lord's 'sign' that His apocalyptic plans for the boy will soon be made clear. Hines takes the Paulist position that women, as vessels of sexual evil, make it possible for men to fall prey to the sins of lechery and fornication.

493:38 **madam** The head of a whorehouse is a 'madam,' the term Hines uses to refer to the matron who runs the orphanage.

494:10 **the weight of the Lord's remorseful hand** Hines means that the dietitian has felt remorseful for the past three days, waiting for whatever punishment may come, not that the Lord feels remorse for whatever punishment he is going to inflict: Hines's God shows no compassion for anyone, especially sinful women.

494:12 **my sin is greater than your sin . . . To what I done. . . . I done bore mine five years** Hines is explaining why he works as janitor at the orphanage—as a kind of mortification for his sin. That sin is unclear. Perhaps he feels guilt for having allowed his daughter Milly to die in childbirth five years earlier. Or maybe he considers it a sin to have fathered a daughter who would sleep with a circus hand and give birth to a Negro bastard. This happened, according to his wife in chapter XVI, because he was in jail for fighting when his daughter was born, and she warned him then that one day the devil might appear to 'collect his toll' (674). In any case, his self-assigned penance has been to watch over the "damned" child. He brags that the dietitian's suffering has been nothing compared to his: 'I done bore mine five years.' His pride is perverse, but it is also the only sign that he feels remorse, or at least that he recognizes his behavior as sinful. Significant or not, Hines's eyes are gray in color—symbolic of the mortification of sins: "Brown and gray, lifeless colors, the color of ashes, are used in religious habits to signify mortification, mourning, and humility."°

494:17 **handful of rotten dirt** A 'handful of rotten dust' is what Hightower imagines will be left of him after his idyllic life as a minister in Jefferson ends (753). Hines uses the expression in a different context, but in both cases it connotes mortality and insignificance. It is also a possible allusion to Eliot's *The Waste Land*: "I will show you fear in a handful of dust,"° and to Genesis 3:19, "for dust thou art, and unto dust shalt thou return."

494:19 **womanfilth** Hines uses this term to denote what he deems the dietitian's filthy and trivial doings—filthy because she seeks to hide her fornication with the doctor, trivial because she is a woman. In a larger sense Hines uses the term to denote the sexual evil of women, especially as symbolized in menstrual blood. Hines and Christmas both regard women as sexually evil predators who connive to tempt and devour men. Joe is repulsed when he discovers that Bobbie Allen is tainted by such filth, and he kills Joanna Burden, among other reasons, because he feels she has drowned him in a 'whispering of gutter filth' (477).

494:31 **nigger orphanage** In Memphis, Tennessee, in the late 1890s (the time of chapter VI), orphanages, like practically everything else, were racially segregated. The dietitian knows that if she reveals the child is a Negro, he will immediately be sent from the orphanage for whites to one for blacks. Conditions at white orphanages were more comfortable.

495:2 **she began to open her legs and close them slowly** The dietitian engages in this masturbatory behavior as a kind of emotional and physical release after deciding how to deal with the child she believes will betray her.

495:7 **her body open to accept sleep as though sleep were a man** Metaphorically, her body waits for sleep to enter her as a man would enter her during intercourse. See entry 477:35.

95:21 **Dont you know that they . . . .** Don't you know that those in charge of the orphanage don't allow us to have men in our rooms?

495:31 **she was like a puppet** This metaphor foreshadows the figure of the pawn moved by the Player in the nineteenth chapter, 741:7.

495:31 **in some burlesque of rapine and despair** She is, in effect, overacting, like the suffering heroine of silent movies or vaudeville.

495:33 **as if the puppet in the midst of the scene had gone astray within itself** as if the puppet had begun to act on its own, independent of the puppeteer; or, as if the strings controlling it have tangled, and the puppet falls in on itself, motionless, as the dietitian is here

496:3 **If the Lord Himself come into the room of one of you . . . you would believe He come in bitchery** Hines thinks the dietitian believes he has come to her for fornication; in fact, she is distressed at his intrusion while she is undressed.

496:13 **Dont lie to me, to the Lord God** Hines believes himself a prophet, God's representative.

496:21 **Jezebel** whore. In the Old Testament, Jezebel is the Phoenician queen of Ahab, king of Northern Israel. She was a zealous worshipper of Baal. Her religion, as well as the sexual practices associated with it, accounts for her promiscuous, licentious reputation among Biblical historians.° Since the seventeenth century Jezebel has been used as an epithet for "wanton whore" (OED).

496:24 **the eyes released her and enveloped her again** an extension of the metaphor first introduced in 496:10 ('those bright, still eyes that seemed not to look at her so much as to envelop her') and developed further in 496:20 ('his eyes seemed to contract upon her shape and being'): the eyes of Doc Hines become an hypnotic, controlling agent which the dietitian cannot escape until he releases her.

496:37 **At breakfast time the next morning the janitor and the child were missing** The janitor takes the child away because he believes God has appointed him to watch over the boy. The dietitian has just agreed that if the child is black he will be removed from the white orphanage to a black one.

The janitor knows that in such an event he won't be able to watch over the boy. He thus takes him to Little Rock and tries to place him in another orphanage where he can continue his strange vigilance.

497:11 **She looked as if she had not slept** The matron, not the dietitian. Faulkner makes this clear in the following line, but the temporary ambiguity emphasizes the dietitian's serenity.

497:15 **Little Rock** capital of Arkansas, about 135 miles from Memphis.

497:27 **sat in the door yonder . . . watching that child** The word for Hines's job, janitor, derives from the Latin for door or gate, and thus from the name Janus, the two-faced Roman God of doors and gates.

497:32 **the night . . . they found the baby on the doorstep** See 682–83 for Doc Hines's account of this night.

497:33 **When Ch—** When Charley. The dietitian starts to call her lover by his first name but stops when she realizes that such familiarity might make the matron suspicious.

498:28 **jellied look** worried, confused, fatigued look

498:28 **as if she were trying to force them to something beyond their physical cohesiveness** as if she were trying to make them see beyond their ability to see; as if she were struggling to understand beyond her ability to understand

499:1 **We must place him. We must place him at once** 'place' = 'find a family that will adopt him.'

499:23 **perhaps because of it** that is, perhaps he liked her because she mothered him

499:24 **adult women who ordered his eating and washing and sleeping** ordered = regulated, controlled. This is another point at which Faulkner carefully establishes the origins of his protagonist's misogyny. The next line makes clear that the boy regards such women as his enemy.

499:29 **suffering her** tolerating her

499:32 **memory had forgotten her** He had consciously forgotten her.

499:38 **secret sibilance in which a half dozen young girls**

prepare the seventh one for marriage A 'sibilance' is a soft 's' or 'sh' sound, as the 'sh' in "hush." A 'secret sibilance' is a quiet whispering. The narrator compares the adoption of an orphan to a wedding, but the boy experiences it as a leavetaking, a death and funeral.

500:2 **batebreathed** The prepositional phrase "with bated breath" has been changed to an adverb meaning "spoken with shortened or moderated breathing"—spoken in a whisper while attempting to suppress their excitement.

500:39 **furnace room door** See entry 497:27. The association of Hines with a furnace room adds a diabolical element to his character, echoed later by the description of his 'tobaccostained goat's beard and mad eyes' (672).

501:38 **The car came up ... humming while they entered** the distinctive sound of electricity in a trolley car pausing to pick up or discharge passengers

503:9 **It was two weeks before Christmas** Joe was conceived in December 1895 (675), taken by Hines to the Memphis orphanage in December a year later ('two days before Christmas'—680), and in five more years adopted by McEachern in December 1901. See the Chronology.

503:15 **Perhaps memory knowing, knowing beginning to remember; perhaps even desire** An elaborative echo of the chapter's opening. Perhaps Joe's memory, remembering the night Alice disappeared, senses what is about to happen; perhaps he half-consciously begins to remember similar episodes; perhaps he consciously begins to desire the same to happen to himself.

503:17 **since five is still too young to have learned enough despair to hope** A child can want something, but without the experience of despair (the result of *not* having something he wants), cannot hope for it.

503:30 **a blunt clean hand shut ... into a fist** The 'blunt clean hand,' the 'fist,' is one of the defining images by which Joe remembers McEachern.

503:33 **polished by hand** Faulkner stresses here the deliberation with which McEachern cares for his appearance, by

which he lives his life. These carefully polished shoes contrast with the clumsily polished shoes for which McEachern
later whips his foster-son Joe at the beginning of chapter VII.

503:38 **yet not deliberately harsh** The first of a number of
hints by which Faulkner suggests that McEachern is not in-
tentionally harsh or cruel but is himself the victim of a harsh
spiritual upbringing and environment.

504:5 **his parentage** Like Doc Hines, McEachern assumes
that most orphaned children are illegitimate. The matron is
arranging for the adoption of Christmas by white parents,
despite the dietitian's insistence that he is a Negro. To do
otherwise would be to admit that her orphanage had har-
bored a Negro.

504:9 **he was left on the doorstep here on Christmas eve will
be five years this two weeks** On Christmas Eve, two weeks
from now, it will be five years to the day since he was left
here.

504:34 **McEachern** There are quite a few McEacherns (with
variant spellings of the name) in Faulkner's native Lafayette
County. Most of them now pronounce the name *Mc-ECK-
ern*, with the second syllable accented.°

504:37 **with us he will grow up to fear God** Ecclesiastes 12:
13: "Fear God, and keep his commandments: for this is the
whole duty of man." According to Jesse Coffee, the Hebrew
word for 'fear' means "reverence." McEachern, however, intends the literal English meaning, "to be afraid of."°

504:38 **abhor idleness and vanity** McEachern is echoing
such biblical admonitions as Ecclesiastes 10:18 ("Through
idleness of the hands the house leaketh") and Acts 14:15
("Ye should turn from these vain things unto the living
God").

504:38 **despite his origin** his probable illegitimacy. See entry 504:5.

504:39 **the promissory note which he had signed with a tube
of toothpaste on that afternoon two months ago was recalled**
The 'promissory note' is the punishment Joe still expects for

being caught in the dietitian's closet (see 490:4). In a promissory note, one promises to pay a debt at some future time. When payment is demanded, the note is 'recalled.' With McEachern's arrival Joe's note is recalled. In payment for the 'promissory note' which he 'signed with toothpaste,' Faulkner's Joseph is sold into the McEachern wilderness. By allowing the "sale" to occur (he had little choice), Christmas becomes the executor of his own fate—an analogy whose hollowness Faulkner implies in the adjective 'oblivious': that is, Christmas did not know what was happening to him when he was adopted. He remains a victim of the debt incurred by the toothpaste incident, which he will spend the rest of his life paying off.

505:4 **frozen and rutted lane** See 483:24 and 740:2.

505:9 **pointing up the lane with a mittened fist which clutched the whip, toward a single light which shone in the dusk** Christmas's first image of home is joined to the 'fist' and 'whip,' symbols of the uncompromising authority that will be the main element in McEachern's relations with the boy.

505:13 **rocklike** Faulkner applies this word to McEachern four times: 507, 516, 549. It is apparently related to McEachern's first name, Simon, the first name of the Apostle Peter, to whom Christ said "Thou art Peter, and upon this rock I will build my church" (Matthew 16:18). The Greek *petras* means "rock" and is employed here in the well known pun on Peter's name, which Faulkner may be exploiting in his characterization of McEachern. Unfortunately, applied to McEachern, 'rocklike' means stubborn inflexibility and unswerving faith.

505:16 **And he was not old enough to talk and say nothing at the same time.** He was not old enough to know the skill of idle social small talk, of how to acknowledge politely statements that call for no real response.

505:21 **two abominations are sloth and idle thinking, the two virtues are work and the fear of God** Proverbs 19:15 ("Slothfulness casteth into a deep sleep; and an idle soul shall suffer hunger"); Psalms 111:10 ("The Fear of the Lord is the beginning of wisdom"); Proverbs 16:6 ("By the fear of the Lord men depart from evil").

505:31 **eagering, homing, barning** becoming more eager, perking up as they approach the home and barn which they know means food, water, and rest

505:34 **when memory no longer accepted his face, accepted the surface of remembering** when he could no longer remember the man's face, or the superficial details of the episode, but could still recall the moment that made the greatest impact on him: McEachern's decision that Christmas was a heathenish name that would have to be changed

505:38 **Christmas. A heathenish name. Sacrilege** McEachern feels that his adopted son's last name violates the Third Commandment: "Thou shalt not take the name of the Lord thy God in vain" (Exodus 20:7). It is nonetheless ironic, and a mark of the unyielding rigidity of McEachern's faith, that he regards the word Christmas as heathenish.

506:15 **There was no need to bother about that yet. There was plenty of time.** Because he is wholly secure in his identity as Joe Christmas, because he does not fear that McEachern might strip that identity from him, Joe does not need to worry yet over what he knows his new foster-father will try but will fail to accomplish.

CHAPTER VII

507:1 **memory knows this; twenty years later memory is still to believe** *On this day I became a man* Christmas looks back to the experience about to be recounted—his resistance to learning the catechism and to accepting Mrs. McEachern's offer of food and sympathy—as the day he achieved manhood. Significantly, manly behavior here means rebellion against both male authority and mothering women. Moreover, the specific reference to twenty years and the verbs 'believe' and 'know' suggest that he remembers this episode well. The chapter focuses on Joe's resistance to any force that might violate his integrity—his foster parents, love and sex, religion. In this sense the opening sentence applies to each of the episodes it recounts.

An alternative reading: the day Christmas remembers as the one on which he became a man may refer specifically to the night he brained his foster father McEachern with a chair at the schoolhouse dance. In this reading, the attack on McEachern, which Christmas remembers as the culminating event of his childhood and adolescence, is prepared for by the narratives of chapters VII and VIII and their emphases on rebellion against affection, religion, and authority.

507:6 **melodeon with its pedals** a small keyboard organ which produces sound when a bellows, driven by foot-pedals, forces air through reeds. To play, one sits on a chair or bench in front of the melodeon, pumps the pedals, and presses the keys.

507:7 **larkspur** delphinium, a biennial flower grown for its tall, brightly colored, spike-like blooms.

507:9 **nickel lamp** a nickel-plated kerosene lamp°

507:15 **Presbyterian catechism** A catechism is a handbook composed of a series of questions and answers by which one learns and recites the tenets of a particular religion. Presbyterian clergy use a Large Catechism while a Shorter Catechism is intended for children—probably the one McEachern is trying to make his foster son learn. The Presbyterian catechism emphasizes the Calvinist concepts of predestination and Original Sin, concepts central to the Presbyterian faith and, ironically, ones Christmas learns all too well.°

507:17 **glazed shirt** a shirt so heavily starched and ironed that it appears to be 'glazed'

508:3 **beaten face** See 521:13.

508:6 **dress of rusty yet often brushed black** Mrs. McEachern's church-going dress, probably made of a wool twill cloth dyed black. Such cloth, with much wear, takes on a rusty appearance. She has 'often brushed' it to keep it presentable.

508:9 **she saw or heard through a more immediate manshape or manvoice, as if she were the medium and the vigorous and ruthless husband the control** She is like the spiritual medium in a séance, through which a stronger force (her husband) speaks and acts. Hence, she is her husband's puppet, carrying out his will without question.

508:33 **harness strap** a strap of heavy leather°

509:13 **You would believe that a stable floor, the stamping place of beasts, is the proper place for the word of God:** McEachern forgets that Christ was born in a stable.

509:21 **rapt, calm expression like a monk in a picture** a face of piety and devotion, the expression of a martyr, superior to the pain he suffers

509:29 **pamphlet** the catechism

510:25 **faded mother hubbard** loose-fitting, shapeless dress. Mrs. McEachern's change of clothes indicates her awareness that the struggle between father and son, which has lasted most of the morning, will not be resolved in time for church.

510:26 **cedar bucket** Cedar is a wood resistant to rot and decay, an important property for a bucket used in a well.

511:9 **not the overalls in which he went to the field** because he does not work on Sundays

511:21 **cutdown underwear** The boy is wearing the under-clothes of a grown man, reduced in size to fit him.

511:26 **an orphan, who was dear to God** "In thee the fatherless findeth mercy," Hosea 14:3 (Revised Standard, "In thee the orphan finds mercy").

511:38 **the man's hand appeared now as if it had been dripped in blood** Literally, the light from the lamp shines through and around McEachern's hand, making it appear red.

512:13 **weak and peaceful** Joe feels 'weak' from the morning's ordeal and the lack of food; he feels 'peaceful'—calm and unthreatened—because he has resisted McEachern's efforts to make him learn the catechism.

512:15 **full dark** In the South, the period immediately after sunset, while some light still lingers, is 'first dark.' The arrival of complete darkness is 'full dark.'

513:1 **her hands folded into her apron** Whether she has placed her hands in the apron pockets, or has 'folded' and pleated the apron up so that it covers her hands, this posture signifies her nervous concern for Joe, her desperate desire to convince him that she is on his side.

513:6 **calm as a graven face** A 'graven face' is one carved from wood or stone. The ordeal of the catechism has served as an initiation for Christmas, strengthening in him his foster-father's traits of stubbornness and rigidity. Throughout the episode McEachern has been described as 'rocklike' (507), as having a 'bearded face as firm as carved stone' (509), 'a nose, a cheek jutting, granitelike, bearded to the caverned and spectacled eyesocket' (512). Now the boy, reposed in the attitude and form of a carved effigy, assumes this appearance himself. See 517:1.

513:9 **He dont know it. I waited until he was gone and then I fixed it myself** Mrs. McEachern tries to win the boy's favor by sympathizing with him, taking his side against her husband. She has also brought him supper. Yet he views her food and sympathy as a greater threat to his manhood than the catechism. His resistance to her is an important aspect of his entrance into manhood. This scene is directly linked to the aftermath of the primal scene in the dietitian's room in chapter VI. He views all food offered by women as corrupted by the female desire to smother and devour him. Throughout the novel he refuses food that women offer him.

513:13 **dumping the dishes and food and all onto the floor** See chapter XI, 574, where Christmas throws against the wall the food Joanna Burden has fixed for him.

513:15 **monstrance** transparent or glass-faced container which holds the consecrated Host—the bread, blessed and declared sacred—used in the ritual of holy communion

513:28 **memory knew what he was remembering** Memory understood; that is, he understood what he remembered.

513:31 **outraged food** 'outraged' = the food's splattered appearance on the floor. Faulkner often uses 'outraged' to signify something violently disturbed or disrupted from its natural state.

514:23 **womanshenegro** In this coined word Faulkner embodies the two things Christmas most fears and hates—women and blacks—thus partially explaining the violence with which he reacts to the girl on the shed floor.°

514:27 **he seemed to look down into a black well and at the bottom saw two glints like reflection of dead stars** The 'black well' is the girl's face, specifically her eyes. This image suggests that Christmas sees himself in her eyes: not merely in the reflection, but in his recognition of racial kinship. That is, as he stares at her he perhaps half-consciously senses that he is staring at someone of what he believes to be his own race. This helps account for the violence of his reaction: against sex, women, and Negroes as well; in another sense he reacts in shame to the degradation to which the boys have submitted the girl. This is a doppelgänger image similar to the one at the end of the fifth chapter; see entry 485:21.

514:34 **enclosed by the womanshenegro** the embodiment of his worst fears. Joe experiences his characteristic reaction to women here: he feels that by having sex with the girl he will in some way permit her to capture and devour him. His feelings are complicated by the fact that she is black.

514:38 **rage and despair** at how his reaction to the girl totally overwhelmed him, his behavior before his friends, and the emotions he experienced as he looked down at the girl on the shed floor

515:36 **The evening star was rich and heavy as a jasmine bloom** The evening star is the planet Venus, symbolic of spiritual, physical, and romantic love. Its appearance, just after Christmas's sordid first sexual encounter, is a brooding ironic force. Christmas has entered another stage in his rebellion against McEachern and authority. The evening star possesses a particularly ambiguous, multivalent symbolism. The jasmine is a fairly small shrub-like plant that blooms in the evenings and whose blossom exudes a heavy fragrance. Venus blooms bright and low in the sky just as the jasmine blooms fragrant and low against the ground.

516:39 **a post or a tower upon which the sentient part of him mused like a hermit, contemplative and remote with ecstasy and selfcrucifixion** Christmas does not suffer from McEachern's punishment: he receives it in a kind of 'ecstasy' of suffering because his ability to endure pain signifies his successful resistance to McEachern's will. Physical torture thus becomes for Joe a substitute for religion.

517:3 **As they approached the kitchen they walked side by side** The beating administered and accepted, as both McEachern and Joe deemed right and proper, they now go to the house together, unified: 'he and the man could always count upon one another, depend upon one another' (516). Joe feels comfortable with McEachern, who behaves according to a consistent and logical pattern, while he finds Mrs. McEachern more difficult to understand, thus more dangerous.

517:33 **forenoon** late morning, a term not much heard anymore

518:2 **unrecking** unconcerned, unthinking

518:7 **come up** come in from the fields

518:18 **McEachern was sitting on a wooden block in the door** like the orphanage janitor who sits in the door and watches Christmas on the playground (500–01)

519:17 **the responsibility of the owner to that which he owns under God's sufferance** 'sufferance' = permission, toleration

519:38 **almost of a height** almost equal in height

520:13 **belike** perhaps, most likely, like as not

520:15 **He heard his mouth say the word with a kind of shocked astonishment** as if his body had betrayed him, and he were not really responsible for the lie

520:38 **butter money** money earned through the sale of butter she churned herself, like Mrs. Armstid's egg money in chapter I

520:39 **Simon** McEachern's first name, also the first name of the apostle Peter, to whom McEachern is at points implicitly compared: see entry 505:13

521:9 **neat screw of graying hair and the skirt** Throughout the novel, gray or graying hair is associated with women: Mrs. Armstid (411), Joanna Burden (465, 576), Mrs. Hines (655, 655), and Mrs. McEachern. Joanna Burden's graying hair links her to the vaguely remembered image of his foster mother.

521:14 **an attenuation** gradual weakening caused by her husband, whose treatment has 'hammered [her] stubbornly thinner and thinner like some passive and dully malleable metal.' To attenuate means to make thin by extending or stretching out.

521:27 **Kneeling before him she was trying to take off his shoes . . . she fetched a basin of hot water . . . . 'I done washed just yesterday,' he said** Foot washing is a religious ritual practiced by such fundamentalist Protestant sects as the Pentecostal, Holiness, and Brethren groups, and by the

Churches of God. Not observed by any of the major Protestant churches, it demonstrates one's humility and desire to serve fellow Christians. Its source is John 1:1–17, where Christ washes the feet of his disciples, explaining "Know ye what I have done to you? Ye call me Master and Lord: and ye say well; for so I am. If I then, your Lord and Master, have washed your feet; ye also ought to wash one another's feet."

522:15 **He was waiting for the part to begin which he would not like, whatever it was, whatever it was that he had done. . . .** He remembers the episode in chapter VI of the dietitian, who was kind to him only because she wanted something of him (something he didn't understand then either). He interprets Mrs. McEachern's sitting beside his bed as the precursor of the punishment he will suffer for whatever he has done wrong.

522:19 **It began on that night.** 'It' = Mrs. McEachern's unceasing attempt to win him over, which Joe interprets as her attempts to weaken him, to 'make me cry' (523)

522:31 **he thought that he would tell her . . . who in her helplessness could neither alter it nor ignore it** that 'McEachern has nursed a nigger beneath his own roof'

522:33 **the man whose immediate and predictable reaction to the knowledge would so obliterate it as a factor in their relations that it would never appear again** McEachern would refuse to believe that his foster-son was part-black, because that would mean having to admit that he had made a serious mistake in adopting the boy. But if 'their relations' means the relations of McEachern and his wife, the passage can be paraphrased: McEachern would react to the knowledge that his foster-son was part-black by permanently casting him out of the house, and refusing to mention him ever again, thus 'obliterating' him as a factor in his relations with his wife (much as Hines apparently did with his daughter Millie after her death).

523:6 **a woman's affinity and instinct for secrecy, for casting**

a faint taint of evil about the most trivial and innocent actions Compare with the dietitian's 'natural female infallibility for the spontaneous comprehension of evil,' 492; see entry 492:1.

523:16 **terrific nickels and dimes (fruit of what small chicanery and deceptions with none anywhere under the sun to say her nay he did not know)** The coins are 'terrific'—astounding, awesome, significant, terror-filled—because of the difficulty and stealth with which Mrs. McEachern collected each one of them, because of the attempt they represent to seduce Joe. Joe regards Mrs. McEachern's deceptions as examples of a woman's instinct for secrecy and evil.

523:22 **making a secret of the very fact which the act of trusting was supposed to exemplify** Trust is supposed to involve honesty and openness, yet Mrs. McEachern trusts Joe not to reveal the secret acts by which she deceives McEachern, thus implicating him in the deception.

523:32 **moonlight** Christmas and moonlight are associated frequently. See especially 524, 538, 554, 563, 591: Moonlight is the light of unreality, of shadows, and is another signification of Christmas's separation from the world. The moon is closely associated with the night "maternal, enveloping, unconscious and ambivalent because it is both protective and dangerous and the pale quality of its light only half-illuminating objects. Because of this, the moon is associated with the imagination and the fancy as the intermediary realm between the self-denial of the spiritual life and the blazing sun of intuition."°

523:33 **the steady murmur of the man's voice as it mounted the stairway on its first heavenward stage** This deliberately archaic metaphor of climbing stairs towards heaven or perfection characterizes McEachern's whole attitude towards religion, life, and redemption: blind adherence to Biblical law and principle and no allowance for human nature and frailty.

523:35 **they would have had me** They—his foster-parents—

would have defeated, overcome, overpowered him. Christmas believes that what made him a man (note the chapter's
first sentence) was his resistance not only to learning the catechism but also to Mrs. McEachern's attempts at kindness. Resisting a woman—as well as his father, and God—
made him a man.

CHAPTER VIII

524:1 **Moving quietly, he took the rope** In contrast to chapter IX, related from McEachern's perspective, chapter VIII is narrated from Christmas's perspective. See entry 547:1. This opening scene occurs on the evening of the day that McEachern confronts Joe about the missing heifer. The chapter recounts the events leading to that confrontation, focusing mainly on Joe's affair with Bobbie Allen.

524:4 **with more than a year of practice** The text suggests that Joe's affair with Bobbie Allen lasts only a few months, not more than a year. See the Chronology. He was probably crawling out the window for other reasons before he met Bobbie: to see his friends, to hunt, or to do other things his foster parents would disapprove of.

524:6 **the shadowlike agility of a cat** Christmas is compared to a cat six times: here, 565, 567, 568, 568, 601. The comparisons emphasize his nocturnal nature (see entry 475:19) and his separation from the routine of normal human beings.

524:9 **spider skein** strand of spider web

524:17 **He found it** The details of this discovery are inconsistent with 517–18, where McEachern finds the suit on the morning of the day he first strikes his son with his fists. Here it is nighttime. Christmas has crept from the house to the barn to learn that his father knows of the suit. Thus, while chapter VII clearly states that McEachern found the suit and told his son so later the same day, chapter VIII implies that Christmas learned of the discovery himself, at night after his parents were in bed, when he finds that the suit in its hiding place in the barn has been disturbed. Moreover, the next paragraph refers to the 'uproar about the heifer' (524). This is one of the few inconsistencies in the novel.

524:21 **after all the uproar about the heifer** the uproar of McEachern's discovery that Joe had sold the heifer, and of Mrs. McEachern's intercession on Joe's behalf. See entry 524: 17. This reference reveals that McEachern's discovery of the missing heifer, related on 517–521, has already occurred.

524:32 **dollar watch** probably a large Ingersoll pocket watch, which for years did sell for a dollar and which continued to be called a 'dollar watch' long after the price increased. The boy's purchase of the watch, along with the suit, is a sign of his growing independence, and of his desire to arrive on time for his date with Bobbie Allen. Joe's new watch is not running, because he has forgotten to wind it.

525:4 **highroad** the main road or highway

525:19 **movement among the shadows** See 547:34.

525:32 **did not look more than seventeen too** She looked to Joe as old as he was: seventeen. He is eighteen when his affair with her begins the next spring. See Chronology.

526:1 **always downlooking** This attitude may suggest to Joe that she is a shy and demure woman, but it is also a typical characteristic of the Madonna in painting and sculpture— an ironic inversion, for Bobbie Allen is no Madonna. According to G. G. Sill, "the figure of the mourning Mary develops into a subject of devotion called the Pietà . . . . In the famous example by Michelangelo, Mary is in the traditional pose of the grieving woman, her eyes downcast, head bowed, her body numb." Mary is traditionally depicted as 'downlooking' in pictures where she is holding and looking down upon the infant Christ.°

526:3 **Her eyes were like the button eyes of a toy animal: a quality beyond even hardness, without being hard.** a metaphor that characterizes without explaining the effect on Bobbie of her years as a prostitute. Her life has been so different from Joe's that there is no chance that he, with his inexperience, could ever comprehend the person she is.

526:11 **It began in the fall** Joe's acquaintance with, love
for, Bobbie Allen, began in the fall, though the actual love
affair did not commence until the following spring. See
Chronology.

526:17 **dinnertime** time of the midday meal

526:21 **and then at the sun** Like many farmers, McEachern
can estimate the time of day by looking at the sun's position
in the sky, and he probably trusts sun time over clock time.
He thus looks at the sun here to be sure that the clock is
right.

526:24 **examining and weighing the boy** judging whether
he is sufficiently mature to expose to the more sordid aspects
of adult life. The text raises the question of how McEachern
knows about the sordid character of the cafe. He has apparently visited it before, and has perhaps even confronted the
temptations hidden behind its inner door. But his parsimony
compels him to overlook the evils of the place in hopes of a
cheap meal.

526:26 **It cant be helped now** It's lunch time, we did not
bring our lunches with us, and there's nothing else to do now
but to buy and eat lunch in town. McEachern may take Joe
to the cafe because it is the least expensive place in town to
eat.

526:27 **The town was a railroad division point** "a town in
which a railroad division headquarters is located," a division
being "a large administrative unit (and area of the network)
of a railroad." Evidently, this is also the point where crews
change shifts, boarding and disembarking, the 'transient . . .
population of men . . . whose intermittent presence was pan-
dered to like that of patrons in a theatre' (526). This detail
in particular makes tempting the possibility that this town is
based on the actual town of Water Valley, which lies nineteen
miles south of Oxford and is itself the probable model of
Mottstown in the novel. According to the *Mississippi Guide*:
"Early identified as a railroad town, Water Valley experienced an overnight development when, after the [Civil] war,

the Illinois Central System absorbed a number of smaller railroads and located the main division points here. Until 1929, when the [repair and refitting] shops were moved . . . the town, entirely dependent upon its railroad, drew from them a comfortable prosperity."° If Mottstown *is* the town near which Christmas grew up, then his return there at the end of chapter XIV, where he thinks he has 'made a circle' (650), is a logical final stage in the pattern of circular repetition that has characterized his life, in contrast to the straight line of Lena Grove.

527:9   **not farmers and not townsmen either**   men who would frequent this sort of place: gamblers, bootleggers, potential customers of a prostitute

527:24   **brasshaired**   hair the color and hardness of brass, dyed with a garish blonde color easily recognized as artificial, in a hard set which leaves it impervious to wind or rain

527:25   **belligerent and diamondsurfaced respectability**   a respectability worn as if a flag, a 'shield,' which almost dares one to challenge it, whose meticulously crafted design ('the false glitter of the careful hair, the careful face') cannot be broken or penetrated (because it is 'diamondsurfaced')

527:33   **equivocal men**   equivocal in that their purpose for being there is unclear

527:34   **slant their hats and their thwartfacecurled cigarettes** They wear their hats at a more rakish angle than is customary in a small North Mississippi community. Their cigarettes dangle down at various angles from their mouths. The cigarettes are 'curled' because the smoke spirals across ('athwart') the faces of the men and into the air. Christmas will soon adopt this casual, arrogant appearance. See, for instance, his first appearance in Jefferson, 421.

528:5   **That is the business of the town and not of yours.**   By refusing to explain, by implying that such matters are the concern of adults only, McEachern further enhances the restaurant's allure.

528:30   **the long, barren, somehow equivocal counter with the still, coldfaced, violenthaired woman at one end as though**

guarding it This scene with the woman, surrounded by the smoking men, standing guard at the end of the counter figuratively suggests the entrance to Hell: Bobbie Allen's sexuality, the sexuality of women, which Christmas has been raised to regard as evil, which he half-consciously senses in the bar's atmosphere, and to which he is attracted. The counter is 'equivocal' because Joe senses that considerably more goes on behind it than the mere serving of food.

Robert M. Slabey sees Mame, the 'woman at the end of the counter,' as the mythological figure of Demeter, and Bobbie Allen as Persephone: Bobbie's "'rape' takes place in a field; as a goddess of fertility her rites involved menstrual lunar aspects."°

529:4 **believing** *I do not know yet that in the instant of sleep the eyelid closing prisons within the eye's self her face* a deeper layer of thought, 'believing' before 'knowing': When I close my eyes to sleep I imprison the image of her face behind my eyelid ('within the eye's self'), and so I can 'see' (in my mind's eye) nothing but her face. The face his closed eye "sees," as the following passage reveals, is *'demure, pensive'*; *'tragic, sad, and young'*; *'waiting, colored with all the vague and formless magic of young desire,'* which means that he believes, with his eyes closed for sleep, that she holds the same feelings for him as he does for her.

529:8 **sleeping** *I know now why I struck refraining that negro girl three years ago and that she must know it too and be proud too, with waiting and pride* Joe half-consciously believes that he can explain why he lashed out, three years before, when his turn came with the black girl: he was saving himself for Bobbie, and he thinks that Bobbie must sense this too, and be proud of him and herself for having waited to share their first sexual experience with one another.

529:11 **love in the young requires as little of hope as of desire to feed upon** Love for the young is so much a condition of naive and romantic imaginations that realistic considerations (the fact that Joe did not expect to see the waitress again) do not temper it in the least.

530:1 **with a cigarette burning in one corner of his mouth . . . Joe was to acquire one of his own mannerisms** Note the description of how Joe smokes when he first arrives in town, 421.

530:7 **when life had begun to go so fast that accepting would take the place of knowing and believing** i.e., when he lost his idealism

530:10 **in a dirty apron which he wore as a footpad might assume for the moment a false beard** He did not look like a man accustomed to wearing an apron, as if he wore it as a disguise; 'footpad' = highway robber, an archaism.

530:11 **The accepting was to come later, along with the whole sum of entire outrage to credulity: these two people as husband and wife, the establishment as a business for eating, with the successive imported waitresses clumsy with the cheap dishes of simple food** Joe was later to understand and accept what he now does not realize: that the cafe is a front for prostitution, and probably other illegal activities, that his sexual 'holiday' with Bobbie Allen (he never wonders about her easy willingness to have sex with him) is a function of her profession. The 'successive imported waitresses' are 'clumsy,' of course, because they are not trained waitresses; they are prostitutes.

530:31 **Bobbie** When the proprietor calls for the waitress by this name, Joe believes for a moment she has been replaced by a man. See entry 540:31.

531:17 **because of her smallness partook likewise of that quality of his, of something beyond flesh** Joe sees Bobbie's smallness as a sign of innocence and vulnerability.

532:10 **his spirit wrung with abasement and regret and passionate for hiding** so humiliated he wanted to hide. Joe is embarrassed that he did not have enough money to buy pie and coffee, that he did not know how much they would cost, and most of all that the woman whom he loves and wants to impress had to come to his aid.

532:16 ***It's terrible to be young. It's terrible. Terrible.*** terrible to be young and naive, subject to the sort of embarrassment Joe has just experienced. Compare this agonizing complaint with Gail Hightower's romantic glorification of youth on 633.

532:26 **gramophone record . . . worn threading which blurred the voices** Old phonograph records were made of hard wax. Their grooves became worn after repeated playings, blurring and distorting the sound.

532:30 **misdoubt** mistrust

532:40 **it was again too fast and too complete to be thinking: *That is not a gift. It is not even a promise: it is a threat*** Joe instinctively knows that McEachern is daring him with the calf to fail at the responsibility of owning it. Once again the narrative explains Joe's unconscious thoughts in order to qualify the significance of what he consciously thinks: 'I didn't ask for it. He gave it to me. I didn't ask for it.'

533:32 **He heard, not hearing; he saw, not looking.** Though he was not consciously aware of them, the sights and sounds in the room nonetheless made an impression on him.

533:37 **Jack** a conventional, mildly contemptuous way of addressing a stranger

533:40 **unwinded by any movement** unstirred by air currents

534:3 **Hiram** short for Hiram Hayseed, another term of address for an anonymous stranger, this one implying the stranger is a hick, a country bumpkin

534:3 **Maybe you can make a girl there with a nickel** suggesting that Joe wants to buy the favors of a prostitute with a nickel. To 'make a girl' = to have sex with her.

534:5 **the coin sweating his hand, larger than a cartwheel, feeling** Again badly embarrassed, Joe is so conscious of the returned coin that his hand becomes moist with perspiration and the coin feels enormous, too large to hide.

534:19 **Can you tie that** Can you beat that?

534:21 **To another they must have looked like two monks met during the hour of contemplation** The 'hour of contemplation' is the "greater silence" of monastic life, when monks observe complete silence. It begins after the final liturgical prayer of the day and extends into morning hours.° Compare this sentence with 531:11: 'they must have looked a little like they were praying.'

534:26 "It's not McEachern," he said. "It's Christmas." Compare with 541:19, where Joe tells Max his name is McEachern. Joe believes that with Bobbie Allen he can be wholly honest, so he asserts his true identity and rejects the adopted name.

534:31 They were associated with Sunday and with church. So he could not notice them. Already women and religion form a potent combination in Joe's mind. He is as stubborn in his rejection of religion as is McEachern in trying to force him to accept it.

534:36 "They all want to," he told the others, "but sometimes they cant." They all want to have sex, but during their menstrual periods they cannot.

535:1 They thought differently They believed that women did not like sex.

535:6 ceremony suggesting the mystery with which the boy cloaks the facts of menstruation

535:9 to be discerned by the sense of smell and even of sight The boy draws on the mistaken notion that one can identify a menstruating woman by her odor or appearance.

535:11 the temporary and abject helplessness of that which tantalised and frustrated desire 'that' = vagina. In Joe's mind menstruating women are helpless, unable to have sex, trapped by the physical inconvenience of what is happening to them.

535:12 the smooth and superior shape in which volition dwelled doomed to be at stated and inescapable intervals victims of periodical filth Faulkner epitomizes in this image the paradoxical nature of woman in this novel, especially as Joe Christmas regards her. She is an ideal, 'a smooth and superior shape in which volition dwelled.' She controls her own life, especially her sexual availability. This on the one hand is what makes her 'superior' to men. Yet at moments she falls victim to a biological force beyond her control that renders her helpless and unavailable to men, who thus also fall victim. Note *The Sound and the Fury* (147): "Delicate equilibrium of periodical filth between two moons balanced with all that inside them shapes an outward suavity waiting for . . . liquid putrefaction." Although Faulkner emphasizes that such views are the distorted views of characters, he often seems unable to escape them.

535:18 **Joe was hidden in the barn. He stayed there all that day.** Joe hides to avoid confronting the boys who learned about female biology at the same time as he. So doing, he can evade temporarily the significance of what he has learned. He is also, we may assume, considering how to react to this new knowledge.

535:22 **he shot a sheep . . . Then he knelt, his hands in the yet warm blood of the dying beast, trembling, drymouthed, backglaring** Joe's precise motives in this passage are unclear, as is the meaning of this strange ritual, with which he seeks to buy immunity from knowledge of the menstrual cycle and the impurity of women. He acts irrationally, reacting to the trauma of what seems a horrible knowledge. He also appears quite frightened, probably of being caught ('trembling, drymouthed, backglaring'). One possible explanation for this behavior might lie in the Biblical symbolism of his ritual. In the Old Testament, the sacrifice of a sheep or lamb is a show of faith in God. Yet Christmas seeks to cleanse himself of the knowledge of sin (female sexuality) with the sheep's warm blood. In this sense the sheep is the symbolic Lamb of the New Testament, Christ. John the Baptist addresses Christ as "the Lamb of God, which taketh away the sin of the world" (John 1:29). Revelations repeatedly calls Christ "the Lamb," and describes the redeemed as those "who have come out of the great tribulation; they have washed their robes and made them white in the blood of the

Lamb." Hence, one "washed in the blood of the Lamb" has been "saved," or redeemed from sin.

McEachern has indoctrinated his foster son to believe that sexuality is evil. To rid himself of this evil, Christmas slays the sheep in a reenactment of the archetypal pattern of sacrifice and redemption. The text later clarifies this sacrifice when the narrator explains how Joe hoped that 'With the slain sheep he had bought immunity from it [knowledge of female sexuality]' (537). His abhorrence of blood—the blood that sustains life, that results from the process that insures life's continuation—symbolically and literally is an abhorrence of life evident in his misogyny. For Christmas, being washed in the blood of the lamb means being saved not from sin, but from life.

It is also possible that, rather than trying to immunize himself, he is simply seeking to habituate himself to menstrual blood by washing his hands in the blood of the slain sheep, in effect engaging in a sort of self-imposed initiation. ('Then he got over it, recovered. He did not forget what the boy had told him. He just accepted it. He found that he could live with it, side by side with it'—535:27)

535:31 **in the sense that a fact is forgotten when it once succumbs to the mind's insistence that it be neither true nor false** A fact (i.e., the fact of menstrual blood) can be forgotten when the mind can convince itself to ignore it.

535:34 **He met the waitress on the Monday night following the Saturday on which he had tried to pay for the cup of coffee** This refers to the preceding section, where Christmas meets Bobbie on his way out of the cafe and, presumably, makes a date with her (see 534). Why does she become interested in him? She may be impressed that he has come to the restaurant specifically to pay her the nickel he believes he owes her—probably one of the more chivalrous acts she has encountered in either of her professions. She is also flattered that he likes her and thinks her attractive. She may also be drawn to his innocence.

536:3 *To not let her find out that I dont know, that I will have to find out from her* Joe is anxious that Bobbie not learn he is a virgin.

536:16 **It's five miles.** five miles from the street corner to the McEachern farm

536:18 **a year later, remembering that night, he said, suddenly knowing** *It was like she was waiting for me to hit her* Because she is menstruating, Bobbie believes the boy will not want to have sex with her, that he will become angry and strike her. As she makes clear on 537 ('I forgot about the day of the month'), she should have known ahead of time that she would be menstruating and scheduled their meeting for another night. To her, as to Joe, sex and violence are closely linked.

536:21 **He could smell her, smell the waiting** a way of expressing his intense anticipation of what he believes will soon follow. Similar to the expression, "I was so close [to some unattained goal] I could almost smell it."

536:22 **still, wise, a little weary** Bobbie Allen, the prostitute, from much experience knows what to expect from this boy and is even a little wearied by the thought of it.

536:26 **I thought maybe they would be waiting for you.** 'they' = Max and Mame, whom Joe believes to be Bobbie's parents

537:1 **the fact** that women menstruate

537:2 **With the slain sheep he had bought immunity** immunity from the knowledge of female biology, and the sinful, impure nature it implies to him. The "buying" of immunity is a form of redemption to which the novel frequently alludes. According to Francis J. McConnell, "The idea of redemption in the [Old Testament] takes its start from the thought of property. Money is paid according to law to buy back something which must be delivered or reserved. From this start the word 'redemption' throughout the [Old Testament] is used in the general sense of deliverance. God is the Redeemer of Israel. . . . In the [New Testament] the idea of redemption has more a suggestion of ransom. Men are held under the curse of the law [Galatians 3:13], or of sin itself [Romans 7:23f]. The Redeemer purchases their deliverance by offering himself as payment for their redemption [Ephesians 1:7, 1 Peter 1:18]."° See entry 535:22.

537:3 **So he could not at first understand what she was trying to tell him** Having lived so long with what the boy had told him, and with the immunity he believed he had purchased by killing the sheep, he had put all knowledge of menstruation out of his mind, so that he did not recognize what Bobbie was telling him.

537:19 **How sick** What kind of sickness? In *The Sound and the Fury* 'sick' refers to Caddy Compson's pregnancy; here it refers to Bobbie's menstrual period. In both instances it characterizes a male character's distorted view of female biology.

537:36 **She told him** about menstruation

538:16 **the hard trunks, the branchshadowed quiet, hardfeeling, hardsmelling** The tree trunks are intensely masculine images in opposition to the feminine plants growing in the furrows through which he has run. These contrasting images suggest Joe's attraction to the masculine, his repulsion by the feminine. Note also the opening section of chapter VIII, where he moves towards the fateful schoolhouse dance down a lane 'bordered on each side by trees' casting shadows diagonally across the road. Throughout the novel he is typically surrounded by masculine elements whose influence he clearly prefers over the feminine.

538:18 **he seemed to see a diminishing row of suavely shaped urns in moonlight, blanched. And not one was perfect. Each one was cracked and from each crack there issued something liquid, deathcolored, and foul** This Platonic/Freudian vision of broken urns signifies Christmas's conception of female decay and depravity. Urns are a classic Freudian sexual symbol of the Female, yet the ones Joe imagines are cracked, with foul liquids flowing from them. His vision is stimulated by the furrowed earth through which he runs, 'with something growing in furrows.' The growing plants are the product of fertility—burgeoning life. Life repulses Christmas, for it involves sexual realities he cannot bring himself to acknowledge. Among the clearly phallic trees, 'the branchshadowed quiet, hardfeeling, hardsmelling,' he seeks shelter from these symbols of female fertility. His reaction here—vomiting at the vision of the urns—recalls his reaction to the toothpaste in chapter VI, where he also envisions 'ranked tubes of toothpaste, like corded wood.'

Elsewhere in *Light in August* the Keatsian urn is a symbol of timeless purity and natural harmony. In the first chapter it is associated with Lena Grove, whose quest for Lucas Burch is 'like something moving forever and without progress across an urn' (404). Women are 'the smooth and superior shape' of an urn (535). Christmas's negative perception of the urn ('Each one was cracked and from each crack there issued something liquid, deathcolored, and foul') clearly suggests the profound confusion of his life and personality.

539:2 **half dragged among the growing plants, the furrows, and into the woods, the trees** Christmas drags Bobbie Allen through the feminine furrows of growing plants into the phallic, masculine trees. His first sexual experience is an act of near-rape and self-centered lust that denies the normal purposes of sex—love and procreation. See entry 528:30.

539:21 **the woman** Bobbie Allen

539:24 **he had watched for years Mrs McEachern hide money in a certain place** In Sherwood Anderson's *Winesburg, Ohio*, in the chapter "Death," George Willard's mother hides money for him in a plastered-over hole in the wall, but she dies before telling him about it. Faulkner knew this novel well, and there is a clear similarity between how Mrs. McEachern conspires to deceive her husband and how Elizabeth Willard more openly opposes her husband Tom, as well as in each woman's relationship with her son.

539:33 **punching board** a gambling board frequently found in country stores at the time of this novel. A 'punching board' is a thick 'board' of layered paper with numerous small holes punched through it, often in patterns. The holes are covered on each side by sheets of paper. For a nickel or ten cents, the gambler buys the right to punch out one of the holes with a small key-shaped instrument and to remove the piece of paper inside. If the number on the paper matches one of the winning numbers printed on the front of the punching board, the customer wins a prize, usually money, a doll, or candy.

540:7 **John Jacob Astor** a name synonymous with wealth and prestige, referring either to the first American member of the Astor family, John Jacob Astor I (1763–1848), a fur merchant and capitalist who built what was thought to be the largest fortune of his day (some $20,000,000 at his death); to his grandson, John Jacob Astor III, also a fur trader, financier, and the wealthiest man of his time, who lived from 1822–1890; or to his great-grandson, John Jacob Astor IV, a New York hotel magnate, who died in the 1912 sinking of the *Titanic*

540:9 **She had covered herself** Though she is a prostitute, she is still modest enough to not to want Max to see her undressed. She has other shreds of decency and likely speaks truthfully when she says that she sees Joe because 'Maybe I like him' (540:20).

540:12 **A setup for hayseeds** a cozy arrangement ideal for the bilking of young, inexperienced lads from the farms

540:13 **Memphis** a large city in the southwestern corner of Tennessee, on the Mississippi River. In 1900 its population was 100,000 but had swollen to 250,000 in 1930.° Memphis in Faulkner's fiction is usually a city of prostitutes and liquor. In both *Sanctuary* and *The Reivers*, a Memphis whorehouse is a significant setting.

540:13 **Maybe I'd better start giving away grub too** Since you (Bobbie) are giving to Joe free what you are supposed to be selling, maybe I should follow your example by giving away food at the restaurant.

540:15 **I'm not doing it on your time** Bobbie argues that because she is seeing Joe during her off hours her affair with him costs Max nothing.

540:18 **good jack** a lot of money

540:27 **Romeo and Juliet** the young lovers of Shakespeare's 1595 play. Max invokes their names sarcastically.

540:28 **For sweet Jesus** an expression Joe later takes as his own. See 568, where he discovers the sweet peas and molasses Joanna has left in her kitchen.

540:31 **Max Confrey presenting Miss Bobbie Allen** This is the only time in the novel Bobbie is called by this name. It may be her name. Or it may be a joke: Max, the manager of a whorehouse, sarcastically announcing his star attraction, as P. T. Barnum might announce Tom Thumb. Faulkner borrowed the name from the title of the well known English and Southern Appalachian folk ballad about a young man who dies of love for a hardhearted woman. Faulkner uses the name ironically: unlike the woman of the song, Bobbie is neither young nor beautiful.

540:32 **the youth's companion** Max alludes to *The Youth's Companion*, a popular juvenile magazine published between 1827 and 1929.° Bobbie is no fit companion for youths.

540:34 **I just brought her change for a nickel** Max refers to the nickel that, earlier, Joe had come to the restaurant to pay back to Bobbie Allen. This event spawned a series of jokes from Max about how Joe is trying to 'make a girl . . . with a nickel' (534). He won't let go of the idea that the prostitute he brought to this town to make money is sleeping with a farm boy who's paying her nothing.

541:11 **She began to laugh** Bobbie laughs at Joe's gift, specifically remembering Mame's earlier question, 'Does he ever pay you' (540) and Max's general complaining about her relationship with the boy. She now calls both Max and Mame in to share the joke by proving that Joe really does pay her, in his own way.

541:19 **My name's Joe McEachern** Joe has just been addressed as Romeo, and he does not recognize either the lit-

erary allusion or the sarcasm, so he corrects Max by giving
his real name. He obviously considers 'McEachern' his public
name, the one under which he was raised and by which he is
known. See entry 534:26.

541:27 **Sometimes Christmas lasts a good while** A pun on
Joe's last name, ridiculing his gift of candy to Bobbie; also
perhaps a pun on his sexual prowess. Max jokes that although it is early summer (see Chronology), Bobbie is still
receiving 'Christmas' presents.

541:30 **on his face an expression a little placative and
baffled though not alarmed** Joe is probably 'baffled' over
why Max, who has just called him 'Romeo' for a second time,
can't get his name straight. His face is 'placative' in expression as if he does not want to anger Max, as if he wants to
allay whatever suspicions or doubts the man might have
about him.

541:32 **inscrutable and monklike face** an expressionless face,
one whose thoughts and emotions Joe cannot understand

542:5 **a drink on the house** In light of Max's involvement in
prostitution, the fact that he offers alcohol to Joe suggests
that he is also a bootlegger.

542:9 **Dont hold him in suspense because of his past behavior** Mame has just offered a drink, and Joe has not yet accepted. Max tells Mame to tell Joe the drink will be free, on
the house, so that he won't hesitate to accept it. See entry
540:34.

542:12 **Never tried anything on the house . . . For sweet
Jesus** Max's amazement that Joe has never had anything on
the house stems from his consternation that the boy has been
having sex with Bobbie for nothing, or almost nothing.

542:18 **the man, without looking at him, had never ceased**
Max kept his eye on the boy, studying him carefully, every
second he was in the room.

542:26 **It's all right** Joe is trying to reassure Bobbie about
Max's ribbing, to show he's not bothered by it either.

542:36 **even then he did not even know that he had not**

known what to expect to see   Joe was unaware that he did not know what a naked woman would look like.

542:40   **So this is it.**   So this is love; this is what it's like to be naked in bed with a woman.

543:21   **night now known, not to be desired, pined for**   Joe has now discovered the secrets of lying in the dark in bed with a woman, so he does not need to desire or long for them any longer.

543:27   **"I got some nigger blood in me."**
   Then she lay perfectly still, with a different stillness. Later in life Joe will make a habit of telling women he has slept with that he has 'nigger blood.' But this is the first time he has ever done so. Bobbie's 'different stillness' indicates she is carefully considering what he has told her, deciding whether to believe it and how to react. Although Joe 'does not seem to notice' her reaction, he will later use this revelation to horrify and enrage his sexual partners, to provoke arguments and fights, and to avoid having to pay prostitutes.

544:8   **More than p—More than Mr McEachern**   More than pa—. Although she addresses her husband in private as Simon (for example, see 520), before her foster-son Mrs. McEachern uses the more formal and respectful form of address. Thus she changes 'pa' to 'Mr McEachern.' She might also sense that the boy himself does not think of the man as 'pa.'

544:18   **Mrs McEachern may have told him so**   At the end of this paragraph on p. 205 of the typescript, Faulkner added, and then deleted: 'A month afterward, McEachern gave Joe the heifer calf.' Apparently this addition was meant to explain further why McEachern gave Joe the calf, as a response to what the man took to be the boy's desire to earn money for himself. Faulkner may have deleted the sentence because he felt it was unneeded, or because it showed McEachern in an uncharacteristic kind light.

544:24   **not for the actual fact, but because of his presence there**   not for the fact of his having sex with the woman he believed to be their daughter, but because he was having sex with her in their own house

544:31 **he had suggested it** He had suggested they meet somewhere other than her room. He never thinks it odd that he spends most of his time with Bobbie somewhere other than her house, her place of work, or that she might have reason for keeping him away from the house.

545:7 **He knew then what even yet he had not believed** Only through a violent expression of anger does Joe achieve understanding of why he is angry. When he strikes Bobbie he accepts the significance of his discovery that she earns her living by sleeping with men for money, knowledge he has been trying to avoid for two weeks.

545:12 **Even the reason for striking her was gone now** Having vented his anger and disbelief, Joe no longer has a 'reason' or need to strike her.

545:16 **telling him** explaining to him her job as a prostitute

545:21 **odorreek of all anonymous men above dirt** Listening to Bobbie, Joe imagines he can smell every man she has slept with, which to him means all the living men in the world ('above dirt' = not dead). The image encloses his discovery of the nature of evil in the world, the reality of sexual relations between men and women, the specific reality of Bobbie and her life.

545:29 **Two weeks later he had begun to smoke, squinting his face against the smoke, and he drank too** See 530:3. Joe's smoking, his squinting (in imitation of Max), and his drinking signify his disillusionment and his entry into the adult world where he now tries to ape the manner of other adult men.

545:34 **waitresses** waitresses during the day, prostitutes at night

545:39 **his loud, drunken, despairing young voice, calling her his whore** The word 'despairing' undercuts the new character Joe contrives to assume. He takes on this role because it seems to him the only one available, since he clearly does not consider McEachern's a feasible alternative. The 'despairing' voice is the result of Joe's disillusioning discovery that Bobbie is a whore, a disillusionment he almost immediately begins to hide.

546:4 **Once they had to put him to bed, helpless** because he was drunk

CHAPTER IX

547:1 **McEachern lay in bed** The first five pages of this chapter are narrated from McEachern's perspective. They form a narrative block that covers the same period of time as the first three pages of the previous chapter, which is narrated from Joe's perspective. Both chapters, for instance, describe Joe sliding down the rope from his window, but from different perspectives.

547:9 **some adjunct to sinning** some aid to the commission of sin

547:22 **Thus bigotry and clairvoyance were practically one, only the bigotry was a little slow** McEachern reached his conclusions about Joe's sinning through the combined forces of his bigotry (severe moral opposition to sin) and clairvoyance (intuition founded in his confident knowledge of the 'theatring of evil'—547:20). His fierce opposition to sin makes him sure he knows how it is committed. But his 'bigotry was a little slow' to account for all the possible ways sin might be accomplished. He is surprised to see Joe sliding down a rope outside his window because he had not imagined this particular method of the 'theatring of evil.'

547:30 **something of that pure and impersonal outrage which a judge must feel were he to see a man on trial for his life lean and spit on the bailiff's sleeve** outrage at the disrespect shown by a person on trial for his life to the very court on which he must depend for fair and merciful judgment. Earlier that day McEachern confronted Joe about the new suit. One would think that Joe would be on his best behavior, refraining from any act that would confirm McEachern's suspicions about the suit's purpose. Instead, Joe openly displays his disregard (and contempt) for McEachern by setting out on his way to commit the very crime he had earlier been accused of.

547:34 **Hidden in the shadows of the lane**   See 525:19. When Joe twice thinks he hears something in the bushes, he is obviously hearing McEachern.

547:37 **Possibly he did not even care**   Through much of the novel the narrator relates the thoughts of the character he is describing, but in this chapter, first with McEachern and later with Joe, he assumes a considerably less omniscient stance. Repeatedly he qualifies his narrative with 'possibly' or 'perhaps,' suggesting that he is less than certain of his account. The narrative thus assumes a more detached tone towards these characters, who themselves do not always seem in control of their actions. (McEachern pursues Joe 'as if he believed . . . he would be guided by some greater and purer outrage' [548] while Joe finds his foster-father's horse 'with something of his adopted father's complete faith in an infallibility of events' [551]).

548:8 **greater and purer outrage**   God's outrage

548:9 **carpet slippers**   "house slippers made of carpet material,"° like the carpetbags after the Civil War

548:10 **braces**   suspenders

548:17 **in juggernautish simulation of terrific speed**   A 'juggernaut' is a massive, inexorable force destroying all in its path. See entry 739:36.

548:23 **He rode . . . straight to the place which he sought and which he had found out of a whole night**   Frequently in this novel characters seem to act in accordance with the will of some force or agent outside themselves. In the first chapter Lena Grove comes from Alabama to the very town where Lucas Burch is living; in chapter XVI Doc Hines rides without guidance through the dark and rain straight to the carriage that holds his daughter and the circus "Mexican"; Percy Grimm in chapter XIX pursues Christmas with 'blind obedience to whatever Player moved him on the Board' (741). See entry 739:36.

549:2 **some militant Michael Himself** The archangel Michael is mentioned twice in the Bible as an angelic warrior for the Lord (Daniel 10:13, Revelations 12:7–10). Revelations 12:7–10 describes the war that Michael and the angels wage against Satan and the rebellious angels.

549:6 **incipient pandemonium** In *Paradise Lost*, Milton coined the term 'pandemonium' to name the capital of Hell and Satan's palace. Its literal meaning is "all demons." In light of the earlier allusion to Michael, and another soon to come (where McEachern imagines himself face-to-face with Satan, 549:34), it is unlikely that the use of this word is coincidental. 'Pandemonium' also simply means a loud noise or racket.

549:18 **Jezebel** See entry 496:21.

549:24 **he seemed to himself to be standing just and rock-like . . . about the actual representative of the wrathful and retributive Throne** The analogy extends the earlier comparisons of McEachern to the archangel Michael. The 'wrathful and retributive Throne' is the throne on which, according to Revelations 20:11–12, God will sit at the Last Judgment and judge the sinful and virtuous.

549:28 **Perhaps they were not even his hands which struck at the face** Perhaps McEachern is at this moment so completely God's instrument that he is not really acting for himself. His hands are really God's hands.

549:33 **it was not that child's face which he was concerned with: it was the face of Satan** McEachern believes he is battling not against Joe but against the forces of evil, against Satan. Compare with the chapter III description of Hightower as he leaves his church after his wife's funeral: 'his teeth were tight together and his face looked like the face of Satan in the old prints' (448).

549:37 **exaltation of a martyr who has already been absolved** A martyr feels 'exaltation' because, dying in service to God, he knows he has been forgiven for his sins ('absolved') and is thus redeemed, ready to enter Heaven.

549:39 **into nothingness** Whether McEachern is killed is unclear. Joe thinks his foster-father is dead ('Stand back! I said I would kill him some day! I told him so!' [551]), but the narrative states only that McEachern appears 'indomitable even in repose' (550), which could mean either death or unconsciousness. As with the more significant questions about Joe's racial heritage and the outcome of Byron's courtship of Lena, the novel does not provide an answer.

550:14 **writing and struggling, her hair shaken forward . . . her mouth a small jagged hole filled with shrieking** The image evokes both the head of the mythological Medusa, with its writhing snakes, and a painting entitled *The Scream* by the Norwegian expressionist Edvard Munch, which Faulkner must surely have known.° See entry 590:31.

550:24 **stiff offcolors** relatively new (thus starched, 'stiff') dresses of a fabric whose 'offcolors' (poorly dyed colors) allowed it to be bought for less than the normal price.°

550:25 **boardlike garments** heavily starched, stiff

550:32 **clodhopper** a farmer, a redneck, one who plows fields for a living and, thus, 'hops clods.'

551:30 **Faustus** subject of many medieval tales, protagonist of Christopher Marlowe's *Dr. Faustus* and Goethe's *Faust*, a German scientist and astrologer who bargains with the devil in return for youth, power, and the secrets of the universe. Faulkner compares what Joe feels after assaulting McEachern to what Faust feels when he rejects God and his law (the 'Shalt Nots') and stands ready to relish his freedom. Both men exult in their freedom from God (to Joe, McEachern and God have become indistinguishable). Both exult in what becomes, after all, their damnation.

551:31 **the Shalt Not** the power of moral law, embodied in the Shalt Nots of the Ten Commandments (see Exodus 20).

551:33 **I have done it! I told them I would!** I have killed McEachern.

552:3 **His face looked as McEachern had seen it as the chair fell. Perhaps she could not see it good yet.** The face McEachern saw 'as the chair fell' was 'the face of Satan' (549).

Faulkner implies that if she had seen Joe's face, she would have reacted in horror.

552:19 **vanishing upward from the head down** Mrs. McEachern stands at the bottom of the stairs. As Joe runs up the stairs into the attic, first his head and then torso disappear, the opposite of how he would disappear if he were descending into a hole.

552:29 **It was as though she were a phantom obeying the command sent back by the absent master.** McEachern is the 'absent master' whose spell controls her. A similar image occurs on 508:10.

554:29 **spurned road** By running, choosing not to stand still, Joe 'spurns' (rejects) the road as it passes beneath his feet.

554:31 **small, random, new, terrible houses** terrible because of the banal and meaningless lives of the people within them, 'people who came yesterday from nowhere and tomorrow will be gone wherenot' (554:32).

555:11 **during his heydey in the house** when he was welcomed in the house, at least by Bobbie

556:2 **the Beale Street playboy** Another of Max's sarcastic epithets for Joe. From the nineteenth century until its buildings were razed around 1970, Beale Street was a nationally famous Memphis district of whorehouses, bars, and nightclubs featuring jazz and the Beale Street blues—similar in spirit and notoriety to Bourbon Street in New Orleans. Because Beale Street was mainly a black night-life center, Max likely intends by calling Joe a 'Beale Street playboy' to suggest that he is not only a regular whorehouse customer but also a black man. On 560 we learn that Bobbie has told someone, probably Mame, that Joe believes he is part black.

556:4 **Come in and meet the folks** a sarcastic greeting, as if 'the folks' are the parents of the bride-to-be, and Joe is meeting them for the first time

556:5 **moving toward the door which he knew** the door to Bobbie's room

556:7 **Beale Street . . . in comparison with which Harlem is a movie set** The narrator comments that Harlem, the black district of New York City, was in the 1930s (when the narrator tells this story) a tame imitation of Beale Street. Harlem then was a 'movie set,' a tourist attraction with cleaned-up night clubs that catered to whites who wanted a taste of the exotic black night life. Beale Street was more authentic.

556:17 *I didn't think she would have that many* Joe believes that all the bags belong to Bobbie and that she is packed to leave with him. He doesn't know that Max and Mame are packed to leave too, fearful that the school-house incident will bring the authorities down on them.

556:27 **He was running now; that is, as a man might run far ahead of himself and his knowing in the act of stopping stock still.** One of a number of instances in this chapter where Joe's mind and body act independently of one another. The sentence says literally that though Joe had physically come to a stop, in his mind he still thinks he is running: that is, he is not fully aware of what he is doing. He is frantic, overwhelmed by his attack on his foster-father, fearful of arrest, urgent to find Bobbie and take her away.

556:39 **thought went faster than seeing** He was still preoccupied with his plan to go off with Bobbie, paying no attention to his surroundings. See entry 556:27.

557:2 **He and Max might have been brothers in the sense that any two white men strayed suddenly into an African jungle might look like brothers to those who lived there** Neither Max nor the other man looks like the kind of man who would live in a small town such as this one. That is the source of their "brotherhood."

557:10 *Ask him* Ask him whether he killed the old man. They are mainly just curious: they want to know whether they are running away because of a murder or a brawl. In either event, they can't risk the attention the incident may bring.

557:16 *He might know.* whether he killed McEachern

557:18 **Though Joe had not moved since he entered, he was still running** running from what he did at the schoolhouse. He was still thinking fast, uncomprehendingly, without seeing.

557:25 **croaked him** killed him

557:26 **You don't want to get Bobbie in a jam** in trouble with the law.

557:27 **"Bobbie," Joe said, thinking *Bobbie*. *Bobbie* He turned running again** All Joe hears of what Max is asking him is Bobbie's name, which returns him to his purpose—to take Bobbie away with him.

558:21 **Do you think that I——** Do you think that I would run away without coming to get Bobbie first?

558:33 **I've got.** I've got money.

558:34 **Then the wind blew upon him again, like in the school house three hours ago** the uproar of screaming voices. See 550: 'Then to Joe it all rushed away, roaring, dying, leaving him in the center of the floor . . . looking down at his adopted father.'

559:2 **his voice alone quiet enough to register upon the air** With Bobbie (and perhaps others) screaming around him, the only voice Joe can hear and is aware of is his own.

559:5 **she struggled and shrieked, her hair wild with the jerking and tossing of her head; her face, even her mouth, in contrast to the hair as still as a dead mouth in a dead face** The image again evokes both the mythological Medusa, with her writhing hair of snakes, and a painting entitled *The Scream* by the Norwegian expressionist Edvard Munch.° See also 550:14.

559:9 **that always treated you like you were a white man** Bobbie, who has just called Joe a 'bastard' and a 'son of a bitch,' now calls him a Negro. But she probably does not really believe he is a Negro. In Mississippi in the early decades of the 1900s few white women would have accepted a black man as a lover. Nor would Max and Mame have permitted Joe to come to their house, or to see Bobbie, if they believed he was black.

559:11 **even yet it was just noise . . . just a part of the long wind** The 'wind' that began just after he knocked Mc-Eachern down in the schoolroom (550:4), continued during his ride to steal Mrs. McEachern's money (551:33), followed him to Bobbie's house (558:26, 558:34, 559:18), and did not stop until the stranger beat him up (559:34). When Joe much later realizes that Joanna Burden has lied about her pregnancy, a 'long wind of knowing' rushes down upon him (603:34). In that instance, as here, the 'long wind' is a gradually dawning realization that catches him unawares. Here the realization involves traumatic change, the collapse of his plans, his betrayal in love.

559:13 **at the face which he had never seen before** the face of anger and hatred

559:18 **Then she too seemed to blow out of his life like a third scrap of paper** blown by the wind (see entry 559:11). The two other scraps are Max and the stranger: 'the two men were blown as completely out of his life as two scraps of paper' (558).

559:28 **There'll be a cop out here soon. They'll know where to look for him.** Mame means that the police will be looking for Joe and that because they know he frequents their house, she, Max, Bobbie, and the stranger had better leave soon. The local police have apparently tolerated Max and Mame's establishment, but now the schoolhouse brawl will force them to take action.

559:32 **f.ing** fucking. Faulkner spelled it 'f.ing' in both manuscript and typescript.° The intended pronunciation could be "effing," a fairly common euphemism.

559:34 **swinging his hand as though it still clutched the chair** the chair with which he struck McEachern at the schoolhouse

559:37 **with something of the exaltation of his adopted father he sprang full and of his own accord into the stranger's fist** See 549: '[McEachern] walked steadily toward it . . . in the furious and dreamlike exaltation of a martyr who has already been absolved.' See entry 549:37.

560:7 as immobile and completely finished and surfaced as a cast statue a statue made by pouring molten metal, usually bronze, into a mold. When the metal hardens, the mold is broken away, the statue emerging 'completely surfaced and finished.' The smooth, hard surface of Mame's hair is not ruffled by the uproar. She is smooth and hard—like a cast statue. This is the second sculpture metaphor in this chapter: Joe was earlier compared to 'an equestrian statue strayed from its pedestal' (554).

560:12 *bitching up* messing up, ruining

560:12 *as sweet a little setup* 'sweet' = lucrative, profitable; 'setup' = an ideal situation. The small town with its unwitting citizens made it easy for Max, Mame, and their associates to earn illegal money without getting caught, since few who were not customers themselves could suspect the presence of prostitutes.

560:14 *He was born too close to one* The stranger means that his mother was a bitch, a woman, and that he's a son of a bitch.

560:19 *We'll see if his blood is black* We'll discover if he really is a Negro. The stranger doesn't mean this literally. He just wants an excuse to continue beating him. Not coincidentally, as Christmas dies at the end of chapter XIX, the blood flowing from his wounds is described as 'pent black blood' (743).

560:29 *This one is on the house too* This next blow is free too. Max alludes here to the free drinks he earlier offered Joe (542), and to his general contention that he was cheated by all the free sex Bobbie gave to Joe.

CHAPTER X

561:1 **Knowing not grieving remembers a thousand savage and lonely streets** These lines echo the opening of chapter VI as well as of chapter VII. The opening of chapter VI suggested that although Joe does not clearly remember the events it relates, they deeply influenced his life nonetheless. 'Knowing not grieving remembers' makes clear that Christmas consciously and clearly recalls the events this chapter relates, the 'thousand savage and lonely streets,' but that he does not 'grieve' over them. He simply accepts them, whatever misery they might have involved. See entries 487:1, 507:1.

561:6 **as though in the house where all the people had died** The bulb burns with the same 'aching and unwavering glare' that Joe remembers from when, in the previous chapter, he stood knocking at the front door and heard the house suddenly fall silent.

561:10 **volition and sentience** will and consciousness. Joe's awareness ('sentience') of his location is not linked to his ability to do anything about it ('volition').

561:15 *chicken feed* small amount of money. Perhaps literally it means "not enough to buy a handful of chicken feed."

561:16 *must have tapped the sunday school till on the way out* on the way out of the schoolhouse—Max's sarcastic comment about the money he's found in Joe's pocket. A Sunday school collection plate typically would not contain much money. What Max or the stranger is referring to is almost certainly the collection plate that holds the fee that each per-

son attending the dance was required to pay before entering—they believe Joe has stolen it.

561:18   *keep it as an installment*   as a payment towards the
money Max would claim Joe owes him for the sex he had
with Bobbie

561:21   *helped to rot one hole pretty big for its size*   an obscene
joke about the size of Bobbie's vagina. The speaker sarcastically suggests that Christmas's affair with Bobbie has ruined
her sexually, and he is irritated that Christmas never paid
for his time with her. He is also angry that the schoolhouse
brawl guarantees that Bobbie will earn him no more money
in this town.

561:23   *like hell you will*   Mame is fed up with Max's cynical
jokes and his continuing victimization of Joe.

561:29   *jack*   money

561:30   *f.ing*   "effing," fucking

561:35   **fob pocket**   small pocket on the front of a man's
pants, just below the belt, originally intended to hold a
pocket watch but often used to hold one or two folded bank
notes

562:12   **Then the two wireends knit and made connection**
'wireends of volition and sentience' (561).

562:16   **thinking said *Not yet***   Though his body sits up and
looks into the mirror, his mind tells him he is not ready to
begin functioning.

562:36   **the whiskey began to burn in him and he began to
shake his head slowly from side to side, while thinking became one with the slow, hot coiling and recoiling of his
entrails**   This scene echoes the chapter VI toothpaste episode in the dietitian's bedroom, especially through the word
'coiling' (488). 'Coiling' and 'recoiling' suggest the motion of
the 'cool invisible worm' from chapter VI.

563:4   *If I can just get it outside, into the air, the cool air*   'it' =
Joe's body. If I can just get my body outside, the cool air will
revive me.

563:8   **It never would have opened a window and climbed**

through it His body, bruised and numbed by the beating, could not have managed the coordination to do this. The narrator notes a few lines above that Christmas's head 'was clear' but that his body 'would not behave' (562–63).

563:16 **cheap and brutal nights of stale oftused glasses and stale oftused beds** Note the faint echo of T. S. Eliot's "The Love Song of J. Alfred Prufrock": "Of restless nights in one-night cheap hotels."°

563:20 **the street which was to run for fifteen years** a continuation of the road imagery introduced in the 'unwinding road' (see entry 404:27) of chapter I. These images imply that the fate of anyone on such roads is already determined. This road runs out, as we are soon to see, at the house of Joanna Burden, when Christmas is thirty-three (565)—as the narrative says and as evidence in the text allows us to deduce. He is eighteen at the time of the schoolhouse brawl. For a full discussion of his age, see the Chronology.

563:34 **spurious board fronts of oil towns** the artificial façades often affixed to the front of hastily erected buildings to give them a permanent and respectable appearance.

563:36 **bottomless mud** the mud of oil-fields, 'bottomless' because there is no apparent end to it

563:40 **gold** oil

564:4 **gambling tout** one who sells "inside" horse racing information to prospective bettors. If the horse he recommends wins, he has a claim to a share of the bettor's profits.

564:8 **beneath the dark and equivocal and symbolical archways of midnight he bedded the women** He slept with prostitutes in whorehouses. 'Equivocal' means of uncertain reputation. 'Symbolical archways of midnight' suggests the red-lighted doors of the establishments where he slept— ones which necessarily function mainly at night, under the protection of darkness.

564:12 **For a while it worked; that was while he was still in the south.** In the 1920s Southern whorehouses, like all Southern institutions, were segregated. Black houses would accept white clients but white houses would not accept black ones. Since Christmas looks white, he had no difficulty being admitted to white houses.

564:18 **Because one night it did not work** In some Northern brothels white prostitutes catered to both black and white clients.

564:20 **wop** an Italian; by extension, any dark-skinned foreigner. A deprecating term, though the prostitute apparently means no offense.

564:23 **shine** a black man, another deprecative racial epithet, though not a Southern one.° The girl means that she does not care what Christmas's race is and that his skin is not so dark, especially compared with that of the 'shine' who was her previous customer.

564:24 **turned out** let out

564:26 **what do you think this dump is anyhow? the Ritz Hotel?** the Ritz Hotel in Paris. Its name became a catch phrase for anything lush, fashionable, and expensive—as in "putting on the Ritz." The prostitute implies that only at such a hotel could Joe expect to find prostitutes who refused black customers.

565:1 **He now lived as man and wife with a woman who resembled an ebony carving** Christmas's behavior during this phase of his life resembles that of Charles Etienne de Saint-Valery Bon in *Absalom, Absalom!* (1936). Thought by Quentin and Shreve to be the son of Charles Bon and his mulatto New Orleans wife, he seeks to live as a Negro, though he is white in appearance. He marries a black woman ("a coal black and ape-like woman," 257) and frequently provokes fights with Negroes who often badly beat him. Both he and Christmas pursue such an existence as a way of denying the white elements of their racial identities.

565:9 **his nostrils at the odor which he was trying to make his own would whiten and tauten, his whole being writhe and strain with physical outrage and spiritual denial** The 'odor' refers both to the supposed physical smell as well as to

'the dark and inscrutable thinking and being of negroes.'
Christmas tries to make himself a Negro, to convince himself
that he has already become one, but the effort makes his
'whole being writhe and strain with physical outrage and
spiritual denial' because he despises what he is trying to become. The 'odor' that he here tries to breathe into himself is
analogous to the 'black tide' (650) which later creeps up his
legs from the shoes of a Negro woman as he rides into Mottstown at the end of chapter XIV.

565:13 **catlike** Like a cat, Christmas developed no attachment to any one place, however long he might have stayed.
See entry 567:24.

565:16 **he might have seen himself as in numberless avatars,
in silence, doomed with motion, driven by the courage of
flagged and spurred despair; by the despair of courage
whose opportunities had to be flagged and spurred** He
could envision numerous scenes and episodes, all of them
more or less similar, in which he moved on, always doomed
to remain a wanderer, never to stop in one place and settle
down. The rest of the passage can be paraphrased only in
the most abstract sense: Christmas is driven in his wan-
derings by his willingness to accept that his life will never
change, driven also by his hope that it might: his despair
sometimes lessened ('flagged') and slowed him down ('flagged
him') if he thought things might improve, and sometimes
worsened ('spurred') and prompted him to continue wandering ('spurred' him on) if he thought they would not improve. When he felt the desire to remain in one place too
long, he had to combat it and move on; he also had to per-
suade himself to stay in one place long enough to take advantage of whatever opportunities might await him there.
The second phrase, 'by the despair of courage whose opportunities had to be flagged and spurred,' suggests that
Christmas had to keep himself from feeling too hopeful
('flag his courage') and keep himself willing to continue wandering ('spur his courage'). In general, the passage means

that Christmas was careful to cultivate the despair, the sense of total estrangement from anything and anybody, that in a significant way helped him to define his identity as a wanderer, a man with no home and no past.

565:17 **avatars** See entry 404:1.

565:20 **He was thirtythree years old** The manuscript reads "He was 30 years old." In the typescript Faulkner revised Christmas's age to thirty-three, perhaps, as Joseph Blotner suggests, to avoid over-emphasizing possible parallels with the Christ story.°

565:30 **grove of trees** See entry 486:5.

566:2 **tin bucket** a lard bucket used as a lunch pail, like those of the mill workers in chapter II. It is late afternoon and the boy is probably on his way home from work.

566:4 **Miz Burden** Joanna Burden; see entry 424:33 for a discussion of her full name. In Southern dialect, 'Miz' is how Mrs., the term of address for a married woman, is pronounced. Joanna, of course, is not married. The black man uses it as a respectful term of address for an older white woman.

566:11 **Colored folks around here looks after her.** Christmas knows that in the rural South a white woman living alone and looked after by 'colored folks' will necessarily be an isolated, perhaps eccentric soul. This information informs his judgment as he approaches the house.

566:14 **It was as if the boy had closed a door between himself and the man** As soon as the man asks a question about Joanna's relations with Negroes, the boy refuses to say anything more. He knows the subject of a white woman's relations with black people is one that might get him into trouble, especially with a strange white man.

566:19 **Christmas** From the time he lived in the orphanage up until now, the text has referred to Joe Christmas as Joe. But now he becomes 'Christmas,' his name through the rest of the novel.

566:32 *Say dont didn't.*
        Didn't dont who.
        Want dat yaller gal's
        Pudden dont hide.

Calvin Brown observes: "This bit of doggerel is obviously one of the unintelligible children's, and especially Negroes', songs which either arise as nonsense or, often, are corrupted beyond recognition . . . by a long process of rote repetition without understanding. . . . Pudden ('pudding') is sometimes used (like the Negro jelly-roll) in the sexual senses (both anatomical and abstract) of 'pussy.' That seems to be the meaning here." The expression 'yaller gal,' says Brown, means "yellow girl, a very light mulatto woman," that is, one with both white and black ancestry.° Light-colored skin in a black woman supposedly makes her more sexually attractive to black and white men alike. Whether the boy means the sexual connotations of his song to have a connection to the single woman who lives alone in the house is unclear.

567:1 **the house bulked** the large shape of the house loomed

567:12 **He could feel the neversunned earth strike, slow and receptive, against him through his clothes: groin, hip, belly, breast** A few lines later the earth is 'fecund.' The presence in the house of a woman who 'aint old' has turned Christmas's thoughts to sex.

567:22 **now dimensionless bulk of the house** Christmas is so close to the house that in the darkness it seems huge, without shape or dimension.

567:24 **cat** See entries 481:6 and 524:6.

567:26 **the crickets . . . keeping a little island of silence about him like thin yellow shadow of their small voices** As Christmas walks through the grass, his noisy movements frighten the crickets into silence. Around him, then, is a 'little island of silence,' like the 'thin yellow shadow' around the base of a burning candle, which isn't really a shadow at all but light, an inverse shadow ('island') of refracted light in the darkness.

567:29 **with that tiny and alert suddenness** This phrase modifies the sudden cessation of sound from the crickets, not the movement of Christmas.

568:3 **Then he climbed into the window** He enters through the window rather than the unlocked door as an assertion of his independence. Though he probably would be welcomed into the house, even fed and sheltered, if he chose to enter it as a black man (the unlocked door, along with the fact that 'Colored folks . . . looks after her' [566] tell us this), or as someone willing to accept the owner's charity, he enters as an intruder, leaving himself indebted to no one, and making no declaration of a racial identity.

568:4 **a shadow returning without a sound and without locomotion to the allmother of obscurity and darkness** Christmas is entering the primordial darkness of which he himself, 'a shadow,' is a part. His entrance into an unknown woman's kitchen is a symbolical return to the womb. He knows he stands in the kitchen of a single woman who lives alone; he knows what a man's unwanted intrusion into her house potentially signifies. He must also be aware of his own suspicion of women, of what he believes to be their desire to feed, mother, and control him. The kitchen thus offers him some degree of safety, but also potential danger and complication.

568:10 **like the cat, he also seemed to see in the darkness as he moved unerringly toward the food which he wanted as if he knew where it would be; that, or were being manipulated by an agent which did know** We have two choices here, either that Christmas is being driven by animal instinct towards the food, or as if some external agent, like God, moves him. This scene in which a character moves as if under the guidance of a foreign agent is one of the paradigmatic moments of the novel. Elsewhere, McEachern rides to the site of the school house dance as if guided by 'clairvoyance' (548), after attacking the old man Joe finds his horse 'with something of his adopted father's complete faith in an infallibility in events' (551), in chapter XIX Percy Grimm pursues Christmas 'as though under the protection of a magic or a providence' (740), and the final pursuit seems controlled by a 'Player' (741) moving game pieces on a board. Such facts would suggest that the characters of this novel lack free will, that their fates are predetermined, were it not for Lena Grove, who is able to an extent to choose her future, and Byron Bunch, who sloughs off the fossilized habits of an entire lifetime to pursue the woman he loves.

568:19 **five miles even beyond a corner where he used to wait** He remembers the McEachern farm, five miles from the corner where he used to wait for Bobbie Allen

568:21 **someone whose name he had forgot** Bobbie

568:22 *I'll know it in a minute. I have eaten it before, . . . I hear the monotonous dogmatic voice . . . I see the indomitable bullet head the clean blunt beard . . . the hot salt of waiting my eyes tasting the hot steam from the dish* It's peas," he said, aloud. **"For sweet Jesus. Field peas cooked with molasses** Here Christmas struggles to identify by its odor and the memories it evokes the food on the counter before him. The '*dogmatic voice*' and '*bullet head*' belong to Simon McEachern, whom Christmas recalls saying long blessings before each meal. The '*mouth and tongue weeping the hot salt of waiting*' simply means that Joe's mouth watered as he sat at table and thought of the food he would eat when his foster-father finished praying. 'For sweet Jesus' is an expression used by Max Confrey, in chapter VII (542), whom Joe began to imitate in a number of ways after learning that Bobbie was a prostitute. Faulkner characterizes memory here in a curiously naturalistic way, as if it functions independently of the conscious mind, as if the images it contains are not always accessible, though they affect the individual nonetheless. In general this passage seems a specific demonstration of the meaning of the opening to chapter VI: 'Memory believes before knowing remembers. Believes longer than recollects, longer than knowing even wonders' (487).

568:38 **his eyes glowing suddenly** like a cat's, reflecting the inrush of light coming through the suddenly opened door

569:1 **he did not move** his failure to flee at the approach of the house's owner emphasizes his intentions. He has intruded into a woman's house, and he wants her to know that she can do nothing about it, that what might happen to him in consequence does not bother him.

569:12 **If it is just food you want, you will find that** Joanne means that the intruder will get nothing from her but food. She does not know whom she is dealing with. Nor, of course, does he.

CHAPTER XI

570:2 **soft light downfalling** She is illuminated by the candle she carries, 'holding it high, so that its light fell upon her face' (569).

570:2 **softungirdled presence of a woman prepared for sleep** This faintly erotic image strongly affects Christmas. See 571:38: 'the woman at first sight of whom in the lifted candle . . . there had opened before him, instantaneous as a landscape in a lightningflash, a horizon of physical security and adultery if not pleasure.'

570:3 **When he saw her by daylight** presumably the next day

570:7 **it was not that first night, nor for many succeeding ones, that she told him that much even** 'it' = when they talked and she told him she was forty. The phrase 'that first night' may refer simply to the night of Joe's arrival, but it may also mean the first night he forced himself on her sexually. It is unclear whether that assault occurred on the night of his arrival, or a few nights later (there is evidence for either interpretation). In any case, as the passage indicates, she would not have felt kindly enough to talk to him until later in their relationship, probably not until the September evening she appears in his cabin, on 575–76.

570:15 **since it didn't try to and didn't intend to** 'it' = speech that did not *try* or *mean* to convey meaning

570:23 **she would never stay while he ate** Since eating is a social occasion, Joanna's failure to sit with Christmas while he eats signifies her lack of social interest in him. She treats him in this first phase of their relationship as her inferior.

570:28 **a cloth sunbonnet like a countrywoman** Though

Southern city women once wore such bonnets, by the 1920s and 30s only women from the country wore them.

571:15 **When he learned that, he understood the town's attitude towards her** No respectable Southern white woman would employ a black lawyer, let alone an out-of-state one.

571:19 **One day he realised she had never invited him inside the house proper. He had never been further than the kitchen** i.e., he had never been *invited* further than the kitchen, a small room built on to the back of the house, not a part of the house proper. A door leads from the kitchen into the house. He has gone into the house 'of his own accord' numerous times, but never by Joanna's invitation.

571:22 **liplifted** sneering, in anger and contempt

571:26 **as he had entered it that first night** 'that first night' = the night he first assaulted her, perhaps the same night of his arrival, when she found him in her kitchen. His second assault on her thus occurs on the next night (572–73), followed by the 'four or five month' interval in which he ignores her completely, waiting for her to 'make the first sign.' However, there is some evidence that a few days might have intervened between his arrival and his first assault.

571:26 **he felt like a thief, a robber, even while he mounted to the bedroom where she waited. Even after a year it was as though he entered by stealth to despoil her virginity each time anew** Each time he enters her bedroom, Joe feels he is 'despoiling' Joanna again. This passage and others suggest that Joanna assists Joe in this fantasy once their sexual affair begins in earnest. Over the past fifteen years he has taken special satisfaction from sleeping with white women and then telling them he is a black man. He almost certainly told Joanna this the first night he assaulted her. On later nights, when he mounts to the bedroom 'where she waited,' the text makes clear that she awaits him expectantly. She now acts out her own sexual fantasy as she imagines herself the white virgin raped and despoiled by a Negro ravisher. We see this clearly at 590:26: 'in the wild throes of nymphomania, her body gleaming . . . breathing: Negro! Negro! Negro!' Her affair with Christmas is thus the conjunction of two people with opposite but complementary racial and sexual fantasies.

571:35 **A spiritual privacy so long intact that its own instinct for preservation had immolated it, its physical phase the strength and fortitude of a man** 'A spiritual privacy' = the moral, spiritual, and intellectual integrity of her commitment to serve black people in a region that treated them as unworthy, and to preserve her own New England heritage and identity in a community that regarded her as an interloper. 'Immolated' = sacrificed in service to a cause. To defend her privacy she found it necessary to develop 'the strength and fortitude of a man.' Joanna had struggled so long to preserve her identity and heritage that she had somehow in the process forfeited part of what she was trying to defend. She became manlike in her attempt to remain whole and intact.

572:1 **a horizon of physical security** In this woman who lives alone, Christmas envisions the possibility of a long adulterous affair that he can conduct without interference from the outside world. He also believes she would welcome such an affair and would not want or seek help from others.

572:4 **with which he had to fight up to the final instant** As we learn on the following page, Christmas grudgingly respects the sporting, masculine way in which Joanna resists him: 'She had resisted to the very last . . . she had resisted fair, by the rules that decreed that upon a certain crisis one was defeated' (572). And when that moment came, she surrendered with an 'almost manlike yielding' (571), recognizing that to resist any longer was pointless.

572:8 **for which they struggled on principle alone** He struggled on the principle that it was his masculine right to claim her virginity; she struggled on the principle that although it had no real meaning to her he had no right to take it.

572:14 *Under her clothes she cant even be made so that it could have happened* Because she does not react as he would expect a woman to react to assault and loss of virginity, Christmas wonders whether she really is a woman, whether under her clothes there is a vagina to be penetrated.

572:15 **He had not started to work at the mill then** He has just arrived at Joanna's house and has not had time to look for work. His first sexual encounter with her occurs soon after his arrival, perhaps on the first night, certainly no more than a few nights later.

572:19 **'it was like I was the woman and she was the man.' But that was not right, either. Because she had resisted to the very last** He believes she fought him as vigorously as a man would have, almost as if she had been assaulting him. But unlike a man, she kept on fighting until she was overpowered. A man, Christmas believes, would have fought only until the outcome was no longer in doubt.

572:22 **not woman resistance, that resistance which, if really meant, cannot be overcome by any man. . . . But she had resisted fair, by the rules that decreed that upon a certain crisis one was defeated** Christmas believes a woman can always avoid rape if she really wants to: she can kick or wrench or otherwise injure his genitals, which among men would not be fair fighting. Joanna, however, fights a fair fight. She observes the rules of men, which decree that a combatant should surrender when he recognizes he cannot win the fight. By surrendering, she earns Christmas's grudging respect.

572:27 **That night** the second night he entered her room

572:29 **He did not go in eagerness, but in a quiet rage. "I'll show her"** Christmas is angry because on the day after the rape Joanna behaves as if nothing had happened. His purpose on this second night is to prove she cannot ignore his male presence.

572:32 **"Who is it?" she said. But there was no alarm in her tone** as if the person mounting the stairs might equally well have been anyone coming for any purpose. She does not fear Christmas. This angers him still more.

572:38 **she did not flee . . . He began to tear at her clothes . . . I'll show you! I'll show the bitch!"** He'll show her that he is not to be ignored, that he is to be feared and submitted to. The shift from the second-person 'you' to the impersonal, contemptuous 'bitch' suggests that Joe here is reacting not merely to one woman but to all women, to Woman and all that his life's experience has made him believe that word means.

573:7 **'At least I have made a woman of her at last,' he thought. 'Now she hates me. I have taught her that, at least.'** Christmas believes he has made a woman of her by forcing her to submit to sex, by showing her that she had no choice but to submit. He believes she must now understand that men and women are enemies, that she must hate and fear men because she is always vulnerable to them. She has not learned this at all. She never reports his assault to anyone, does not demand that he leave, and the next day prepares another supper for him.

573:14 **'Better blow,' he thought. 'Not give her the chance to turn me out of the cabin too. That much anyway'** 'blow' = leave. Apparently Christmas has realized that he taught her very little the previous evening. Now he believes she will want to make him leave her land. By departing now, he will deny her the chance to inflict a further indignity on him.

573:16 **No white woman ever did that. Only a nigger woman ever give me the air, turned me out** Christmas was apparently not bothered that the black woman turned him out. He has never had to prove his dominance over black women. White women have been his main interest. And he has never allowed any white woman to control him, certainly not to throw him out of her bed or house, as now he fears Joanna might do.

573:18 **waiting for sunset** presumably so he could go to her undetected in the dark

573:21 **fireflies began to drift** This scene occurs in the spring, shortly after Christmas's arrival at the Burden house. Fireflies in the South begin to appear in April or May and remain throughout the summer.

573:25 **the street of the imperceptible corners** the street he entered in Chapter X (563), and which, by implication, he entered at the end of Chapter VI when the McEacherns adopted him. Since its corners are 'imperceptible' but nonetheless still there, and since in Chapter XIV, as he approaches Mottstown, Christmas thinks 'it had made a circle' (650), it must be a circular road, one whose beginning and end points ultimately meet.

573:26 **Yet when he moved, it was toward the house** Why does he go to the house instead of leaving? It has become his habit the last few nights to go there for supper. Perhaps he surrenders to habit, but more likely he surrenders to the woman in the house who refuses to act as he believes a woman should, whom he cannot subjugate through sex and violence as he has subjugated other women, whom he thus finds strangely irresistible.

573:30 **onto the back porch and to the door by which he would enter, that was never locked** Three doors are involved here. The main back door to the house, which enters from the back porch; the door which leads from the outside into the kitchen; and the door which leads from the kitchen into the house proper. The kitchen door to the houses of white Southerners was traditionally used by blacks, who could not use any other entrance, while whites might enter through the back porch door. At least until the second world war, the outer doors to most rural Southern houses, and many city ones, were seldom locked.

573:32 **when he put his hand upon it, it would not open . . . He turned away quietly. He was not yet raging** Joe understands that Joanna has locked the door to keep him from repeating his performance of the two previous evenings. This does not particularly anger him.

573:32 **Perhaps for the moment neither hand nor believing would believe; he seemed to stand there, quiet, not yet thinking** Literally, this variation on the 'memory believes before knowing remembers' motif means that Christmas at first cannot accept what his hand tells him: that the door is locked. 'Hand' roughly translates to 'action.' 'Believing' translates to 'consciousness, awareness.'

573:37 **He went to the kitchen door. He expected that to be locked also** He reasons that if she meant to keep him away from her at night, she would lock the kitchen door too.

573:38 **he did not realise until he found that it was open, that he had wanted it to be** He wanted it to be locked either so that he would have an excuse to break into the house in anger, or so that he would have an excuse to leave.

573:39 **When he found that it was not locked it was like an insult.** Joanna has denied him access to her house and herself by locking the door reserved for whites, but she has left open to him the door for blacks so that he might enter for his nightly handout of food ('*Set out for the nigger. For the nigger*'). She thus puts him in what she considers his place: that of a Negro and her inferior. By accepting the food she has cooked for him, he has willingly played that role, a fact she now reminds him of—perhaps to nullify whatever advantage he might have gained from the previous evening's sexual encounter. But he does not like being so reminded and is enraged even more. That she locks the door for whites after the second rape but not after the first suggests that he told her he was part black on the second night. Ironically, he does not hesitate to tell her he is part black, but he reacts violently when she locks the door as a way of acknowledging that she believes him. Even more ironically, though he has told Joanna that he is part black, when he goes to work at the mill, he presents himself as neither white nor black, though most of the mill workers believe he is white.

574:3 **When he entered the kitchen, he did not approach the** door into the house proper. . . . He went directly to the table where she set out his food   Why? Because he is more interested in confirming that she set the food out 'for the nigger' than in going to her bedroom again.

574:8   **His hands saw**   With his hands he felt the dishes and their warmth.

574:10   **He seemed to watch his hand as if from a distance**   Since it is dark and he cannot see, and since 'He did not need to see. His hands saw,' this means that he 'felt' what his hands were touching.

574:21   *This is fun. Why didn't I think of this before?*   He did think of it before. In a parallel scene in chapter VII (513) Christmas refused Mrs. McEachern's food by throwing it against the wall.

574:29   **he heard the bolt in the door**   He hears the bolt and understands that Joanna had locked the door between the kitchen and the house, furthering the insult she has already given him.

574:37   **The next day he went to work at the planing mill**   Why did he decide not to leave Jefferson? Obviously he feels a strange attraction to Joanna. She is unlike any woman he has known, and she has confounded his expectations about the behavior of a white woman raped by a black man. He stays partly to see what she will do next, but also to wait her out, for he knows now that by leaving he would be surrendering to her. Here begins between Joe and Joanna a struggle for dominance that continues until their deaths.

575:11   **as if he were ashamed of the overalls. Or perhaps it was not shame**   Overalls are the clothing of farmers, manual laborers, and Christmas wants no one to believe he is either. He affects a more urban, swaggering image and dresses accordingly.

575:19   **the first time that he deliberately looked again toward the house, he felt a shocking surge and fall of blood**   Christmas 'believed that he no longer expected' Joanna to 'make the first sign.' In essence, he believes he does not care whether she makes the first sign. But with that 'shocking surge and fall of blood' he discovers that he does care.

575:31 **'You dont bother me and I dont bother you,' he thought, thinking *I dreamed it. It didn't happen*** He is trying to convince himself that there is not now, and never has been, any sexual attraction between them, a belief he will find to be delusion come September.

575:39 **the loose abandon of her hair, not yet wild** A few months later, once the second phase of their relationship begins, her hair becomes 'wild hair, each strand of which would seem to come alive like octopus tentacles' (590:31).

576:5 **Thinking, knowing** first suspecting, then realizing with certainty. Faulkner continues to elaborate on the 'memory believes before knowing remembers' motif.

576:7 **She told him that she was fortyone years old** On 570:5 we learn that 'she told him that she was forty' but that 'it was not that first night, nor for many succeeding ones, that she told him that much even.' Since they do not talk at all after the night he throws his supper against her kitchen wall, this would be her first opportunity to tell him her age. So there is a discrepancy between this reference to her age (41) and the earlier one (40). Perhaps she had a birthday in the interim.

576:26 **Calvin Burden** The first name is probably taken from the last name of John Calvin, the French-born Swiss theologian and religious reformer (1509–1564) whose doctrines of salvation and predestination formed the basis of Puritanism, Presbyterianism, and Unitarianism. See entry 424:33 for the significance of the name Burden.

576:28 **before he could write his name (or would write it, his father believed)** The rebelliousness of this child who refuses (as his father believes) to learn how to write his name parallels Christmas's refusal to learn the catechism in chapter VII.

576:30 **the Horn** Cape Horn, the southernmost tip of South America. Before the building of the Panama Canal at the turn of the century, sea voyages from the eastern to the western American coast had to pass around this stormy and hazardous Cape.

576:33 **Huguenot stock** Huguenots were French Protestants of the sixteenth and seventeenth centuries. Political and religious persecution at the end of the seventeenth century forced many Huguenots to convert to Catholicism or to immigrate to England, Germany, and the United States, as did the ancestors of the woman Calvin married.° He apparently uses her Huguenot ancestry as partial justification for his renunciation of Catholicism on their wedding day.

577:5 **a church of frogeating slaveholders** an insult reflecting Burden's belief that St. Louis Catholics are slaveholders and of French ('frogeating') descent. Actually, in 1838 Pope Gregory XVI "condemned all forms of slavery and the slave trade." In practice in the U. S., "Catholics in the North and South generally took no stand on slavery; those opposed to the institution were mindful that abolitionist leaders were in many instances also anti-Catholic. With the outbreak of the Civil War, Catholics chose sides according to their sections." Calvin's intense anti-Catholicism is thus a reflection of his abolitionism.°

577:11 **Unitarian** Unitarianism believes in a single God rather than in a holy trinity. Related to the Presbyterian Church, by orthodox standards Unitarianism is radical, denying the divinity of Christ and emphasizing his humanity. It stresses reason, intuition, and individual belief over standard doctrine and was an important force in the Abolitionist movement.°

577:18 **the book** probably a Spanish-language bible, or some other religious text, such as a missal, which contains the text of the Catholic mass

577:20 **fine, sonorous flowing of mysticism . . . composed half of the bleak and bloodless logic which he remembered from his father on interminable New England Sundays, and half of immediate hellfire and tangible brimstone** 'immediate' suggests the Puritan belief that hell is only a breath away, that only by God's mercy are we saved from being thrown into hellfire.° Calvin's theology fuses Spanish Catholic mysticism, New England Puritanism, and Southern fundamentalist evangelism. In fact, these elements characterize the New England Puritanism of Jonathan Edwards, whose sermon "Sinners in the Hands of an Angry God" employs both reason and emotion to warn sinners against the fires of hell.

577:24 **country Methodist circuit rider** a preacher assigned to minister to a large rural, undeveloped area, preaching in one place this week, another the next week, following a fixed schedule so that all who desire can hear a sermon periodically

577:26 **Nordic man** a man of North European or Scandinavian descent: tall, with light skin and hair and blue eyes

577:31 **Democrats** most Democrats supported (or at least did not oppose) slavery

578:3 **I'll learn you to hate two things . . . hell and slaveholders** Compare with McEachern's statement to Joe on 505:20: 'I will have you learn soon that the two abominations are sloth and idle thinking.' Both boys are reared by stern, authoritarian men quite certain about the world view they wish to impress on their sons.

578:3 **frail the tar out of** to whip soundly

578:10 **go to their own benighted hell** let their ignorance of the truth damn them to hell; 'benighted' = ignorant

578:11 **I'll beat the loving God into you** 'loving God': love of God. Compare with McEachern's statement to Joe: 'I'll learn you . . . Take down your pants . . . McEachern began to strike methodically, with slow and deliberate force' (509:15). Both men use corporal punishment to discipline and educate. Faulkner means us to recognize the authoritarian violence of these men, but he also makes clear that they are trying in the only way they know to mold the moral substance of their children.

578:15   **frockcoat**   a knee-length, double-breasted dress coat°

578:16   **the collarless plaited shirt which the oldest girl had laundered each Sunday as well as the dead mother ever had**   'Plaited' is an English spelling for 'pleated.' Men's dress shirts until the late 1920s had detachable collars that could be removed and replaced with clean collars. Many men wore their shirts without collars. Dress shirts had several pleats down their front, and ironing them was time-consuming and difficult.

578:19   **once gilt and blazoned book**   a book whose cover was once covered with gold inlay and elaborate drawings or engravings, now worn away by time and heavy use. See entry 577:18.

578:19   **that language which none of them understood** Spanish

578:25   **Old Mexico**   that part of Mexico south of the Rio Grande River, distinct from New Mexico, Arizona, Colorado, Utah, Nevada, California, and Texas, all of which by 1848 had become a part of U. S. territory as the result of the Mexican-American War

578:35   **a troop of partisan guerilla horse in the Kansas fighting**   'troop' = any cavalry unit; 'partisan guerilla' = an irregular soldier usually not in uniform and not a member of any organized military unit but still fighting for one side or another in a war. 'Horse' = cavalry. Kansas was a center of guerilla activity in the years just before the Civil War. Abolitionist John Brown and his five sons rode against pro-slavery forces in Kansas in 1855–56, but the 'Kansas fighting' here probably refers to the activities of the infamous William Quantrill, who for almost four years, beginning earlier than the first battles of the Civil War, led a band of Confederate guerillas in Kansas as they slaughtered civilians and scalped and otherwise mutilated Union soldiers and sympathizers. Since Calvin was opposed to slavery, he may have lost his arm while fighting with Union guerillas attempting to put down Quantrill's forces.

579:2   **You know how them Spanish are about white men,**

even when they don't kill Mexicans Nathaniel's racial attitudes are apparent here and later in the paragraph. 'White men' means Europeans, whom Nathaniel considers racially pure. 'Spaniards' are not so pure, perhaps because of their dark skin color, or because he has heard that they interbred with Arabs, whom he would not consider white. Below the Spaniards are the 'Mexicans,' product of interbreeding between Spaniards and Indians, and thus not pure at all.

579:6 **tenderfeet** people unfamiliar with life in the Old West and Mexico, thus, literally, people whose tender feet make it difficult for them to walk over rough ground

579:7 **corn cakes** thin fried patties or pancakes made of corn meal, sometimes called Johnny cakes

579:8 **sweetening** any sweet flavoring such as corn syrup, sorghum molasses, or sugar

579:9 **noways** anyway

579:11 **with these Easterners already giving the West a bad name** Apparently Nathaniel refers to the stories Easterners tell about the violent, savage West when they return from visits there, and to the often exaggerated accounts of the West in Eastern newspapers.

579:13 **I'll be bound** I'll guarantee it; I'm not surprised

579:15 **yellowbellied** a derisive term suggesting cowardice

579:16 **Reb** Rebel, a soldier of the Confederate Army or any citizen of the Confederate states

579:31 **buckboard** a horse-drawn wagon. It is roofless and has one wide, flat seat at the front, and a cargo space behind the seat extending six or eight feet back. The front wheels are widely separated from the back. A buckboard probably gave a hard, uncomfortable ride.

579:32 **two leather sacks of gold dust and minted coins and crude jewels** probably the source of the Burden family money, later used to buy the big house outside Jefferson (584:27)

579:34 **sod cabin** a cabin built from blocks of turf or sod by pioneers of the American prairie, where sod was plentiful

580:4 **frail** flail. See entry 578:3.

580:5   **Vangie!**   short for Evangeline; see entry 580:30.

580:51   **Beck!**   short for Rebecca

580:30   **Evangeline**   Perhaps Faulkner named old Burden's first wife for the heroine of Henry Wadsworth Longfellow's popular poem *Evangeline*, published in 1847. The name was not particularly popular among New Englanders prior to the poem's publication. Faulkner entitled a story "Evangeline," written in 1931 but unpublished during his lifetime.°

580:34   **Juana**   Spanish feminine name, the equivalent of the English Jane, Jean, or Joan.

580:38   **There were no ministers out there . . . just priests and Catholics**   In Calvin's mind priests do not qualify as ministers able to conduct Christian services.

580:40   **chico**   Spanish for boy

581:2   **a heathen**   Nathaniel regards Catholics as idol-worshipping heathens.

581:2   **to humor her**   to keep her satisfied, to let her have her way. She does not want her child born out of wedlock.

581:7   **white minister**   Nathaniel does not want to be married by a Catholic priest, nor by a Spanish or Mexican minister. He considers Spaniards and Mexicans racially impure. This is the same Nathaniel who married a Mexican and is opposed to slavery.

581:12   **Rangers**   the Texas Rangers, organized as a paramilitary "ranging" force in 1823 intended to oppose marauding Indians. Until the Civil War they patrolled border areas, occasionally harassing Mexican residents. The Mexican-American War (1846–48) secured their reputation as a fearsome fighting unit. Their sensational, romantic image, popularized by dime-store novels and Hollywood, conflicts with the historical fact of their often racist and lawless vigilantism.°

581:19   **Another damn black Burden . . . Folks will think I bred to a damn slaver**   Another Burden who does not, by New England standards, look to be white. Burden's confused notion that Spanish blood makes one a Negro is shared by

Doc Hines. Confused racism lies at the heart of Christmas's ambiguous racial identity. Burden's statement that people will believe he 'bred to a damn slaver' perhaps humorously reflects his conviction that slave owners often interbred with their slaves, producing racially mixed children like Juana's child. According to C. Vann Woodward, such racism was not unusual among many Northern abolitionists.°

581:23 **Damn, lowbuilt black folks: lowbuilt because of the weight of the wrath of God, black because of the sin of human bondage staining their blood and flesh** 'Lowbuilt' = short. God's wrath holds 'black folks' close to the ground, keeps them from growing taller. They suffer His wrath because of the curse of Ham: according to the Biblical story, when Ham looked upon his father's naked body, God doomed his descendants to be slaves, which many have understood to mean Negroes, who are thus referred to as the 'sons of Ham.' See Genesis 4:8–15. Burden's confused logic argues that slaves are black because the sin of their enslavement has stained them over the years. This would explain his notion on 581:26 that once slaves are freed, 'they'll bleach out' in a hundred years. See entry 675:39.

581:26 **we done freed them now, both black and white alike. They'll bleach out now. In a hundred years they will be white folks again. Then maybe we'll let them come back into America** 'We'—Northerners, abolitionists—have freed 'them'—blacks—from slavery, and whites from the sin of slavery. Once the blacks have had a while to enjoy freedom, they will gradually turn white again, and then we can forgive the Rebels for having been slaveholders and can allow them back into the Union. During Reconstruction, many former Confederates who refused to sign a loyalty oath were denied the right of U. S. citizenship and were otherwise prevented from participating in local and state government. Calvin Burden's pronouncement is remarkably similar to a half-sarcastic utterance of Shreve McCannon in the final chapter of *Absalom, Absalom!*: "I think that in time the Jim Bonds [i.e., blacks] are going to conquer the western hemisphere. . . . of course as they spread toward the poles they will bleach out again like the rabbits and the birds do" (471).

581:40 **even if he was dark like father's mother's people and like his mother** The family of Joanna's father's mother were Huguenots, of a Gallic heritage; Calvin's mother was a Mexican. People of Mexican and/or Gallic descent are likely to have dark skins.

582:4 **he was killed in the town two miles away by an ex-slaveholder and Confederate soldier named Sartoris, over a question of negro voting** Joanna's account of the killings generally coincides with the story given by Bayard Sartoris in the "Skirmish at Sartoris" chapter of *The Unvanquished*. See also entry 432:25.

582:25 **Carpet baggers** Southern term for Northerners who came South after the Civil War to take financial advantage of the defeated states and the Reconstruction policies that white Southerners thought were intended to punish them. The term derives from the travel bags made of carpet fabric that Northerners brought with them.

582:26 **still too close for even the ones that got whipped to be very sensible** The Burdens arrived in Mississippi around 1867. Joanna means that the War had occurred so recently that neither Northerners nor Southerners could think reasonably about issues related to it, including the rights of freed slaves. She acknowledges that some Northerners trying to enforce Reconstruction policies, including her own relatives, often seemed to provoke trouble and invite retaliation.

583:11 **the summer, and it would have been too hot** Summer heat and humidity accelerate the decomposition of flesh.

583:16 **the negroes hadn't raped or murdered anybody to speak of** The atrocities that Southern whites thought freed slaves would commit had not occurred. Joanna speaks with some irony: she bemusedly contrasts Southern expectations against post-war realities.

583:24 **at least thirtyfive years old** Joanna's father wants for a second wife a woman who is mature, settled, and willing to stay at home.

583:38 **the veil out of some mosquito netting that a saloon keeper had nailed over a picture behind the bar. They borrowed it from him** The 'picture behind the bar' is probably the traditional saloon picture of a reclining nude woman. The saloon keeper probably pulls the mosquito netting down over the picture to hide it when genteel women or others who might be offended enter his bar.

584:16 **Lincoln and the negro and Moses and the children of Israel were the same** Old Burden asserts the literal truth of the metaphor, popular among blacks and abolitionists, that links Lincoln's emancipation of American slaves to the Biblical story in which Moses freed the enslaved Israelites from the Egyptian pharaoh. See Exodus for the Biblical account.

584:17 **the Red Sea was just the blood that had to be spilled in order that the black race might cross into the Promised Land** In Burden's embellishment, the Red Sea becomes the blood spilled by white soldiers in the Civil War so that slaves could cross to the Promised Land of freedom.

584:23 **a commission from the government . . . to help with the freed negroes** a commission from the Freedmen's Bureau (the Bureau of Refugees, Freedmen, and Abandoned Lands), established March 3, 1865, to aid freed slaves and to administer abandoned land. The Bureau was rife with financial corruption, and most white Southerners viewed even the most honest and dedicated of its agents as carpetbaggers.°

584:28 **what they probably knew all the time was going to happen did happen** The two Calvins were killed.

584:33 **father named me Joanna after Calvin's mother** Joanna is the anglicized form of Juana. Thus, Joanna Burden is the daughter of Nathaniel Burden and his unnamed New Hampshire wife, the granddaughter of the elder Calvin Burden, and the half-sister of the younger Calvin.

584:33 **I dont think he even wanted another son** I don't think he was disappointed that I was a girl. I think he didn't care.

585:3 **something that came from the cedar grove to me, through him . . .** 'something' = the curse and burden of slavery, which the Burden family took as its special obligation to expiate. See 486:5 for a discussion of 'grove.'

585:8 **Your grandfather and brother are lying there, murdered not by one white man but by the curse which God put on a whole race** As Joanna soon explains: 'The curse of the black race is God's curse. But the curse of the white race is the black man who will be forever God's chosen own because He once cursed Him' (586). See entries 581:23 and 675:39.

585:12 **A race doomed and cursed to be forever and ever a part of the white man's doom and curse for its sins** Nathaniel's interpretation of God's curse on the black race is that it is forever bound to the white race, which itself had been cursed for its own sin—the primal original sin—before there was a black race.

585:14 **His doom and his curse** the white man's doom and curse

585:18 **'Not even me?' and he said, 'Not even you.** The father's response to this child who cannot understand why she must be responsible for acts committed before her birth reflects his Puritan belief in original sin and infant damnation: "In Adam's fall we sinned all."

585:18 **Least of all, you** Since Joanna will be the only remaining Burden after her father's death, she especially bears responsibility for the curse. Moreover, by *explaining* the curse to her, her father has insured that she cannot forget it. From now on she must live in its shadow.

585:19 **I had seen and known negroes since I could remember. . . . But after that I seemed to see them for the first time . . . as a thing, a shadow in which I lived, we lived, all white people** Until that day with her father at the grave site, Joanna had regarded Negroes just as another part of her world. But since then, Negroes have been the 'shadow' that darkens her world and determines the course of her life, the shadow in which she believes all whites are forever doomed to live. Joe Christmas himself is frequently described as a shadow.

585:26 **And I seemed to see the black shadow in the shape of a cross. And it seemed like the white babies were struggling, even before they drew breath, to escape from the shadow ...** Joanna imagines the 'black shadow in the shape of a cross' on which she and all other children are crucified—as Christ was crucified, though while He was crucified to redeem the sins of others, she and the children are crucified as punishment for slavery.

The 'black shadow' suggests "the valley of the shadow of Death" of the Twenty-third Psalms. Ronald W. Hoag finds in it the influence of Herman Melville's "Benito Cereno," which Faulkner could have known through Raymond Weaver's edition of *Shorter Novels of Herman Melville*, issued in 1928 by Horace Liveright, who had published Faulkner's two first novels. Hoag observes:

> After Amasa Delano has quelled the slave rebellion on the *San Dominick* and rescued that ship's haggard captain, Don Benito Cereno, he is perplexed by Cereno's failure to recover from his ordeal ... Some months before Cereno's decline ends in death, Delano puts to him the vexed query: 'You are saved: what has cast such a shadow upon you?' To which question the haunted man replies, 'The negro.' ... One central correspondence that underlies both passages is the imaging of a change in consciousness and perspective, a change depicted as the fall of the black shadow. ... Joanna's admission that before her father's lecture she had looked at Negroes as she did at 'rain, or furniture, or food or sleep' attests that she too was oblivious to the continuing rent in the individual and social fabric wrought by racial subjugation. For her as for Benito, the Negro ... must hereafter be regarded seriously as the objectified, returning curse of the slave-system.°

585:39 **You must raise the shadow with you** Thus Joanna Burden lives in Mississippi and has dedicated her life to helping blacks, trying to 'raise the shadow,' struggling to bear her cross. See entry 487:14.

585:39 **you can never lift it to your level. I can see that now, which I did not see until I came down here** 'it' = the shadow, the black race. Nathaniel believed that blacks are inherently inferior and *cannot* be raised to the level of whites. He did not believe this until he had lived in the South where the freed slaves lived. But he still considers it his duty to try to raise blacks as far as they can be raised. Joanna repeats her father's belief as if she agrees, and she is explaining it to Christmas, who himself has told her that he is part black.

586:2 **The curse of the black race is God's curse. But the curse of the white race is the black man** This explains the relationship of the two curses first mentioned on 585:10–14.

586:3 **the black man who will be forever God's chosen own because He once cursed him** 'him' = the black man. In Nathaniel's theology even God must atone for the curse which he placed on Ham's sons. See entry 675:39. Faulkner once suggested that this sentence should read "He once cursed Ham," but typescript and manuscript show 'him'—not 'Ham' or, for that matter, the 'Him' of the 1932 edition.°

586:13 **You would have** She means that Christmas, had he been in her father's place, would have killed the murderer of the two Calvins.

586:18 **You dont have any idea who your parents were?** This non sequitur, Joanna's sudden turn to the question of Joe's racial identity after her long story about her family history, suggests she may see in Joe an opportunity to serve her family's dedication to the black race in a specifically personal way. Thus this entire passage, which explains her family's response to the curse of slavery and its belief that the black race is inferior, bears directly on the relationship she is about to begin with Christmas.

586:20 **Except that one of them was part nigger** In the manuscript, Christmas answered Joanna Burden's query about his parentage with a blunter "Except that one of them was a nigger." In typescript Faulkner revised 'nigger' to 'part nigger,' heightening the ambiguity of his protagonist's race.°

586:25 **I dont know it** Christmas admits that his racial identity is uncertain.

586:30 **If I'm not, damned if I haven't wasted a lot of time** wasted time by living my life on the assumption I am black

586:33 **I had thought of that** of why her father had not killed Colonel Sartoris. But this sentence is sufficiently ambiguous to suggest that she is also agreeing with Christmas that if he had been mistaken about his racial identity then he has indeed wasted a lot of time.

586:34 **I think that it was because of his French blood** Joanna suggests that her father's French blood underlay his understanding of how the inhabitants of an invaded land feel about the invaders, since France had been invaded often enough. She says that her father did not kill Sartoris in revenge because he understood why the man would want to kill "foreigners" trying to force new ways on a vanquished land.

CHAPTER XII

588:1   **the second phase**   of their relationship. Faulkner divides their affair into three phases. The first begins with Joe's
arrival at Joanna's house in the late spring of 1929. This first
phase is a struggle between Joe and Joanna for the possession of her 'spiritual privacy' (571). At first he forces himself
on her, but later, for four or five months, he ignores her
entirely. He wants her to make clear that she needs him
sexually and waits for her 'to make the first sign' (575). The
second phase begins in September 1929 when she comes to
his cabin and surrenders 'in words' (576), telling him her life
story. During this phase Joanna gives in to Joe completely,
immersing them both in a frenzy of lust that to Joe is like 'a
sewer' (588). Over a two-year period the lust diminishes and
the second phase gradually gives way to the third, which begins in earnest in February 1932 when Joanna asks Joe 'Do
you realise . . . that you are wasting your life?' (597) and
begins trying to reform him.

588:1   **It was as though he had fallen into a sewer**   Christmas
feels corrupted by the passion and lust of this second phase
of his affair with Joanna. The 'sewer' image is the controlling
metaphor of this episode.

588:3   **that first hard and manlike surrender**   on the night in
chapter XI when he forced his way into her room and raped
her. See 571–573.

588:15   **He washed and changed to the white shirt and the
dark creased trousers**   In chapter IX (550:32) Max Confrey called Joe a 'clodhopper.' Years later, though he wears
overalls to his job at the sawmill, Joe dons the more formal

shirt and trousers in the evening to insure he will never suffer that insult again.

589:20 **breaking down something and leaving it corrupt** breaking down her New England-bred resistance to lust and sexuality, so that what once had been aversion to sex now becomes obsession

588:28 **paths . . . which radiated from the house like wheel-spokes** one of several wheel images in the novel (see entry 760:12), like the wheels of the wagon in chapter I and the wheel of Hightower's thinking in chapter XX. The Burden house is a center, a haven to which black women come for help and advice.

588:33 **headrags** a cloth wrapped around the head like a turban, often worn by black women at work°

589:1 **He believed that during the day she thought no more about him than he did about her** This seems to contradict 588:24, where we are told that Joe thought about Joanna all day long. However, if we understand 'no more' as 'no more often,' this statement means that Joe believed Joanna thought about him no more often than he thought about her, that is, that they thought about one another intensely; in any case, the wording is vague.

589:12 **perhaps with foreboding and premonition, the savage and lonely street which he had chosen of his own free will** the street that 'was to run for fifteen years' which he entered in chapter X (563:21). Joe wonders whether he ought still to be traveling that street instead of settling down to domestic comfort with Joanna. On the 'street' he could determine his actions and his fate. With Joanna, that freedom is denied him.

589:14 *This is not my life. I dont belong here.* Christmas feels this way because of the strangely domestic pattern his life has taken, the fierce sexuality of his relations with Joanna, and Joanna herself. He has spent his life fleeing and fighting these things; now he almost feels he has surrendered to them.

589:16 **the New England glacier exposed suddenly to the fire of the New England biblical hell** See entry 577:20.

589:18 **Perhaps he was aware of the abnegation in it** 'abnegation' = denial, a giving up. Joe thinks she is giving up the hope of salvation, that she attempts to make up for all the 'frustrate and irrevocable years' of sexual repression by sinning with an 'imperious and fierce urgency' that will, according to the doctrine of her forefathers, damn her to hell.

589:20 **frustrate and irrevocable years** years of repressed sexuality that cannot be changed or recovered

589:31 **without any feminine fears at all** without the fears that a woman living alone might suffer: of loneliness or of rape.

590:17 **that house which no white person save himself had entered in years** a reference only to Joe's white skin color, not to his ambiguous racial identity

590:23 **her eyes in the dark glowing like the eyes of cats** Lust effects an animalistic transformation in Joanna. Many folk tales and myths relate the transformation of women into cats and of cats into women.° Interestingly, Christmas himself is repeatedly compared to a cat. See entry 567:24.

590:29 **a Beardsley of the time of Petronius** Aubrey Beardsley (1872–1898), English artist whose highly stylized, often erotic drawings and paintings depicted women of the Bible and classical literature and of the late nineteenth century. Faulkner's early admiration for Beardsley is apparent in his illustrations for *Marionettes* and in his portrayal of feminine eroticism in Cecily Saunders and Margaret Powers of *Soldiers' Pay*. Gaius Petronius (?–66 A. D.) described the licentiousness of Rome during the time of Nero. His most famous work, *The Satyricon*, includes a description of an orgy.

590:30 **close, breathing half-dark without walls** 'close' = suffocating, claustrophobic

590:31 **her wild hair each strand of which would seem to come alive like octopus tentacles** an image linking Joanna to the Medusa of Greek myth, an aggressive, sexually threat-

ening gorgon with writhing snakes for hair and whose glance
could turn men to stone. Joanna, like the Medusa, is decapi-
tated.° A similar image describes Bobbie Allen after McEachern accosts her in the schoolhouse (550:16).

590:33 **Negro! Negro! Negro!** Joanna revels in what she regards as her own degradation—making love with a man she
considers a Negro. Despite her work for the welfare of
blacks, she is clearly a racist.

590:37 **The corruption came from a source even more inexplicable to him than to her** Joanna's lust is stranger to Joe
than it is to her because he lacks any essential understanding
of female sexuality and emotions. As the person who feels
sexual desire, Joanna at least has some understanding, however confused, of its origins.

590:40 **He began to be afraid.** Because he does not understand what is happening to Joanna, he is losing control of
their relationship, in which he is supposed to be the cor-
rupter. There are echoes throughout this passage of 'the
suavely shaped urns' from which 'there issued something liquid, deathcolored, and foul' (538) in chapter VIII.

591:4 **the street lonely, savage, and cool** The street is 'cool'
because it allows Christmas freedom from threatening rela-
tionships that inflame his passions and threaten his isolation.
The street is 'savage' because it allows him escape from domesticity and order (see 561:1, 589:13).

591:8 **But something held him, as the fatalist can always be
held** Since Joe, a fatalist, believes that events will ultimately
come to an unhappy end, he is easily dissuaded from deci-
sive action that he believes will do him no good.

591:10 **imperious and overriding fury of those nights** 'imperious,' which also occurs on 589:6 and 589:19, suggests
that Joe feels he has lost control of his relationship with
Joanna, that she and her lust are now dictating the affair's
course

591:12 **the two creatures that struggled in the one body . . .
upon the surface of a black thick pool beneath the last moon**

a nightmarish, apocalyptic, perhaps demonic image. The 'two creatures' are the warring aspects of Joanna's personality—her Puritan self struggling against her lust-obsessed self. The 'thick black pool' is the pool of filth, of sin, in which Christmas feels he is drowning. The 'last moon' deepens the unreality of the image and suggests that Joanna is rushing to experience as much lust and pleasure as she can before the onset of menopause and age.

591:16 **that still, cold, contained figure of the first phase who, even though lost and damned, remained somehow impervious and impregnable** In the 'first phase' of her relationship with Joe (described on 572:4), she merely submitted to sex. But she was doomed to begin to enjoy it and thus was 'lost and damned.' Because she had not yet openly surrendered to the sexual forces within her, she remained on the surface 'impervious and impregnable,' by which Faulkner means that her spirit had not yet been corrupted. He compares the progress of the affair to the phases of the moon, which illuminates the nighttime encounters, and to the "phases" of Joanna's body, her menstrual cycle and the approach of menopause. See entry 588:1.

591:29 **but she dont know how to do that either.** Christmas paraphrases his earlier comment: 'She's trying to be a woman and she dont know how' (576).

591:30 **She had begun to get fat.** The preceding passage, which emphasizes Joanna's 'struggling' in the 'black thick pool' of her lust, would seem to suggest that she is losing control over her body, that she has fallen victim to gluttony as well as to lechery. 593:30 reveals that 'She had never been better; her appetite was enormous.' Weight gain can also be a sign of age. All three explanations probably serve here.

591:35 **shadows before a westering sun, the chill and implacable import of autumn cast ahead upon summer; something of dying summer spurting again like a dying coal, in the fall** These images may have been influenced by Shakespeare's Sonnet 73, especially lines 5–10:

In me thou seest the twilight of such day
As after sunset fadeth in the west;
Which by and by black night doth take away,
Death's second self, that seals up all in rest.
In me thou seest the glowing of such fire,
That on the ashes of his youth doth lie.

Ilse Dusoir Lind suggests that Faulkner may have read a book entitled *The Glands Regulating Personality*, by Louis Berman (1921). Of women about to enter menopause, Berman writes: "It is as if the ovaries and the accessory sexual internal secretions erupt into a final geyser before they are exhausted." Faulkner may have incorporated the "final geyser" in his image of 'dying summer spurting again like a dying coal.'° Joanna's sexual excitement is the result of 'an actual despair at frustrate and irrevocable years' (589). She is, quite literally, trying to make up for lost time, to compress the sexual life of twenty years into a few months.

592:17 **articulate beneath the clean, austere garments . . . that rotten richness ready to flow into putrefaction at a touch** Joe views Joanna's female sexuality as corrupt and dangerous. The fact that she menstruates makes her unclean to him, and he associates every aspect of her sexual existence with that uncleanliness. All he need do to arouse her is to touch her, and then she flows 'into putrefaction.' See also entry 538:18.

592:39 **mistral** a strong cold and dry wind that occurs in southern France; it may blow for several days at a time, often at a speed of more than 60 miles per hour.

593:10 **talking of still a third stranger** There are three strangers here: Joe, Joanna, and the child she wants to have.

593:18 **ruined park** the overgrown yard surrounding the house

593:36 **that it would overtake and betray her completely, but she would not be harmed . . . she would be saved, that life would go on the same and even better, even less terrible** 'betray' here means "change drastically, do something to her she could not expect." Before the second phase of the affair, Joanna regarded menopause as the end to her childbearing days and her sexual existence (both of which would seem to her Puritan mind as 'terrible'), thus 'saving' her from temptation and making her life 'better.' Now at the height of her affair with Christmas and her sexual awakening she does not want to be saved.

594:2 **wild with regret** an allusion to Tennyson's "Tears, Idle Tears": "Deep as first love, and wild with all regret; / O Death in Life, the days that are no more."°

594:4 **Dont make me have to pray yet. Dear God, let me be damned a little longer** Joanna's prayer recalls a passage in the *Confessions* of St. Augustine: "'Grant me chastity and continency, but not yet.' For I was afraid lest thou shouldest hear me soon, and soon deliver me from the disease of concupiscence, which I desired to have satisfied rather than extinguished."°

594:6 **far and irrevocable end** The 'end' of the tunnel is Joanna's past, before Joe's arrival and her sexual awakening. It is 'irrevocable' because it cannot be relived or changed.

594:7 **her naked breast of three short years ago ached as though in agony, virgin and crucified** 'naked breast' is metaphoric rather than literal: it means the heart of her bare soul, which ached from loneliness and lack of fulfillment. She had never known passion: her 'naked breast' was 'virgin.' It was 'crucified' because she had sacrificed her opportunity for love by devoting herself to the black race that, as her father told her, was 'doomed and cursed to be forever and ever a part of the white race's doom and curse for its sins' (585).

594:29 **If I give in now, I will deny all the thirty years that I have lived to make me what I chose to be** The manuscript reads that he spent thirty years building "the edifice of the self-made pariah,"° a sufficient explanation of what he fears he would deny here. The temptation of domestic life is another parallel between Joe's life and Christ's. See Matthew 4:1–11, which narrates Satan's tempting of Christ in the wilderness.

594:38 **He discovered now that he had been expecting her to tell him that for three months** because she has been talking for three months, since September, about the possibility of a baby

594:40 **he knew that she was not . . . she also knew that she was not** not lying. Both Joe and Joanna believe she is pregnant. Neither realizes that she has missed a period because she has entered menopause.

595:9 **A full measure** Justice is served. She believes that her suspected pregnancy with a 'negro bastard child' serves a 'full measure' of justice to, and is the logical consequence of, her family's abolitionism. She may also be thinking of the 'curse' that her father described to her when she was four years old, 'the curse of every white child that ever was born and that ever will be born' (585). Here that curse takes form in the child she believes she carries.

595:10 **I would like to see father's and Calvin's faces.** The prospect of her half-Negro illegitimate child would outrage them, and this gives her pleasure because that child is the result of her fidelity to her father's enjoinder in chapter XI that 'You must raise them up' (585:36).

595:14 **that final upflare of stubborn and dying summer upon which autumn, the dawning of halfdeath, had come unawares** Although earlier (591:35) this metaphor implied the approach of age and menopause, here Joanna uses it to denote the end of passion. Hence the sentence that follows: '"It's over now," she thought quietly; "finished."'

595:17 **the waiting, for one month more to pass, to be sure** Joanna has missed one menstrual period. She will wait one month more to be sure of her pregnancy before telling Christmas. However, she forgets that missed menstrual periods also signal the onset of menopause. Faulkner links the advent of menopause to the coming of autumn, a symbolic parallel between seasonal and human biological cycles.

595:22 **accomplish** pass

596:8 **quilted, lintpadded covers** quilted blankets stuffed for warmth with small bits of cotton

596:30 **This was when the third phase began** The third phase marks the end of their sexual affair and the beginning of Joanna's struggle to reform Joe. This phase ends in her murder seven months later in August 1932.

596:32 **a kind of tacit apology** for her indifference to him

596:33 **He was prepared to go that length, even** He was prepared to go through the motions of trying to win back her affections, if this would allow the resumption of their affair.

596:38 **It wont hurt the kid** Joe, who still thinks Joanna believes she is pregnant, assures her that sex will not hurt the child.

597:1 **a single word** No.

597:3 **Do you realise . . . that you are wasting your life** Joanna has given up the idea that she is pregnant and has embarked on a new relationship with Joe, whom she now intends to reform as a sign of her salvation and her victory over desire.

597:37 **During the first phase . . . ; during the second phase . . . ; now he was in the middle of a plain** In the first phase of their relationship Joe sought to be welcomed into Joanna's house, to enjoy her companionship and passion; in the second phase, he encounters a passion for which he was unprepared and that he believes corrupts him; in the third phase he feels utterly drained of passion and desire. See entry 588:1.

598:4 **He began now to be afraid** of the direction their relationship may take, and of his partner Brown's loud mouth

598:11 **I know now that what makes a fool is an inability to take his own advice** Christmas refers to himself. He regrets having taken Brown as a partner. The 'advice' he did not heed was his unstated but obvious belief that the best way to stay out of trouble is to avoid all entanglements.

598:39 **I have got to do something. There is something that**

I am going to do   Here Christmas begins to realize that he will have to do something to end the tension and the impossible state of relations with Joanna. He doesn't know yet what the 'something' will be. Note the link with Chapter V, where Christmas stands on the verge of murdering Joanna: 'Maybe I have already done it' (481); *Something is going to happen to me. I am going to do something.*'

599:31   **he believed he knew what the message would be, would promise**   an invitation to her bedroom and the resumption of their affair

600:5   **whiphand**   the upper hand, the power

600:5   **All that foolishness**   all that 'talking about niggers and babies' (599:34) that caused the lull in their relationship

600:23   **truely: something in minor**   in tune and in a minor key; 'truely' as a musical term is spelled correctly.

601:4   **The table was set for him in the kitchen.**   Since for two months he has been eating his meals in town (597:31), Joe apparently takes the meal Joanna prepared for him as proof of what he believes the note says.

601:22   **tomcat**   "to prowl around at night in sexual pursuit of women."°

601:40   **yellowbellied wop**   See entries 564:20, 579:15. Although this ethnic slur takes note of Christmas's 'foreign' appearance, it stops short of calling him a Negro.

602:16   **severe garment**   plain, unadorned garment, like work clothing

602:20   **wart on a diseased bough**   a symptom of advanced age in trees, metaphorically reflecting Joanna's age, appearance, and personality

602:24   *you should have read that note*   Joanna's appearance in the spectacles and 'severe garment'—she is not prepared for bed—makes Joe realize that he might have been mistaken about what he supposed the note to say.

602:25   **I am going to do something.**   See entry 598:39.

602:29   **calm enormity**   Joanna's (to him) preposterous scheme

602:32   **thinking fled smooth and idle**   Though he seems to listen to and even repeat Joanna's words, he is not thinking about what she says at all.

602:40 **Peebles** her Negro lawyer in Memphis, previously referred to but not named on 571:12

603:5 **Then I will turn over all the business to you . . . So that when you need money for yourself you could. . . you would know how; lawyers know how** Joanna tells Joe that he would be able to use for his own purposes money from the funds she supervises—funds that support Negro charities and scholarships, thus the money of the very people she has spent her life serving. This is the most substantial temptation Joe faces. Frederick Asals believes it parallels the third temptation of Christ: "She is in a very real sense offering to him both her 'kingdoms,' earthly and heavenly, if he will surrender to her. The parallel to the third temptation of Christ is evident"; see Matthew 4:8–9.°

603:14 **promptive** asking her to respond

603:18 **"Tell niggers that I am a nigger too"** Throughout his life Christmas has delighted in telling people, especially white women with whom he has just had sex, that he is a black man. But he has done so voluntarily. One of the most dangerous things Joanna could do is try to compel him to accept his blackness.

603:32 **in that long blowing wind . . . long wind of knowing** the wind of dawning awareness

603:37 **it happened to you** it = menopause

604:2 **the words which she had once loved to hear on his tongue** obscene words that she enjoyed hearing during their lovemaking

604:18 **briefer than epitaphs** Before the notes held promise of love and pleasure; now they signify the death of their passion.

604:26 **When have I sat down in peace to eat.** By 'peace' Joe apparently means freedom from the tension and strain of his relationship with a woman.

604:31 **monotonous steady voice** the same voice with which McEachern prayed. See 511:24, 568:25.

604:33 **He dared not try to distinguish the words. He did not dare let himself know what she was at.** He does not want to hear her pray because he might be driven to an act he is not ready for.

605:1 **it would seem to him that he could distinguish the prints of knees** from where she had been kneeling on the floor. Compare with 512:18. As a boy Joe knelt while his foster-father McEachern prayed, but he did not pray himself; nor does he pray now.

605:8 **Your soul . . . . Expiation of . . . . hell . . . . forever and ever** Joanna repeats to Joe the contents of her prayer for the redemption of his soul. She prays for him perhaps because she feels responsible for the sins they committed together.

605:15 **he would not even go away** Why not? Because he is bound to her as closely as she to him. There has been passion between them. He feels entrapped by their own mutual past.

605:22 **saying what and to what or whom he dared not learn nor suspect** Again Joe resists thinking that Joanna is praying to God for his salvation. See entry 604:33.

605:23 **And so as he sat in the shadows of the ruined garden on that August night and heard the clock in the courthouse two miles away strike ten and then eleven** The retrospective account of Christmas's life that began in chapter VI ends here, and the narrative has moved up to the present time of August 1932 and the night when he kills Joanna. This narrative point in time corresponds to the end of chapter VI.

605:24 **ruined garden** the overgrown garden near Joanna's house: metaphorically, the ruined Edenic garden of their love. It is tempting to view the garden as Christmas's Gethsemane, where he wrestles with what he believes to be his fate.

605:26 **he believed with calm paradox that he was the volitionless servant of the fatality in which he believed that he did not believe** He believes he is acting with free will, but at the same time he feels he has no choice but to kill Joanna. He is rationalizing his own fatalism.

605:29 *She said so herself* She had said it first three months
before: 'Maybe it would be better if we both were dead'
(604:7). Two nights before this night she had said: 'Then
there's just one other thing to do' (606:21). Joe contrives to
believe, as part of the rationalizing logic that drives him, that
they both think he should kill her. See entry 606:21.

605:38 **her attitude of formal abjectness a part of the pride,
her voice calm and tranquil and abnegant in the twilight**
She took pride in her humility, in her full and calm acceptance of what she has surrendered. Faulkner used both 'abject' and 'abnegant' earlier in a related passage: 'the abject
fury of the New England glacier' (589:16), the 'abnegation'
of which Joe was perhaps aware.

606:2 **finished a period** paused at the end of a sentence

606:18 **This time she did not even ask the question** i.e.,
'Will you pray?'

606:21 **"Then there's just one other thing to do."**
"There's just one other thing to do," he said. Joanna
and Christmas are both saying aloud, though not necessarily to each other, more likely to themselves, that the only
thing left to do is to kill each other: Joanna intends to kill
Christmas with the pistol; he intends to kill her with the razor. Unlike her, however, he does not intend to kill himself
afterward.

606:23 **So now it's all done, all finished** Here the time shifts
from 'two nights ago' to the night Christmas kills Joanna. He
is in the same place at the same time—outside her house, at
midnight—where he was at the end of chapter V (486).

606:27 **But that was in another time, another life.** an often-
quoted line from Marlowe's *The Jew of Malta*:

> Thou hast committed—
> Fornication?—but that was in another country;
> And besides, the wench is dead. [IV.i]

Christmas thinks this while he is sitting in one of the places
where he had met Joanna 'on one of the wild nights two

years ago' (606). But that was 'in another time, another life,' and besides in his mind the 'wench' is already dead (605: 29).°

606:29 **the voices** all the voices of his life, mentioned before in Chapter V: 476, 478, 483.

606:31 **tomorrow night, all the tomorrows . . . tomorrow to- be and had-been would be the same. Then it was time.**

He rose. He moved from the shadow There are clear echoes here from the famous soliloquy in *Macbeth*, that begins, appropriately enough, "She should have died hereafter," and then continues:

> To-morrow, and to-morrow, and to-morrow
> Creeps in this petty pace from day to day,
> To the last syllable of recorded time;
> And all our yesterdays have lighted fools
> The way to dusty death. Out, out, brief candle!
> life's but a walking shadow . . . .

The notion that 'tomorrow to-be and had-been would be the same' reflects Faulkner's belief in the unbroken linearity of time—in the links between past, present, and future—that he held to the end of his career. In a 1955 interview, he stated: "There is no such thing as was—only is."°

607:1 **It was as if he were not thinking of sleep, of whether she would be asleep or not** a reference to the previous night in chapter V (476:37) when he wondered whether she were asleep. At 486:6, Joe thinks: *'Maybe she is not asleep either.'*

607:7 **He held the razor in his hand** Joe goes to Joanna's room intending to kill her. He delays the act, puts the razor down on the table, perhaps to learn whether she will say something that will change his mind.

607:21 **I dont ask it.** Joanna means that God, not she, asks Christmas to kneel. If she plans to kill him and then herself, then she is giving him a chance to repent of his sins.

607:23 **old style, single action, cap-and-ball revolver** probably a Colt Army Revolver (six-shot, .44 caliber, 14 inches long), "the principal revolver used in the Civil War."° It used old fashioned balls and black powder rather than modern cartridge ammunition. The caps were wrapped in paper that deteriorated over time, a fact that probably explains why the pistol does not fire.

607:31 **They were calm and still as all pity and all despair and all conviction** Joanna feels 'pity' toward Joe and 'despair' for herself but is convinced she is doing what she must.

607:33 **the shadowed pistol on the wall** The shadow on the wall takes the form of a snake about to strike, and Christmas is transfixed by that image of his impending death.

608:12 **as fear gained courage as it were** Fear gains courage only when the situation becomes desperate, as the girl believes it has here.

608:23 **naming the same town which the negro boy had named to him on that afternoon three years ago, when he had first seen Jefferson** See 566:18–21. Neither here nor in chapter X is the town named, but Mottstown, the nearest town of any size other than Jefferson, would be a likely choice. In Mottstown Christmas will be captured a week later, closing the circle of his life (see 649–50), and there is at least circumstantial evidence that the small farm where he grew up with the McEacherns was close to Mottstown. See, for instance, entries 573:25, 651:8, 681:7. So his desire to go there on this particular night, when he has just killed a white woman, is significant, perhaps a sign of his intention to surrender to the fate he feels is inevitable.

608:26 **cap'm** captain: an ingratiating term of respect

609:1 **recapitulant** See entry 460:26.

609:39 **the now impalpable dust** The dust is 'impalpable' not because he cannot feel it but because he cannot see it: the car headlights no longer illuminate it.

610:11 **the ancient thing with its two loaded chambers** the cap-and-ball revolver

610:15 **For her and for me** Joe is thinking of the 'two loaded chambers' of the pistol he is about to throw into the undergrowth. One was loaded with a bullet meant for him, 'the one upon which the hammer had already fallen' and which had misfired; the other with a bullet intended for her.

CHAPTER XIII

611:1 **Within five minutes after the countryman found the fire** We first learn of the fire's discovery in Chapter IV, 464–65, when Byron Bunch tells Hightower about it. Chapter XIII begins with that discovery, which loosely parallels Lena Grove's approach to Jefferson in the first chapter: she sees the smoke from the fire as her wagon mounts the hill overlooking the town (420). The end of Chapter XII thus marks the conclusion of the seven-chapter "flashback" of Christmas's life leading up to Joanna Burden's murder.

611:6 **corporal's guard** small band

611:11 **blatting** making a lot of noise. Faulkner may have intended another meaning: the crying of a calf or sheep.

611:14 **with that static and childlike amaze with which adults contemplate their own inescapable portraits** i.e., with bewilderment and wonder. In Joanna's corpse, they see proof of their own mortality.

611:31 **Presently the fire truck came up gallantly . . . hatless men and youths clung with the astonishing disregard of physical laws that flies possess** The 'hatless men and youths' are the Jefferson volunteer fire department. This farcical description suggests the film antics of the Keystone Cops, still popular in the early 1930s.

612:1 **opera hats; only there was now nothing for them to spring to** The crowns of opera hats collapse for easy storage and spring open 'at the touch of a hand' (611) for wear. The ladders have nothing to spring to because the Burden house has burned down.

612:2 **telephone trust advertisements** 'trust' = company,

syndicate. Telephone company advertisements frequently depicted coils of telephone cable as evidence of the company's competence and commitment to the public good.

612:15 **emotional barbecue . . . Roman holiday** an excuse for excitement and uproar. Faulkner compares the gathering of townspeople before the burning house to the practice in ancient Rome of giving citizens a holiday to watch public executions.

612:17 **Not that. Peace is not that often.** Peace does not come that easily, even in death.

612:18 **believing that the flames, the blood, the body that had died three years ago** onlookers believe that the murdered body demands revenge, not realizing that in death it has achieved peace. The 'body that had died three years ago' refers to the destructive passion of her sexual relationship with Christmas that killed her true self, corrupted her soul, long before he killed her body with a razor. These words are clearly linked to 594:7: 'her naked breast of three short years ago ached as though in agony, virgin and crucified.'

612:19 **had just now begun to live again** Joanna's body lives in the imagination of the crowd as it speculates about her death.

612:20 **not believing that the rapt infury of the flames and the immobility of the body were both affirmations of an attained bourne beyond the hurt and harm of man. Not that.** 'rapt infury': a furious concentrated turning inward. The flames are self-feeding, self-consuming. The crowd does not understand that the fire and Joanna's lifeless body signify that she has achieved a place of safety from the harm men can do her. The archaism 'bourne' means an endpoint or place of final rest, the "undiscover'd country from whose bourn no traveler returns" (*Hamlet* III.i.56).

612:23 **Because the other made nice believing. . . . Better than the musty offices where the lawyers waited . . . or where the doctors waited . . . And the women too** 'the other' = the belief that Joanna was ravished both before and

after her murder; see 611:20. Her death, the crime that demands vindication, becomes a focus of mystery and meaning
in the otherwise meaningless lives of the people in the mob.

612:34 **believing . . . that they labored for that end whose
ultimate attainment would leave them nothing whatever to
do** Doctors believe they labor for the public health, but if
they attained that goal, they would have 'nothing whatever
to do.'

612:37 **women . . . with secret frustrated breasts (who have
ever loved death better than peace)** Women need the excitement which Joanna's murder offers. They love 'death
better than peace' because death—the events and people
who caused it—offer excitement, while peace offers nothing
of interest to them.

612:38 **hurried garments** hurriedly donned clothes

612:40 **to print with a myriad small hard heels . . . periods
such as perhaps *Is he still free? Ah. Is he? Is he?*** 'myriad' = many; 'periods' = both the small round marks left by
the heels of women's shoes, like the periods at the end of
sentences, and the rhetorical divisions of speech. Thus, as
they walk about the scene of the murder, the points of the
women's heels punctuate and emphasize their passionate
questions about the murderer. They believe, Faulkner seems
to suggest, that if the rapist-murderer is still at large, then
rape remains a possibility that they find preferable to the
banality of their lives.

613:8 **It seemed to him that that by and because of which
he had had ancestors long enough to come himself to be,
had allied itself with crime** the antecedent of the second
'that' is 'fire.' The sheriff thinks that fire, whose discovery
figured importantly in the evolution of the human race and
ultimately brought about his own existence, now conspires
against him, on the side of criminals.

613:12 **that heedless monument of the color of both hope
and catastrophe** the burning house. The red color of fire
is the color of 'catastrophe'—in a general sense as well as the

more specific sense of Joanna's fate. Fire as a beacon is the color of hope, but again more specifically it signifies the secret fantasies of those who gaze with fascination on Joanna's body and her burning house.

613:22 **A white man?** Why does the sheriff ask this question? The countryman just remembered having seen a man in the Burden house. In the South of the 1930s, a 'man' is a white man. A black man is a 'black man' or 'nigger.' Because the countryman doesn't say he saw a 'black man' in the house, the sheriff knows he saw a white man, and by his question seeks to confirm that fact. The sheriff knows it would not be unusual for a black man to be seen near Joanna Burden's house, but a white man's presence there is unusual.

613:23 **Blumping** blundering and bumping

613:33 **done for her** finished her off, murdered her

613:34 **Get me a nigger** The sheriff assumes that all blacks in the vicinity will know what he wants to know about the Burden place, and that one black will be as good as any other.

613:37 **Mr Watt** Watt Kennedy, the Sheriff. The black man addresses him as 'Mr' followed by his first name, the accepted racial etiquette of the day.

614:3 **apotheosis** the moment an individual is deified. Here it suggests that the individual members of the mob fuse into a single mass organism, one whose words seem to come out of the air or wind—as a god's would.

614:12 **the dying fire roared, filling the air though not louder than the voices and much more unsourceless** 'voices' refers to the italicized lines above on 614 and immediately following this line. The voices burn with the desire to do violence, to find a victim on whom vengeance can be inflicted; they possess a destructive potential as dangerous as the flames. How is the fire 'unsourceless'? How it started is unclear. To the onlookers it burns with a symbolic fury far more meaningful than any rational explanation would allow. It is a primal destructive force.

614:20 **Nigger lover! Nigger lover!** a term of grievous insult in the South of the 1930s, reserved especially for meddlesome outsiders. The insult sometimes bore sexual overtones as well.

614:29 **He was watching the sheriff's face as a man watches a mirror** that is, to see by the look of the sheriff's face whether his own face is betraying him. He also watches the sheriff's face for the gesture that will signal the deputy to strike the strap across his back.

615:2 **white folks** a form of address directed by a black person toward one or more white people whom he does not personally know, or whom he chooses not to recognize

615:3 **Mr Buford** Buford is the deputy's first name.

615:13 **I aint playing. Let alone them folks out there** The sheriff relies on the nearby mob, and the threat of a lynching, to frighten the black man into telling what he knows.

615:29 **any man in Jefferson that his breath smelled right** any man whose breath smelled of whiskey

615:36 **It was as though he carried within him ... the scent itself: that which moved and evoked them as with a promise of something beyond the sluttishness of stuffed entrails and monotonous days** 'Evoked' = provoked, raised the hope of (in the context of this passage). 'Sluttishness' = sordidness. 'Stuffed entrails' = filled human bellies. The crowd felt that the sheriff carried the secret of the murder, which they hope will bring meaning and excitement to their dull lives.

616:5 **impregnable as a monument which could be returned to at any time** The smoke is 'impregnable' because it hides, metaphorically, the solution to the mystery of the murder, also because the murder it signifies has now become a permanent part of community memory and tradition. The townspeople can return to it at any time by remembering and talking about it.

616:13 **young woman ... of advanced pregnancy** Lena Grove arriving in Jefferson at the end of Chapter IV, 473:8–10

616:25 **Exeter, N. H.** a town in New Hampshire, located near Portsmouth and the Massachusetts state line

616:28 **What do you want me to do?** Because the paper directs that a 'nigger lawyer' be notified, because it was written by a woman regarded in the town as a 'nigger lover' and outsider, the white cashier does not feel bound by it. He indicates this to the sheriff, waiting for him to say whether the paper should be honored or whether other steps should be taken instead.

617:2 **Then it began to piece together.** Then the pieces of the story began to fall into place.

617:17 **So they took Brown to the jail for safekeeping** He is, after all, their only suspect. He might decide that the reward money isn't worth the trouble and run away, and he is the sheriff's prime source of information on the probable murderer.

617:25 **Sunday morning** the Sunday morning immediately following the Saturday on which Joanna's murder was discovered

617:28 **fast train** an express train°

617:32 **two gaunt and cringing phantoms whose droopeared and mild faces gazed with sad abjectness** an accurate description of bloodhounds that conveys the eerie quality of the early morning scene

617:35 **ringing them about with something terrible and eager and impotent** The men hope the dogs will relieve them of the frustration they feel over failing to capture the fugitive.

617:38 **something monstrous and paradoxical and wrong, in themselves against both reason and nature** The murder upset the calm order of the world. All 'subsequent' actions appear 'monstrous and paradoxical and wrong.' Nothing can be set right again until the murderer is caught and justice done.

618:11 **made another cast** sent out the dogs again to find the scent

618:13 **fulltongued** baying at top voice

618:28 **he told how he was about to trick the man into permitting him to drive right up into his own front yard** The boy neglects to mention the girl who was with him that night. He intended to drive right up into her front yard, not his own. See 609. He distorts the facts, probably at his father's urging, to improve his chances for the reward money.

618:39 **apparent infallibility for metal** unerring attraction to metal. The irony is strong here: these are sorry bloodhounds.

618:40 **two loaded chambers** Chambers are receptacles for cartridges in a rifle or pistol. A revolver has several chambers in a cylinder, which as it rotates brings each one in line with the barrel.

619:1 **Civil War, cap-and-ball pistols** See entry 607:23.

619:2 **One of the caps has been snapped** When struck by the hammer, the cap, or detonator, explodes and causes the powder to ignite. In this case, the hammer has been released, 'snapping' the cap but failing to ignite it, probably because the cap was old or damp.

619:11 **apparently the animals could not hear either** Preceding events have established that the dogs cannot smell (except for metal—see entry 618:39); now we are told they cannot hear.

619:22 **the darkness after the hot day is close, still, oppressive; as soon as Byron enters the house** The narrative here switches to present tense. It is Tuesday night, three days after the murder.

619:27 **static overflesh** fat which is the result of inactivity

619:28 **well nigh** close to, almost

619:32 **It is the odor of goodness. Of course it would smell bad to us that are bad and sinful** an oblique reversal of Thoreau's observation in *Walden* that "There is no odor so bad as that which arises from goodness tainted."°

620:1 **Where she can . . . .** Byron apparently means to end his sentence with 'where she can give birth to her baby in private,' but what he really means is 'where she won't hear people talking about Lucas Burch and the murder of Joanna Burden.'

620:3   **Why must she move? When she is comfortable there, with a woman at hand if she should need one?'**   Hightower at first interprets Byron's silent, downcast look as an indication that Mrs. Beard has objected to the prospect of a bastard child being born in her boarding house. See the next two entries.

620:8   **Man performs, engenders, so much more than he can or should have to bear . . . That's what is so terrible. That he can bear anything, anything.**   Apparently Hightower means that humankind has an immense capacity for suffering. As bad as life might become, people can endure it, only to discover that they can endure much worse. He refers specifically here to what he takes to be Mrs. Beard's lack of compassion in refusing to have the unwed Lena Grove give birth in her boarding house.

620:16   **A room where it will be quiet when her time comes, and not every durn horsetrader or courtjury that passes through the hallway. . . . . . .**   Apparently Mrs. Beard's boarding house often lodges traveling horsetraders and jurors when court is in session. Byron claims that he doesn't want anyone to tell Lena about Brown and his involvement with Christmas and the murder.

620:21   **makes to speak**   starts to speak

620:29   *I know what he is thinking*   I know he thinks I have shameful reasons for the plans I'm about to explain. Byron never really admits to himself that his motives are less than honorable, that he wants to get Lena out of town so that she won't meet Lucas Burch and he can have her all to himself (he still refuses to acknowledge her full-term pregnancy).

620:36   **laborpurged face**   Years of hard work have purged Byron's face of its youth and vitality.

620:40   **It's just that I thought maybe . . . .**   you would tell me what to do

621:2   **When it's a matter of not-do, I reckon a man can trust**

himself for advice When it's a matter of knowing not to do something wrong, a man can trust his own conscience.

621:8 **I am not in life anymore** My isolation from life disqualifies me from advising Byron. Thus Hightower rationalizes his desire to avoid involvement.

621:12 **you told me she knows that he is here** Hightower feigns innocence of Byron's intentions in order to make him talk more about them. But he fully understands that Byron doesn't want Lena to hear about Brown, and he reminds him so.

621:20 **three days** three days since Lena arrived in Jefferson

621:22 **Christmas** Byron is completing the sentence he began: 'About him and the ——' (621:19). He is is about to say 'nigger' but remembers that Hightower corrected his use of that word once before, at 464:6.

621:33 **to lie it smooth** to lie without detection

622:8 **Nonsense** Hightower's judgment on Byron's explanation of Lena's confusion, and on his plan to get her out of town.

622:13 **I reckon not** Byron's quick response suggests he has better plans in mind for Lena than sending her back to Alabama.

622:29 **Buck Conner** marshal of Jefferson. See also 471:28.

622:36 **struck a trail** picked up a scent they could track

624:1 **running with dogs** tracking with dogs

624:12 **that cabin is the last place in the world he would want her to ever see** The cabin is a squalid dwelling where slaves once lived, hardly the sort of place the braggart Brown would want a woman to know he lived.

625:6 **just how far evil extends into the appearance of evil? just where between doing and appearing evil stops?** Hightower suggests that the distinction between the 'appearance of evil' and its reality is obscure enough that Byron may stumble into evil if he carries out his plan.

625:9 **as if he too were waking** Hightower throughout this talk has been 'waking' to the deceptions and dangers of Byron's deepening involvement with Lena; the 'too' suggests that Byron himself is glimpsing those dangers: in the next sentence he insists that he is trying 'to do the right thing.'

625:11 **by my lights** according to my conscience

625:23 **And he'll run.** exactly as Byron wants him to do

625:28 **suffused** flushed with excitement

625:32 **myriad silence** The only sounds are the usual night sounds of crickets and other insects—a 'myriad' of sounds of no significance, thus a 'myriad silence.' At 633:35 Hightower hears 'the myriad and interminable insects.'

625:33 **You are attempting to come between man and wife** violating the injunction "Those whom God hath joined together let no man put asunder"°—an ironic statement for Hightower in light of the outcome of his own marriage.

625:35 **Byron has caught himself** Byron suppresses his look of 'exultation' (625:24), but not before Hightower has seen it. A sentence later he tries unsuccessfully 'to catch his voice too.'

626:4 **Like enough** likely enough

626:7 **what do you think we—I ought to do?** By 'we,' Byron means himself and Hightower, as the next paragraph makes clear. He effectively involves the older man by discussing the situation with him, despite all his protests that he doesn't want to drag the older man into his problems.

626:16 **And the devil is looking after *him*, too** The time is the next day, Wednesday, about noon. The italicized '*him*' refers to Christmas, about whom we learn Hightower has just been talking with the shopkeeper, as the following paragraphs reveal.

626:22 **white lawn cravat** a necktie made of lawn, a fine linen or cotton fabric used in handkerchiefs, blouses, and curtains

626:37 **That bah—** That bastard. The storekeeper stops short when he remembers that Hightower is a minister.

627:8 **And they have. . . . . .** What Hightower can't bring himself to say, what he prods the storekeeper to confirm, is that 'they have caught and killed him.' This is not yet true.

627:11 **like the earth itself were rocking faintly** Hightower's emotional and physical reaction to what he believes to be the news of Christmas's death. In fact, he *hopes* Christmas is dead, for then he will not have to involve himself, a prospect he continues to resist at 627:17.

627:17 **I have bought immunity. I have paid.** Hightower is the second person in the novel (Christmas is the other) to think it possible to buy immunity from the world. See entry 535:22 for a full discussion. Hightower views his punishment by the town after his wife's death, especially his exclusion from the church and his years of solitude, as the price he has paid for immunity.

627:20 **out to the church** The Negro church that Christmas terrorized, an episode we learn about in Chapter XIV, 637–40.

627:35 **You already paid.** An ironic echo of Hightower's earlier thought, 'I have paid!' (627).

628:7 **giving to the familiar buildings about the square a nimbus quality, a quality of living and palpitant chiaroscuro** The buildings seem to shimmer in the summer heat rising from the asphalt, so that they take on the quality of a three-dimensional 'chiaroscuro,' a picture in shades of black (the dark doorways and windows, the shadows, the asphalt) and white (the lighter-colored buildings), except that the image is not a picture but reality itself, and is thus 'living and palpitant.'

628:11 ***And him too*** The narrative has returned to the moment with which it began on 626:16. There this section began with Hightower on his way home, then jumps back to his conversation in the store, then follows him out of the store and toward his home until it arrives at this moment.

628:18 **it goes on beneath the top of his mind that would cozen and soothe him** 'it' = his fear that he will have to involve himself with Christmas and Lena, a fear that the 'top of his mind'—his conscious, reasoning mind—deceives him into thinking is groundless.

628:22 **I just wanted peace** See Joe Christmas's protest that

'All I wanted was peace' (481, 484). The similarity of the two comments cannot be coincidental: Christmas wanted peace after fifteen years of wandering while Hightower wanted to be left alone by the townspeople.

628:26 **a finality which abrogates all logic and justification and obliterates it like fire would** At 627:17 Hightower argued that because he had 'paid' for his immunity he need not involve himself. That argument was 'justificative.' Now he simply abandons logical argument and flatly refuses involvement.

628:27 **I *will* not! I *will* not!** I will not get involved.

628:29 **When, sitting in the study window in the first dark** This is Wednesday evening, twenty-four hours after Byron and Hightower last talked (on 619–626). 'First dark' = twilight.

628:34 *It is not in him to support even the semblance of evil* I Thessalonians 5:22: "Abstain from even the appearance of evil."° Hightower at first believes that Byron has abandoned his plan to move Lena to the Burden cabin.

628:35 **he started, sat forward** Hightower is not surprised by Byron's visit on Sunday night: *'I had an idea he would come.'* He *is* surprised at Byron's new demeanor, his confidence and determination, his failure to stumble on the front stoop.

629:3 **Tonight** Wednesday evening after the murder

629:12 **he didn't offer to tell me . . . I would have listened** Actually, Byron *did* tell him, on the previous evening. Hightower's statement derives from his consternation at the change in Byron's countenance and the fact that Byron has gone ahead and acted. See 623–26.

629:35 **In other words, you can offer no hope** no hope that you have decided against involving yourself with Lena and compromising yourself morally.

631:4 **what will she be getting from the white women of Jefferson about the time that baby is due** Byron echoes Armstid's thought in Chapter I: 'womenfolks are likely to be good without being very kind' (408:1).

631:10 **she aint going to be married** As long as Joe Brown is alive, Lena will persist in her determination to marry him, and he will continue to flee her.

631:23 **And for the third reason** the third reason why you don't like my plan to install Lena in the Burden cabin

631:34 **even if she wasn't——if it wasn't for——** even if she wasn't pregnant, if it wasn't for the fact that she wants to marry someone else

631:35 **I know you said that** Actually, all Hightower said is 'Ah, Byron, Byron,' but in that exclamation and its likely tone Byron hears disapproval—the antecedent of 'that.'

631:37 **in the attitude of the eastern idol** in the manner of statues of Buddha, sitting upright, stomach protruding, gravely listening. See entry 464:18.

631:40 **this terrible, terrible place** Jefferson, which in Hightower's own experience proved extremely intolerant of immoral and scandalous situations. He is worried at what might happen to Byron if he persists in his present course of action.

632:1 **You will tell me that you have just learned love; I will tell you that you have just learned hope.** Hightower means that Byron has discovered not love but the hope that he will have love. Hightower has learned from his own experience that hope inevitably means disappointment. The distinction for him is important: love means happiness. Hope means despair.

632:19 **No woman who has a child is ever betrayed** A woman always has the child to love, and so she is not betrayed even if her husband deserts her.

632:19 **the husband of a mother, whether he be the father or not, is already a cuckold** The husband is 'cuckolded' either by the real father of the child or, metaphorically, by the child itself, who suddenly commands all the mother's attention.

632:21 **Give yourself at least the one chance in ten** of having a good marriage

632:25 **God didn't intend it so when He made marriage.
Made it? Women made marriage** Hightower's contempt
for women and marriage reflects his own bitter experience.
Because he regards marriage as an institution in which men
inevitably suffer the domination of women, he says that
'women made marriage,' meaning they formed it to their
own interests, which are not the interests of men.

632:27 **Me the sacrifice. It seems to me the sacrifice——**
Byron feels he would be making no sacrifice at all by marrying Lena. Instead, this 'woman wronged and betrayed'
would sacrifice her own happiness by marrying someone she
does not love to give her child a legal father.

632:28 **Not to her** Hightower does not think she would regard marriage to Byron a sacrifice. For her marriage is a
matter of moral self-preservation, and she would take advantage of whatever willing man happened to be available.

632:32 **in their cups** drunk

633:4 **I used to walk it myself, now and then** This cryptic
comment suggests that Hightower used to visit the Burden
house. The novel never reveals why.

633:27 **people who no longer live in life** an echo of Hightower's earlier statement: 'I am not in life anymore' (621)

633:31 **God bless him. God help him.** God bless him because he is a good man doing the best he can. God help him
because he is weak and naive and about to get himself in
trouble.

633:36 **hot still rich maculate smell of the earth** The earth
is 'maculate' because fertility (and sexuality) in Faulkner's
world is always tainted.

633:39 **Then the ground, the bark of trees, became actual,
savage, filled with, evocative of, strange and baleful half
delights and half terrors** Now the night means for Hightower only emptiness and the sounds of 'insects.' But 'when
he was young' it was real for him, full of pleasures and delights, a thing he could actually experience. This passage
suggests the sexual potency of youth and the depth of emo-

tion that accompanies it. Perhaps this is what Hightower is remembering here. When the dark ceases to signify that sexuality for him, when the seminary has influenced him to suppress what the dark once could make him feel, he loses his love of the dark, and he begins to hate it.

634:1 **He was afraid of it. He feared; he loved in being afraid** He loved the darkness because it made him afraid, made him experience emotions and feel alive.

634:10 **Tennyson** British poet, Alfred Lord Tennyson (1809–1892), sometimes unfairly criticized for his galloping rhythms and shallow thought. By making him a reader of Tennyson, Faulkner casts doubt on Hightower's literary tastes and intellect. See 634:12.

634:10 **dogeared** the corners of the pages are folded over where the reader stopped, an indication that Hightower turned often to the book.

634:12 **the gutless swooning full of sapless trees and dehydrated lusts** Tennyson's poetry, which for Hightower becomes a substitute for prayer and the lost emotion of youth

634:15 **like listening in a cathedral to a eunuch chanting in a language which he does not even need to not understand** This pessimistic image describes Hightower more than it does Tennyson. Italian choir boys were frequently castrated to insure they could give long service as adult sopranos (castrati) in the Catholic church (a practice ended in 1878 by Pope Leo XIII). Because the castrati were taught the Eucharistic liturgy by memory, they did not have to understand Latin. They chanted words without understanding them, thus words without meaning. But Faulkner complicates the image by adding that 'they did not even need to not understand' the language they chant in. For Hightower, who has lost his faith and who no longer prays, they are words without faith. Tennyson's words mean nothing to him. His reading is mere habit—nothing more. It is the repetition of the habitual act itself that salves him. The chanting eunuchs in this context are utterly sterile, asexual images of neutrality and meaningless: perfect analogues for Hightower. The sentence may also be a veiled allusion to Tennyson's *In Memoriam*: "What find I in the highest place / But mine own phantom chanting hymns?" See entry 760:33.

Asked at the University of Virginia whether he thought reading Tennyson was like 'listening to a eunuch,' Faulkner replied, "No sir, that was Hightower's opinion, and I'm not responsible for his opinion. . . . when I was younger, I read Tennyson with a great deal of pleasure. I can't read him at all now."°

CHAPTER XIV

635:1 **There's somebody out there in that cabin** It is Thursday, the day after Byron moved Lena to the cabin. After a four-line past-tense introduction, the remainder of the scene is related in present tense ('the sheriff says'—635:9), indicating that the narrative present has moved forward from the last present tense scene (628–634) between Hightower and Byron on Wednesday morning.

635:19 **Said he aimed to tell you** That Byron has delayed telling the sheriff suggests he might feel sheepish about what he has done, and might fear the sheriff's reaction. The sheriff is the source of legal authority in the county, while Hightower is, for Byron at least, the source of moral authority, and Byron has not been quite forthright with him either.

635:30 **It's Christmas, is it?** The sheriff thinks his deputy means that Christmas is the father of Lena's child.

635:34 **"Lucas Burch?" the sheriff says** The sheriff has never heard Brown called Lucas Burch before, and he is surprised that Brown would be anyone's husband (Byron told the deputy that Burch and Lena were married).

636:31 **aint none of my house** It ain't my house and it ain't my business.

637:5 **At three oclock Wednesday morning a negro rode into town . . .** The black man relates an event (Joe's disruption of the revival meeting) that occurred on the previous evening. The sheriff and his posse then track Joe until about noon Wednesday before giving up (643:23). Wednesday morning is four days after Joanna Burden's murder.

637:24 **mourners' bench** pew where worshippers sit who desire to repent their sins and who will present themselves

later in the service to be saved. The name derives from the
fact that they are "mourning" over their sins.

638:16 **he cursed God louder than the women screeching**
This may well be why he disrupted the revival, to curse God
and terrorize the worshippers. Christmas himself appears
'semihysterical,' perhaps from lack of food, loneliness, the
tension of his flight.

638:23 **Roz** diminutive of Roskus, variant of Roscoe and of
the Roman name Roscius°

639:9 **That was what he told, because that was what he knew**
An omniscient external narrator relates the rest of the section, which includes much information the man from the
church lacked.

639:26 **Dont even know they cant see me** Perhaps Christmas means that although they may see his form, they can't
see *him*: can't recognize him, understand who he is. He is
standing in darkness and thinks of himself as invisible, even
invincible.

639:28 **I'll cut a notch in it tomorrow** to record the man he
has just struck down

639:31 **As he struck the match he paused** Christmas arro-
gantly lets the worshippers know that he has beaten Roz, is
showing his face and where he is, daring them to come after
him, perhaps even anticipating the violence they might inflict on him.

639:35 **the good news** of his church rampage; Christmas
sarcastically alludes to the connection between this phrase
and "gospel," derived from the Old English *god* (good) + *spel*
(news).

640:8 **eight oclock the next morning** Wednesday morning

640:23 **one of the party** Brown. Again Faulkner refers, in
ironic fashion, to a previously introduced character as a
stranger. The device serves a comic effect here. It was used
earlier to describe Lena Grove (616).

640:38 **There's a good place there for you to wait in. Cool**
the jail

641:13 **Bufe** Buford, the deputy

641:14 **cast** set to looking for a scent

641:14 **struck** picked up a scent

641:22 **We have been putting dogs on him once a day ever since Sunday** Today marks the fourth time. The first was Sunday morning, just after the arrival of the dogs (618); the second was late Sunday night/early Monday morning, which ends with the dogs crouching frightened in a ditch (619); the third was Tuesday morning (622).

641:36 **lowheaded and eager dogs** Dogs that have struck a scent keep their heads close to the ground to follow it.

641:38 **cotton house** a small building in a cotton field, used to store picked cotton until it can be taken to the gin°

642:7 **Now's your chance to run ahead and catch him and get that thousand dollars** The sheriff toys with Brown's essential cowardice. On 617:16 the sheriff told Brown, 'You catch the fellow that done it, and you'll get the reward.' He is certain Brown will never get the reward.

642:12 **quartering up a hill** climbing along diagonal lines that cross back and forth from one side of the hill to the other, reducing the steepness of the ascent

642:16 **He'll have a gun now.** The sheriff assumes that a gun can always be found in a Negro cabin.

642:28 **a member of the posse** Brown

642:39 **eggsuckers** worthless dogs; an "undisciplined dog may learn to 'suck' (actually, to break and eat) eggs."°

643:25 **At last the noise and the alarms, the sound and fury of the hunt, dies out of his hearing** The first paragraph of this new section recounts the conclusion of the Wednesday cotton house episode from Christmas's perspective, focusing specifically on his reaction to wearing the Negro brogans that confused the bloodhounds. The narrative present time has now moved to Friday morning, a day and a half later. On 647 a new paragraph begins, in present tense, with 'It is just dawn, daylight.' It is followed by a five-page past-tense account of events from the preceding few days. That present-tense, present-time narrative continues without change of tense or day to Joe's arrival in Mottstown on Friday, at the end of the chapter. On 'the sound and fury,' see entry 606:31.

643:30 **They looked like they had been chopped out of iron ore with a dull axe** an accurate description of the inexpensive, stiff, crude ankle-high shoes sold to rural Southern blacks until World War II.

643:33 **he could see himself being hunted by white men at last into the black abyss** the abyss of black identity that has alternately repelled and attracted Christmas almost all his life. He has, until now, insisted on defining his own place in society, refusing to accept a white or black role. But he finds himself now in the archetypal role of a Negro fugitive, pursued by white posse and blood hounds for the murder and (the posse supposes) rape of a white woman. He is 'hunted' and forced into acceptance of a black identity. Thus it seems to him that the battle he has waged for thirty years is now lost, that he must surrender to his black self. It seems logical that now he would allow himself to be captured.

643:36 **bearing now upon his ankles the definite and ineradicable gauge of its upward moving** the brogans of the black woman to whom he traded his own shoes. Donning the shoes, Christmas believes he at last has entered the 'abyss' he has struggled against for thirty years. The shoes, a symbol of black identity, mark how far into that 'abyss' Christmas has stepped: they are a 'definite and ineradicable gauge' of his movement into the abyss, which moves 'upward' along his ankles the deeper in he goes. The 'gauge' is 'ineradicable' because he can never take back the acceptance that wearing the shoes signifies.

644:8 **He has not slept very much since Wednesday, and now Wednesday has come and gone again** The first 'Wednesday' was the one shortly before the murder, the night Christmas refused to pray in Joanna's room, when he realized he would have to kill her (606). The second 'Wednesday' he spent eluding the dogs and posse during the cotton-house episode. It is now Friday morning, six full days after the murder.

644:11 **for thirty years he has lived inside an orderly parade of named and numbered days . . . and when he waked up he was outside of them** At some point in the last week Christmas lost track of time. Soon he will enter Mottstown and allow himself to be captured, a kind of suicide considering the fate he believes awaits him.

644:12 **one night he went to sleep** Here begins a series of recollections of the last few days of his flight. We do not return to time present again until 647:13 ('It is just dawn, daylight').

644:24 **since Friday in Jefferson, in the restaurant** where Christmas ate supper on the Friday evening before he killed Joanna (482).

644:33 **come to the door** came to the door: a typographical error. The manuscript reads 'came,' but the typescript incorrectly reads 'come.'°

645:4 **He thought for a while that he ran because of and toward some destination that the running had suddenly remembered** Perhaps he is unconsciously remembering how in Chapter VIII he ran after Bobbie Allen told him about menstruation, or how in Chapter IX he ran into Max Confrey's house on the night after he clobbered McEachern with a chair. In any event, his physical and mental exhaustion are mirrored in the separation of mind and body.

645:24 **Time, the spaces of light and dark, had long since lost orderliness** This loss of the sense of time contrasts with Christmas's careful attention to time on the day before the murder, when he notes the tolling of each hour by the town clock (485–86).

646:6 **as hard as potato graters** A potato grater is a kitchen implement used for grating potatoes, cheese, cabbage, and carrots. Dry field corn feels and looks as rough as the surface of a grater. It is difficult to eat and digest.

646:16 **resultant crises of bleeding flux** bloody diarrhea

646:32 **there was food before him** Because this meal occurs
on a Thursday (as will be shown), it parallels the Last Supper
of Christ, also on a Thursday.°

646:34 **It seemed to him that he could hear without hearing
their wails of terror and distress quieter than sighs all
about him** Because we know that 'He did not remember'
how he got into the room of the Negro house, it is clear in
this scene that he was not in his right mind. The inhabitants
of the house are terrified at his intrusion. They tried to hide
the sounds of their terror and didn't fully succeed. And
though Christmas heard them, he wasn't aware of what they
really were.

646:38 **Of their brother afraid** To the black people in the
cabins, Christmas is a man wanted for murder, a danger to
them, and he must know that this is how they see him. Yet
his thinking of himself as 'their brother' is further evidence
that he has at last accepted his black identity.

647:1 **without seeming to need the sleep** First he lost his
sense of time (645:24), then his sense of hunger (646:12),
now his need of sleep. This sloughing off of normal human
needs is preparing him for something.

647:4 **he could discover neither derivation nor motivation
nor explanation for it** 'it' = his lack of a need for sleep or
food

647:6 **he had an actual and urgent need to strike off the accomplished days** Joe's gradual casting off of basic human
needs, his desire to know the day as if he needs to prepare
for something, suggests he has in mind some 'day or act' for
which he must ready himself. Probably it is his decision,
whether conscious yet or not, to allow himself to be captured, and to submit to the black identity that his captors will
impose on him.

647:11 **it was so crystallised that the need did not seem
strange anymore** 'it' = the need to fulfill some definite

purpose, perform some definite act, no longer seemed strange to him

647:13 **It is just dawn, daylight.** We have reached again the same narrative moment as at 643:40: time-present, Friday morning. The rest of the chapter occurs on Friday.

647:24 **He follows a straight line, disregarding the easier walking of the ridges** In contrast to the characteristic circular patterns of his earlier movements, he walks with purpose and some haste towards his destination.

648:20 **So he moves back into the bushes.** In the previous paragraph Christmas mused over how when he presents himself for capture his would-be captors run away, 'Like there is a rule to catch me by, and to capture me that way would not be like the rule says.' Perhaps the 'rule' says that the fugitive must be captured while he is still trying to flee: he cannot give himself up. So he moves into the bushes to hide, to play the game by the rules.

649:1 **He had grown to manhood in the country** This sentence, along with the previous reference to 'his native earth,' makes clear that Christmas grew up in the area he is walking through. Thus the McEachern farm must have been somewhere nearby, and Mottstown, the town toward which we soon learn he is heading, must be the one he visited with his foster father in Chapter VIII. Thus, when he learns on 649 that he is headed towards Mottstown, he tells himself that 'the street which ran for thirty years . . . had made a circle. . . . I have never got outside that circle' (650).

649:11 **I dont have to bother about having to eat anymore** because he's choosing capture, choosing the death that he believes will quickly follow, after which he will not need food at all

649:18 **Mottstown** According to Faulkner's map in *Absalom, Absalom!* it is some 20 to 30 miles south of Jefferson on the railroad.

649:19 **You going to Jefferson too?** Apparently this is where Joe intended to be captured.

649:20 **"Dont know whar that is. I gwine to Mottstown."**
"Oh," Christmas says. "I see. You dont live around here,
then." This exchange *may* account for why Christmas believes he can 'let go for a while,' and why he walks right into
the middle of Mottstown: perhaps he believes he is not
known there, that although the news of the murder has certainly arrived there, so few people know what he looks like
that he can walk in safety. But later, at least according to a
citizen of Mottstown, he appears to try to draw attention to
himself so that he will be recognized. See 657–658.

649:25 **yellin calf** yearling calf, at least one but not yet two
years old°

649:28 **'Mottstown,' he thinks. Jefferson is only twenty miles**
away. 'Now I can let go a while,' i.e., after Mottstown, I've
got only twenty miles more to go. I can relax now. I'm almost
there.

649:39 **beyond an imperceptible corner . . . It has made a**
circle beyond a small turn in the road. This is 'the street of
the imperceptible corners' (see entry 573:25) that has been
his life.

650:2 **It had made a circle and he is still inside of it** The
street has come full circle, back to where he first entered it.
We must assume that point is Mottstown. He entered it fifteen years before at the end of Chapter IX. He realizes that
the circular 'street' was the determining pattern of his life,
and that he has never been able to escape it.

650:5 **I have been further in these seven days than in all the**
thirty years In being forced to accept his black identity (see
643), in running from his white pursuers, Christmas has
acted in a way contrary to the habits of his entire existence.
He has changed fundamentally his attitudes towards himself
and his life.

650:10 **dashboard** a plank of wood protecting occupants of
a wagon from water, mud, or snow thrown up by the horses

650:12 **black tide creeping up his legs, moving from his feet**
upward as death moves The 'black tide' that moves 'up his

legs' 'as death moves' makes clear that for Christmas acceptance of his blackness is acceptance of death. He is 'dying'
from the 'black tide' just as a person dies from progressive
circulatory failure, which begins in the feet and lower legs
and proceeds gradually upwards towards other parts of the
body.

CHAPTER XV

651:1 **On that Friday** The manuscript, typescript, and all subsequent texts read 'Friday,' but the novel's chronology makes it clear that Christmas is captured on Saturday afternoon, one week after the murder of Joanna Burden.

651:8 **They came to Mottstown thirty years ago . . .** This account of the Hines's history does not mesh with the one given by Mrs. Hines in chapter XVI, 679–81. This passage contains several references to time which, when compared with other time references in the novel, create real problems unless we regard them simply as the reflection of casual local history. They are not intended as precise: they are how people remember thirty years after the fact. See the Chronology for further discussion.

651:12 **he held some kind of a position in Memphis** as janitor at the orphanage where he left Joe

651:17 **a little touched** a bit crazy. The term originated from the notion that people 'touched' by God were left with prophetic powers and unbalanced minds.

651:32 **forgot or condoned . . . that which in a young man it would have crucified** Because they believe he is crazy, they overlook his consorting with black people. The people of Jefferson cannot so easily overlook Joanna Burden's behavior: she is younger and of stable mind. She is also a Northerner and a woman, an outsider whose violations of racial standards they are unwilling to ignore.

652:4 **twentyfive years** The figure 'twentyfive' does not mesh with the account of the Hines history given in earlier paragraphs. See entry 651:8 and Chronology.

652:15 **Uncle Doc** 'Uncle' was a term of patronizing affection once used in the South to refer to old men, just as Aunt or Auntie was used for old black women. 'Doc' is the diminutive of 'Doctor,' a title which Hines's peculiar reputation as a preacher has perhaps earned him in the town's imagination.

652:24 **he had been better than independent** The meaning of this expression comes clear a few lines below, where we learn that Hines had been the foreman at a sawmill with 'the controlling of lesser men.' That is, he had been in charge, but he had not had to deal with the responsibilities and risks of independence, and when he decided to leave the job, he could do so without hesitation.

652:26 **a man who has had the controlling of lesser men** Hines was foreman at a sawmill in Arkansas for about nineteen years; see 675:1.

653:10 **preclusive expression** an expression that precludes people from talking to him, keeps them at a distance

654:13 **They got him. He cant get away** The crowd attributes Hines's behavior to moral outrage, and they try to calm him by assuring him that the murderer has been captured.

654:16 **men trying to hold a small threshing hose in which the pressure is too great for its size** Carelessly held hoses of any size, but especially high-pressure fire hoses, thresh back and forth when spewing water at high pressure.

654:28 **Kill the bastard . . . Kill him! Kill him!** Onlookers take the epithet 'bastard' merely as an insult. They do not realize that Hines means it literally. His urgent plea parallels Luke 23:21: When Pontius Pilate asks the mob what he should do with Christ, he is answered "Crucify him, crucify him!"

655:17 **Caught who?" she said** Hines remembers the name given to his grandson at the orphanage, and when he learns that a 'white nigger' murderer by that name has been captured, he has good reason to think it is his grandson. His wife does not know whether her grandson is alive. But her query here, her 'grey still expression' as she looks down at the men who have brought her husband home, and her other questions suggests she knows her husband well enough to suspect who the captured murderer must be.

655:22 **the man said to his companion...** The conversation that follows is a tribute to Faulkner's skill in portraying minor, even nameless characters. The two men assume definite personalities, the 'first man' discerning and curious about the Hines couple, the 'second man' witless and unsympathetic.

655:26 **They had to bloody him up some.** Christmas allowed himself to be taken without a struggle, but his passivity and his walking around 'like he owned the town' (658) apparently angered his captors, especially Halliday, so they 'had to bloody him up some.' The speaker intends his statement as humor. He implies that the men didn't have to bloody Christmas up. They merely seized the opportunity to take pleasure in beating him.

655:37 **He belongs to them up there** Jefferson and Mottstown are not in the same county. Christmas committed the murder in the jurisdiction of the Jefferson sheriff, who will thus take custody of him and hold him for trial; 'up there' means Jefferson.

656:7 **Eupheus** pronounced YOU-fuss in Mississippi

656:16 **fifteen years** This particular number seems to have no special significance. The man probably means merely that he has been wondering for a long time.

656:31 **ranklyodored as a cave** Faulkner suggests a beast-like, prehistoric quality in the Hines couple. Earlier he described them as 'muskoxen' and 'two belated beasts from beyond the glacial period' (652). Later he compares them to 'two bears' (671).

656:35 **there was no need to return and lock the front door, which she did** She locks it to shut out the peering eyes and ears of the world, from which she wants to hide the secret she has discovered, that her grandson has come back to Mottstown.

657:4 **strove with it** struggled to control her voice

657:14 **borning** being born

657:26 **they told it again** The remainder of this chapter
(657–66) is told by an anonymous representative of the
town. He seems to be a typical citizen, interested in local hap-
penings, an effective gatherer of gossip and news. He often
cites information reported to him by other townspeople and
seems especially interested in the Hines couple. His story is
a combination of joke and mystery. The result is a lively oral
narrative, like a comic tall tale, which contributes to the novel's overall concern with penetrating the ambiguous motives
of human behavior.

657:27 **must have been the nigger blood** that caused him to
act as stupidly as he did, getting himself caught. See 731,
where Gavin Stevens also suggests that 'nigger blood' can
compel one to behave in a predetermined way.

657:28 **It looked like he had set out to get himself caught**
precisely what Joe set out to do, as the last pages of chapter XIV make clear

657:30 **If he had not set fire to the house . . . tried to lay the
whiskey and the killing both on Brown and Brown told the
truth** This distorted account is the sort town gossip might
produce, but it is largely attributable to the fact that since
Christmas is supposed to be a black man, the townspeople
automatically consider him guilty of all aspects of the crime,
while Brown, a white man, they automatically believe to have
told an honest story.

658:7 **with some of the very money he stole from the woman
he murdered** Nothing in the novel suggests Christmas stole
money from Joanna. Bootlegging was a profitable occupa-
tion, and this was probably his own money. But the townspeople believe that, since he is supposed to be a Negro, since
he killed Joanna in Negro fashion with a razor and since any
Negro who would kill would also steal, theft must have been
one of his motives.

658:17 **he ought to have been skulking and hiding in the
woods, muddy and dirty and running** how the towns-

people believe a Negro murderer should behave. Ironically, this is what he *had* been doing for almost a week, until his conscious decision no longer to resist being black.

659:11 **He said that he had a right to kill the nigger** Hines later tells Hightower that he is 'God's chosen instrument' to watch over the doings of 'That bastard' Joe Christmas (684). He then claims that the Lord, knowing the child is still alive, tells him that 'Your work is not yet done yet. He's a pollution and a abomination on My earth' (684). Hines thus believes it is his obligation and privilege to see the Lord's will done by killing the man just captured.

659:23 **mother hubbard** loose-fitting, shapeless dress

659:25 **She was carrying an umbrella** See 665:4 for an explanation.

660:2 **without** unless

660:4 **like she had got something on him and he had to mind her** What might she have on him? His kidnapping of the child, and his refusal to tell her where the child was and whether it was alive. Moreover, thirty years of marriage to him have taught her how to handle him. He follows her 'like a dog' (664).

660:7 **talking big** inciting the crowd to lynch Christmas

660:13 **Metcalf** Mottstown jailer

660:29 **The plume was nodding now. He could see it nodding along above the fence** Because she is so short, her progress through the crowd can be followed only by the ludicrous nodding of her plume.

660:34 **the courthouse** the county courthouse. The sheriff, the county's chief law enforcement officer, would have his office there. The city's chief law officer would be the chief of police, but most relatively small Southern towns didn't have one, leaving most law enforcement duties to the sheriff, and minor offenses to the town marshal.

660:35 **Russell** Mottstown deputy sheriff

661:3 **Katzenjammer kids in the funny paper** This strip created by Rudolph Dinks in 1897 for the New York *Journal* portrayed the mischievous exploits of two young boys, Hans and Fritz, whose pranks involved a vaudevillian blend of violence and humor.°

661:11 **He might be home taking a nap** Surely the sheriff would not be taking a nap when a man who might be lynched had just been captured. Metcalf and Russell consider Mrs. Hines a nuisance and tell her whatever they think will get rid of her.

661:20 **They came up quick and went in quick** They hurry because they fear what the mob might do.

661:29 **like they were hollering for one another to the dead woman** Each is trying to impress the others with the loudness of his courage and outrage.

661:36 **You better smoke that for a while** stop and think about it for a while

661:37 **Halliday was . . . the foremost one about reason and not making trouble** Halliday was in line to collect the reward for capturing Christmas, and he doesn't want his claim to the reward nullified by a lynching.

661:40 **He aint worth a thousand dead matches to us** a reference to the bonfire that would conclude a lynching, and to the thousand dollar reward

662:5 **Just suppose it was a Jefferson man was going to get it** How would you feel if a Jefferson man was going to get that reward and spend it in his town, instead of here.

662:17 **give back** back off

662:19 **mill from the outside in** As the crowd hears and is influenced by the sheriff's argument against a lynching, the direction of its movement changes.

662:19 **the sheriffs knew it** Both the Mottstown and Jefferson sheriffs sensed the change in the crowd's mood, its flagging desire for a lynching.

662:26 **sulled up** sullen

663:6 **worrying** pestering folks with questions about the captured man

663:15 **A lot of them stayed there, looking at the jail like it**

**might have been just the nigger's shadow that had come
out** Compare with the crowd that, in Chapter XIII, after
Joanna's body is removed from the scene of the fire, continued to look at 'the place where the body had lain' (611).

663:24 **from the look on Uncle Doc's face, home was where
he ought to be** Doc Hines looks 'dazed' (665), 'asleep or
doped or something' (665).

663:28 **The same thing but for different reasons** They both
wanted to go to Jefferson: Hines to see that Joe was killed,
Mrs. Hines to prevent his death.

665:4 **a nickel and dime at a time out of a tiedup rag that she
took out of the umbrella** coins she has scrimped to save,
similar to Mrs. Armstid's egg money and Mrs. McEachern's
butter money.

665:10 **switch tracks** "a connection between two lines of
track to permit cars or trains to pass from one track to the
other track"°

665:12 **southbound** the southbound passenger train

665:14 **drummers** traveling salesmen

666:16 **Bitchery and abomination** 'Bitchery' = Hines's special word for fornication, especially by a woman; 'abomination' = the consequence of 'bitchery,' the bastard Joe, offen-
sive to God.

CHAPTER XVI

This chapter occurs in Hightower's study on Sunday evening, eight days after the murder, and is narrated in the present tense.

667:4 **mulberry tree** large shade tree, sometimes 70′ high and 3′ in diameter, frequently planted around houses

667:13 **And on Sunday again** On the preceding Sunday Byron disturbed Hightower with his talking about what he should do with Lena (chapter IV).

667:13 *I reckon Sunday would want to take revenge on him too, being as Sunday was invented by folks* Since 'folks' have made Hightower's life miserable for twenty years, and since Sunday was 'invented by folks,' it is logical that 'Sunday would want to take revenge on him too.'

667:20 **Hightower's hands are folded, peaceful, benignant, almost pontifical** like the hands of a high priest or bishop blessing his congregation, another link between Hightower and the figure of a religious prophet or mystic. See entry 464:18.

667:28 **the nose which holds invincibly to something yet of pride and courage** Byron imagines that Hightower's nose still reflects the courage and pride the now broken man once possessed.

667:30 **sluttishness of vanquishment** the unattractive aging of the rest of his face and body. See previous usages of 'sluttishness' on 615 and 673.

668:3 **I dont reckon you have heard that any more than you heard about the killing** On Sunday night a week before, Hightower had not yet heard about Joanna Burden's murder, discovered the previous Saturday morning. Byron thus acknowledges Hightower's isolation from the world.

668:10 **And you have come to tell me that he is—that they have . . .** that Christmas has been lynched.

668:14 **All right. You say that he is all right.** 'all right' = safe in jail, not lynched.

668:15 **Byron Bunch has helped the woman's paramour sell his friend for a thousand dollars . . . Has kept the woman hid from the father of her child, while that—— shall I say, other paramour, Byron?** Hightower accuses Byron of wanting to be Lena's lover, and of keeping Lucas Burch busy looking for the fugitive Christmas so that he can keep Lena hidden and improve his chances with her. Byron hasn't done anything to keep Burch on Christmas's trail: the prospect of the reward does that. But the 'other paramour' accusation apparently hits the mark. One day after this scene, Monday, Byron sees that Lena and Burch are reunited.

668:31 **The gainer, the inheritor of rewards, since it will now descend on the morganatic wife of——Shall I say that too? Shall I read Byron there too?** Hightower suggests that Byron is courting Lena for monetary as well as romantic reasons. 'It' = the thousand-dollar reward. 'Morganatic wife' = the wife in a morganatic marriage, in which one spouse is higher in social rank than the other, whose rank does not change and whose children do not inherit the rank or property of the other. Hightower envisions a circumstance in which Brown would be entitled to the reward because he had correctly identified Christmas as the murderer (Hightower hasn't heard of Halliday's role in capturing Christmas), but since Brown is in jail, and probably somehow involved in the crime, the reward would not be paid to him but to his 'almost-wife,' Lena; Byron, her future husband if his plans succeed, would then share in the reward money.

668:36 **it is not right to bother me, to worry me, when I have——when I have taught myself to stay——have been**

taught by them to stay—— It is not right to worry me about the affairs of the town when I have taught myself (and been taught by the town) to stay out of those affairs.

668:39 **reconciled to what they deemed——** have accepted what the town considered my just punishment: expulsion from the church and isolation

668:40 **Once before Byron saw him sit while sweat ran down his face like tears; now he sees the tears themselves run down the flabby cheeks like sweat** Byron recalls Hightower's reaction to the news that Christmas, the supposed murderer of Joanna Burden, was thought to be a Negro (472).

669:3 **It's a poor thing** an inconsiderate act

669:4 **I didn't know, when I first got into it. Or I would have.** I didn't know at first how complicated my involvement with Lena would become, or I would never have made you a part of it.

669:9 **the more than behest** 'Behest' = command; 'more than' refers to the beatings and the other forms of persecution by which the town reinforced the command.

669:12 **with insult and violence upon those who like them were created by the same God and were driven by them to do that which they now turn and rend them for having done it** They (the townspeople, society) treat with 'insult and violence' their fellow man ('those who like them were created by the same God') whom they drove (by their intolerance and mistreatment) to commit the acts for which they (the townspeople, society) now turn against them and punish ('rend') them.

669:20 **them that are good must suffer for it the same as them that are bad** Goodness as well as sin has its price. Byron is about to ask Hightower to pay the price of his goodness, and Hightower knows it. The bill itself is not actually presented until later this same day (687:36).

669:26 **This other one aint lost now. She has been lost for thirty years. But she is found now** A loose paraphrase of the famous line from the hymn "Amazing Grace": "I once was lost but now am found." The 'she' is Mrs. Hines.

669:31 **Waiting, watching the street and the gate . . .** The time is later the same Sunday evening as in the previous section. Hightower waits for Byron to bring Mrs. Hines, as we later learn he must have said he was going to do (672:20, 674:9). He is also 'waiting' for the sound of the music that will signal the start of the evening service at his old church.

669:33 **each Wednesday and Sunday night** when the Presbyterian church holds services or prayer meetings

669:38 **Yet for that reason he has never lost it** Because he no longer *needs* it, he has retained a very clear sense of time.

670:2 **he produces without volition the few crystallizations of stated instances** 'produces' = brings into his mind, remembers; 'crystallizations' = specific memories; 'stated instances' = regularly scheduled times when a service or prayer meeting was to occur. That is, he unconsciously recalls the specific events and schedules that governed his 'dead life' as a minister twenty-five years before.

670:23 **that peace which is the promise and the end of the Church** an allusion to Philippians 4:7: "And the peace of God, which passeth all understanding, shall keep your hearts and your minds through Christ Jesus" or to John 14:27: "Peace I leave with you, my peace I give unto you." This is the same 'peace' that Joe Christmas wants: *'Peace was all I wanted'* (481); 'That's all I wanted . . . That doesn't seem like a whole lot to ask' (484). As he dies at the end of chapter XIX, he looks up 'with peaceful and unfathomable and unbearable eyes' (742).

670:35 **that quality of abjectness and sublimation** Hightower associates the music with the humility before God it encourages, the yielding to the principles of the Church it urges.

671:6 **they took revenge upon that which made them so by means of the praise itself** They took revenge on the religion that made them what they are—puritanical and death-worshipping—through the intense and joyful music (the 'praise') that contrasts so starkly with their somber, passionless, death-worshipping faith.

671:8   **the apotheosis of his own history**   i.e., a religion that
is the summation of the essential characteristics of his life,
heritage, and region

671:9   **environed blood**   those 'people from which he sprang
and among whom he lives'

671:15   *And so why should not their religion drive them to crucifixion of themselves and one another*   Hightower concludes
that Southern Protestantism is a faith of violence whose
symbol of redemption is a violent, painful, martyr's death—
a faith that equates pain and violence with redemption. No
wonder, he concludes, that it drives its believers to abuse
themselves and each other.

671:24   **the doomed man in the barred cell**   Christmas

671:26   **in whose crucifixion they too will raise a cross**   The
'two other churches' will also participate in the crucifixion of
'the doomed man,' 'raising a cross' in self-righteous justification of the morality they claim to represent.

671:30   **Since to pity him would be to admit selfdoubt and to
hope for and need pity themselves. They will do it gladly,
gladly.**   If they pitied Christmas, he thinks, they would have
to recognize their essential kinship with him and, because
they are all sinful beings like him, their need for pity. They
will gladly kill him to show they are not like him.

671:31   **That's why it is so terrible, terrible, terrible**   Hightower mourns that those who will carry out the violent murder of the imprisoned man will do so in the belief that they
act with the sanction of their church and of God.

671:39   **like two bears**   We have already been told that the
Hines house smells like a 'ranklyodored cave' (656).

672:36   **If there is inarticulateness behind it, articulateness
is nullified by the immobility of the face itself**   If the
woman behind the face is inarticulate, it is her immobile,
inexpressive face that makes her so. Either her face is so
inexpressive that it negates the meaning of whatever she
might say, or its inexpressiveness speaks more eloquently of
her experience than any words she might utter.

673:32 **God give old Doc Hines his chance and so old Doc Hines give God His chance too** God gave Hines the chance to expiate the sin of bearing a daughter guilty of the sin of fornication by making him responsible for her abominable child. Doc Hines gave God 'His chance' by allowing Him time to work out the child's fate without need for Hines's intervention.

673:34 **out of the mouths of little children** Hines alludes to the well known proverb "Out of the mouths of children come words of wisdom." Its source is Matthew 21:16: "Out of the mouth of babes and sucklings thou hast perfected praise." See also Psalms 8:2: "Out of the mouth of babes and sucklings hast thou ordained strength, because of thine enemies."

673:40 **sluttishness** Hines means the world's fondness for fornication and other fleshly sins.

673:40 **I have put the mark on him** Hines means that God marked Christmas—his 'parchmentcolored' skin—as he marked Cain (Genesis 4:15: "And the Lord set a mark on Cain, lest any finding him should kill him"). See entry 675:39. Hines may also mean that Christmas bears the mark of the beast of the Apocalypse (Revelations 13:11–18), further evidence that Hines associates his daughter's bastard child with the anti-Christ.

674:27 **try to put on him** try to take advantage of him

674:38 **brakeman** Before the introduction of air brakes in the 1880s, the brakeman was responsible for the general makeup of the train, adding and removing cars, controlling their motion by tightening or loosening the brakes via a wheel at the top of each car. After the 1880s, the brakeman served as an assistant to the conductor.

675:3 **to take God's name in vain and in pride** the Third Commandment, "Thou shalt not take the name of the Lord thy God in vain," Exodus 20:7. Mrs. Hines refers not to her husband's swearing (he doesn't swear) but to his preaching after he returned permanently to Mottstown.

675:4 **Lem Bush** the neighbor who took Milly to the circus

675:9 **quicking** pricking, irritating

675:22 **log tackle** ropes, pulleys, and other apparatus used to position logs so they can be pulled out of the woods by mules

675:23 **It's God's abomination of womanflesh** Hines labels the events about to be described as the result of the sexual "curse" of womanhood: bitchery and abomination.

675:28 **the womansign of God's abomination already on her, under her clothes** Hines knows by the signs of puberty (pubic hair, menstruation) that Milly has reached the age of sexual maturity and the abomination he believes her female nature destines her to.

675:35 **believing she had obeyed the command of the father the Lord had given her** Because God made him Milly's father, it was her obligation to obey his commands. Hines refers to the Fifth Commandment, "Honor thy father and thy mother," Exodus 20:12.

675:39 **already stinking** because already polluted, deflowered

675:39 **Telling old Doc Hines, that knowed better, that he was a Mexican. When old Doc Hines could see in his face the black curse of God Almighty** Though both Milly and the circus owner claimed her lover was a Mexican, Hines claims he could 'see in his face' that he was a Negro. The text suggests that Hines saw Milly's lover only once: when he overtook the buggy and shot 'in the pitch dark' 'the man that might have been a stranger or a neighbor for all he could have known by sight or hearing' (677:13). The 'black curse of God almighty' is the curse on the sons of Ham (Genesis 9: 12–27), often cited before the Civil War as biblical justification for slavery and since the Civil War as justification for white supremacy. According to the account in Genesis, Noah one night became drunk and passed out naked in his tent. His son Ham saw him in this condition and called his brothers Shem and Japheth to look. They covered their father without looking at him and the next morning informed him of Ham's disrespect. Noah cursed Ham and all of his descendants, condemning them to be servants to the descendants of Shem and Japheth. Some interpreters of this episode reasoned that since blacks were slaves, they must be the descendants of Ham, and their owners the descendants of Shem and Japheth. See also entry 586:3.°

676:15 **I reckon she slipped out that night when the circus was stuck** Byron reasons that Milly had two meetings with the Mexican. Her first would have been on the night the 'circus was stuck.' Hines earlier complained that though he 'believed' she had obeyed his command to stay in the house that night, 'he ought to knowed' (674) that she would not obey him. During her first meeting with the Mexican, Milly must have arranged to meet him on the 'next night.' Thus she wears her 'Sunday dress' when she leaves with neighbors to attend the circus the next day and later sends word that she would not be coming home that night because she was spending 'the night with another girl' (676).

677:9 **He rode up on the right side of it** Hines knew the Mexican was sitting on the right side because that is where buggy drivers usually sat.

677:17 **It was raining again, too** Whatever else he might be, Byron is a skilled storyteller. Here he adds his own flourish to this crucial episode.

677:21 **monotonous strophe and antistrophe: two bodiless voices recounting dreamily something performed in a region without dimension by people without blood** In Greek drama the choral ode was divided into sections called strophes and antistrophes, each recited by different parts of the chorus. The 'antistrophe' often contrasted in tone and content with the 'strophe,' and the result was a stylized dialogue. In their telling of the story, Faulkner suggests, the contrasting yet similar 'bodiless voices' of Byron and Mrs. Hines contrast in the manner of a choral ode.

677:26 **watching the lamp. The oil was getting low** Coal 'oil' is kerosene. Mrs. Hines is watching a kerosene lamp of a type common to the time and region.°

678:1 **the devil's laidby crop** A 'laidby crop' is one which has been planted and cared for to the point that it requires no further attention from the farmer until harvest. Hines correctly assumes that the 'Mexican' got Milly pregnant, that she is carrying the 'laidby crop' that the devil will later harvest.

678:2 **I was that tired** I was so tired (emotionally and physically drained) that I couldn't bring myself to do anything but listen.

678:5 **he never fooled her. He never had to.** She didn't care what he was. She just wanted to fornicate.

678:6 **you said once that someday the devil would come down on me for his toll** 'toll' = fee. Hines refers to his wife's warning to him early in their marriage that one day he would have to pay for his rowdy, sinful behavior. He suggests that the 'toll' he had to pay was having a wife who bore him a whore for a daughter.

678:8 **But at least he done what he could when the time came to collect** But at least he (the devil) was fair when the time came to collect: he allowed me to shoot the man who made my daughter a whore.

678:14 **fix it** perform an abortion

678:17 **the trial was over and the circus owner came back and said how the man really was a part nigger** Hines apparently used as his defense the contention that he had shot a black man who had slept with his daughter, which would have made the murder 'justifiable homicide' in the South and other parts of the nation. The circus owner's testimony is at best suspect: exactly what convinced him to return to town to testify? Was he paid to give the information Hines says he gave?

678:28 **a doctor that would do it** would perform an abortion

679:1 **I thought then that he had give up, had seen God's will at last** had seen that it was God's will for the baby to be born

679:7 **had reconciled him like it had on that night when Milly was born** Mrs. Hines convinced her husband that his being in jail on the night of his daughter's birth was a 'sign and a warning' from God that he had better change his life: 'And he took it so himself then, because it was a sign,' putting aside his wild life, moving his family to another town, and getting a job at a sawmill (674–75).

679:25 **looked at the baby and he picked it up and held it up, higher than the lamp** to see if it looks to be part-Negro

679:26 **waiting to see if the devil or the Lord would win** as if the devil and the Lord are fighting for possession of the baby, as if in his own mind the devil is urging him to cast the baby down and kill it, while the Lord is urging him to let it live. Hines is trying to decide which it shall be.

679:28 **looking at his shadow on the wall and the shadow of his arms and the bundle high up on the wall** Mrs. Hines recalls this crucial moment of waiting for her husband to pass judgment on the baby in the same way that Joe watches the shadow of Joanna's pistol on the wall as she readies to shoot him in chapter XII (607).

679:30 **then I thought that the Lord had won. But now I dont know** Because the baby lived, she thought the Lord had won. But now that he's grown up to be a murderer, she's not sure.

679:40 **Eupheus was gone. The man that owned the mill didn't know where** Hines worked at a sawmill when Christmas was born; Christmas works at a sawmill for most of the last three years of his life.

680:5 **Mr Gillman** owner of the sawmill where Hines worked

680:6 **postoffice moneypaper** a money order purchased from a post office

680:17 **he wouldn't tell me** what he had done with the baby

680:25 **tell me what you have done with Joey** Mrs. Hines apparently named the infant 'Joey.'

680:27 **It's the Lord God's abomination** 'It' = the baby

680:31   **he was working in Memphis**   in the orphanage

680:34   **I knew that I would have to wait on Eupheus' will to know**   She would have to wait until her husband decided that she could be told. Her passive acceptance of Eupheus' will, especially after he disappears with the infant, is particularly irritating. Despite the prevailing customs of the time (Christmas was born in the mid-1890s), a man such as Eupheus Hines would not be allowed to take his grandchild away from its grandmother, nor would he have gone unpunished for allowing his daughter to die as she did. Mrs. Hines's failure to report to the authorities the circumstances of her daughter's death or the baby's disappearance is a significant contributing factor to the events in the novel. She must assume some blame for how she has suffered and for the life her grandchild lived. Still, she is a pathetic figure, and the abuse she has suffered in her marriage is part of a larger pattern of male mistreatment of women in the novel: Lena is abused by her brother and abandoned by Lucas Burch; Simon McEachern tyrannizes his wife; Bobbie Allen works for Max Confrey with apparently little say in the matter; and Joe Christmas abuses women throughout his life. Joanna Burden is his last victim.

681:6   **to worry at him**   to bother him with repeated questions

681:6   **it was something that he was there where Joey was, even if I wasn't**   She was consoled that her husband was taking care of the child.

681:7   **after five years he came home one day and he said 'We are going to move' . . . and we come to Mottstown.** Mrs. Hines's claim that she and Doc moved to Mottstown *after* he stopped working at the orphanage does not match the account at the beginning of chapter XV, which relates what the town remembers about the Hineses. Though one might argue that the town memory was simply confused about this eccentric couple to whom it paid little attention, it is unlikely that the town would have known about Doc Hines's working in Memphis, especially his coming home only on weekends, if he and his wife had *not* arrived until after he lost his job at the orphanage. If we accept Mrs. Hines's story that the Hineses did not move to Mottstown until after Joe was adopted, Hines must have decided to move to a place where he could continue to oversee Joe's development. This place is Mottstown. This is more circumstantial evidence suggesting that the McEacherns lived just outside Mottstown, and that the fifteen-year road that Joe traveled did indeed come full circle when he was captured there.

681:33   **to flux instantaneously**   to shift instantly

681:35   **the stare of his apparently inverted eye**   Although he seems enveloped in his own thoughts, he is fully aware of what is happening around him.

681:38   **It was the Lord. *He* was there.**   'It' = the reason why I did what I did: because the Lord told me to. He was there when Milly gave birth, when I stole the child, and in the orphanage.

681:38   **Old Doc Hines give God His chance too**   His chance to work out the child's fate

681:39   **The Lord told old Doc Hines what to do and old Doc Hines done it**   Apparently Hines means that the Lord told him to steal the child, place it in the orphanage, and stay there to watch it.

682:1   **Watch My will a-working**   Watch the pattern of events that will "work out" my plan for this child.

682:2   **mouths of little children**   See entry 493:23.

682:9   **There aint enough sin here to keep Me busy because what do I care for the fornications of a slut . . . the Madam . . . them young sluts**   Hines speaks of the orphanage as a brothel. Rather than selling his Joseph into bondage, he places him in what he considers a den of lechery. Perhaps to Hines this is ironic justice, for lechery begat Christmas. Perhaps also he feels that the bastard child belongs with his own kind, other bastards—the children of the orphanage.

682:14   **chanceso**   coincidence, happenstance

682:15   **My abomination laying wrapped in that blanket**   the
baby Joe. Luke 2:12: "Ye shall find the babe wrapped in
swaddling cloths."

682:18   **chance and call**   opportunity and reason

682:18   **to name him Christmas in sacrilege of My son**
Hines likely believes that Christmas's name violates the Third
Commandment, which forbids taking the Lord's name in
vain. McEachern held the same opinion: see entry 505:38.

682:22   **God's own boiler room**   Since he considers himself
God's appointed servant on the earth, the boiler room in
which he sits and works is God's as well as his own.

682:22   **devil's walking seed**   Christmas, the offspring of fornication, inspired by the devil. Hines regards Christmas as
the devil's spawn, a kind of anti-Christ. See entry 673:40.

682:24   **the working of that word**   'that word' = 'nigger'

682:27   **he was listening to the hidden warning of God's
doom**   At 682:37 this becomes 'hearing and listening to the
vengeful will of the Lord'; 'he' = Joe. Hines believes that the
child had begun to suspect he was different, part-Negro, and
that the Lord had a special fate in store for him.

682:31   **Do you think you are a nigger because God has
marked your face?**   because your skin is darker than the
others? Hines implies there is more to being a 'nigger' than
skin color, that it is a mark of sin and beastliness.

682:34   **the Lord God of wrathful Hosts**   from the term
"Lord of Hosts," frequently used in the Old Testament.

682:34   **His will be done**   from the Lord's Prayer, Matthew 6:10°

683:1   **How come you are a nigger?**   Though the boy might
be asking "Why do people call you a 'nigger'?," more likely
he is asking "Why *are* you a 'nigger'?" What does the word,
the very idea, mean? The boy is attempting not only to understand what 'nigger' means, but to discover the place on
the social ladder to which that word condemns him.

683:4   **You dont know what you are . . . you wont never
know**   At the University of Virginia, twenty-five years after

writing the novel, Faulkner repeatedly stressed the uncertainty of Christmas's racial identity: "I think that was his tragedy—he didn't know what he was, and so he was nothing. He deliberately evicted himself from the human race because he didn't know which he was. . . . that to me was the tragic, central idea of the story—that he didn't know what he was, and there was no way possible in life for him to find out. Which to me is the most tragic condition a man could find himself in—not to know what he is and to know that he will never know."°

683:7   **God aint no nigger**   At 632:34, Joe asks Doc Hines 'Is God a nigger too?' and Hines replies, 'He is the Lord God of wrathful hosts, His will be done.' Here the boy relays that answer to the Negro man.

683:12   **His own Son's sacred anniversary**   Christmas day, when Hines left the infant Joe on the orphanage doorstep

683:29   **Joseph**   The earthly father of Jesus and husband of Mary is Joseph the carpenter. More significant is the Old Testament Joseph, sold by his brothers into bondage in Egypt. Christmas, like his Biblical namesake, is raised by people other than his parents. See Genesis 38–50.

683:32   **It is so in the Book: Christmas, the son of Joe. Joe, the son of Joe. Joe Christmas.**   a parody of Biblical genealogies, specifically Matthew 1:1–16: "And Jacob the father of Joseph the husband of Mary, of whom Jesus was born, who is called Christ."

684:7   **the working of God's will on her**   Hines regards the fear on her face as evidence of how God is working out his plan.

684:10   **You are a instrument of God's wrathful purpose that nere a sparrow can fall to earth**   A variation on the well known proverb that "Not even a sparrow can fall to earth unnoticed by God." The proverb's source is Matthew 10:29–31: "Are not two sparrows sold for a farthing? and one of them shall not fall on the ground without your Father. But the very hairs of your head are all numbered. Fear ye

not therefore, ye are of more value than many sparrows."
Hines means that *everything* is a part of 'God's wrathful
purpose.'

684:14 **like the face of a ravening beast of the desert**
'Ravening' = greedily devouring. Psalms 22:13: "They
gaped upon me with their mouths, as a ravening and a roaring lion"; Isaiah 35:9: "No lion shall be there, nor any rav-
enous beast shall go up thereon, it shall not be found there;
but the redeemed shall walk there." See also Peter 5:8.

684:21 **the Day** the Day of Judgment. Hines tells the dietitian that she has played her role in God's plan and can now
go and commit whatever sins ('abominations') she wishes,
until Judgment Day, when she will answer for them.

684:22 **her rotten colored dirt** her makeup

684:23 **they come and took him away. Old Doc Hines saw
him go away in the buggy** 'they' = the McEacherns. Since
Hines had apparently been fired from his orphanage job
after he tried to kidnap Joe, he must have lurked outside
the orphanage trying to discover what would become of the
child.

684:25 **God come and he said to old Doc Hines 'You can go
too now. You have done My work . . . And old Doc Hines
went when God told him to go. But he kept in touch with
God** Hines says that God released him from his charge to
watch over Joe. But Hines is not sure that his part in God's
plan is over, so he moves to Mottstown to remain near Joe (if
we assume that the McEacherns live near there). He keeps
in touch with God at night, he says, through prayer to be
sure there is no change in instructions.

684:27 **My chosen instrument** Hines, chosen by God to
carry out His will on earth

684:33 **old Doc Hines kept in touch with God and one night
he wrestled and he strove and he cried aloud 'That bastard,
Lord! I feel! I feel the teeth and the fangs of evil!' and God
said 'It's that bastard. Your work is not done yet. He's a
pollution and a abomination on My earth** And God finally

realized I *was* right. The teeth *were* the 'teeth and fangs of evil,' and they belonged to 'that bastard' Joe. So God told me my work was *not* done yet. It was my charge this time not just to watch over Joe but to *eliminate* him. This is Hines's rationalization to Hightower for why he tried to incite the crowd to lynch his grandson in Mottstown and why he wants to encourage a lynching in Jefferson.

685:24 **since he had met them twelve hours ago** We never learn how the Hineses knew to talk with Byron or how he knew to talk with them when their train arrived in Jefferson that morning.

686:20 **like he made them that loved and lost suffer** 'he' = Christmas. This echoes Alfred Lord Tennyson's *In Memoriam*, 27:4, ll. 15–6 (59) "'Tis better to have loved and lost / Than never to have loved at all," (59); 'them' refers apparently to Joanna Burden, though Byron can know little if anything about why Christmas killed her.°

686:29 **without any living earth against him yet** without anyone on this living earth having reason to be against him yet

686:38 **What are they asking of me now?** 'they' = specifically, the Hines couple; more generally, the people of Jefferson, 'the people I live among and who dictate my life.'

687:2 **It will be Byron who will ask it** Byron will 'ask it' because he is the only one of the three able to articulate the question. Moreover, he can impose on his personal relationship with Hightower in a way the Hineses cannot.

687:7 **Ah. Commiseration? . . . Commiseration for me, or for Byron?** Hightower suggests that Byron's apparent sympathy for him might be self-serving, the result of the younger man's sense of guilt and uncertainty over what he has involved himself in.

687:10 **Ah Byron, Byron. What a dramatist you would have made** Hightower sarcastically compliments Byron for the melodramatic scene he has so skillfully constructed. He understands that Byron is trying to impose on their friendship and to lure him into a situation of which he wants no part. Hightower admits that by bringing in the elderly Hines couple, with their pitiful and demented tale of a dead daughter and lost grandson, Byron has built a persuasive case.

687:12 **a drummer, a agent, a salesman** Byron disagrees with Hightower: he is not a dramatist, merely a salesman trying to sell something.

687:24 **I said to you once that there is a price for being good ... it wont be like you haven't done it before, haven't paid a bill like it once before. It oughtn't to be so bad now as it was then** Here Byron plays the salesman. Earlier he told Hightower that there is a 'price for being good' on 669:19. And a good man cannot help but pay, because his own goodness forces him to. Now he argues that it is again time for Hightower to pay the price of being good, and since he has paid it once before, and knows what to expect, Byron says he won't have to suffer as he did then.

687:39 **You could say he was here with you that night ... They would rather believe that about you than to believe that he lived with her like a husband and then killed her** Byron implies that folks would rather believe that Hightower and Christmas were having a homosexual relationship than that Christmas and Joanna were lovers. Moreover, the town has spread similar rumors about Hightower before, at 450:37 and 452:29, for instance. Byron wants Hightower to tell the lie that Christmas was with him on the night he was supposed to have killed Joanna. On 742 Hightower grants Byron's request.

687:40 **the big house** the central house on a plantation

688:8 **very good. Good for all.** Hightower sarcastically summarizes what will be the results of the lie Byron wants him to tell: a murderer will be freed and restored to the grandparents who haven't seen him for thirty years, and Brown will run away, leaving Byron to collect Lena and the reward money.

688:12 **Since I am just an old man who has been fortunate**

enough to grow old without having to learn the despair of love Hightower takes insult at Mrs. Hines's assumption that he is a bachelor who had never known the 'despair of love' (686:8).

688:18 **It's not because I cant, dont dare to . . . it's because I wont! I wont! do you hear?** Why won't Hightower tell the lie that Byron asks of him? He might answer that he does not want to be part of Byron's schemes, or that he does not want to lie. A more fundamental reason is that he does not wish to be involved in life again, with its responsibilities and consequences.

CHAPTER XVII

689:1 **That was Sunday night.** 'That' = the last scene in the previous chapter.

689:13 **I reckon he has not slept much . . . Even if he aint playing—** If playing midwife has not kept Hightower awake, then worrying over the lie Byron asked him to tell has.

689:21 **He had never been deeper into the house than the room where he had last seen the owner of it** Byron's friendship with the exminister has remained formal. They talk in the front room, and there has never been reason for him to go further into the house.

689:28 **they would both have a different name for whoever did the leading** Byron believes Hightower would say the devil is guiding him (he has already said so, on 626:14), while Lena would say that God guides him (as she said on 414:16).

689:37 **There was a quality of profound and complete surrender in it . . . as though he had given over and relinquished . . . that strength . . . which is the I-Am** 'I-Am' = fundamental assertion of self. Hightower is so profoundly asleep that he seems to have lost his very awareness of being alive. Waking him to ask him to do what he clearly does not want to do would be, Byron thinks, 'the sorest injury that he had ever done him.' Cf. Exodus 3:14, "I am that I am."

690:10 **I reckon He has been watching me too lately** watching me as he watches the sparrow. See entry 684:10.

690:26 **Book? My book?** Hightower, slightly confused, at first thinks Byron means his Bible. Byron means the book that explains how to help a woman give birth.

690:40 **failing street lamps** failing because the increasing light of dawn is drowning out their light

691:2 **the façade of its eastern side was in sharp relief against the sky** The silhouetted building fronts on the eastern side of the square stand out against the brightening sky.

691:8 **There was something else behind it, which he was not to recognise until later** 'something else' = a dawning awareness that does not become clear to him until 693−94, where he finally accepts the full meaning of Lena's pregnancy: that she is not a virgin and has had sex with another man, that she is in effect another man's wife. His refusal of these facts caused him to put off finding a doctor until now because doing so would have forced him to acknowledge what he wants to ignore.

691:12 **I got to decide quick** which doctor to ask to help Lena

691:13 **But this is different** This is different because this is a white woman in labor, and I don't want her or her baby to die—this is the woman I love.

691:17 **that will believe the lies that I will have to tell** lies about who she is, whom she is married to, why she is alone in Joanna Burden's cabin, why he waited so long to find a doctor

691:23 **already his decision was made** which doctor to choose

691:29 **at which Hightower had officiated with his razor and his book** Hightower once officiated with regularity at church services and ceremonies. At the birth of the Negro child he 'officiated' in a different way, with a razor to cut the umbilical cord and a book of instructions on childbirth.

691:34 **switch key** the car ignition key

692:23 **gumption** awareness, energy. The entire situation leaves Mrs. Hines very confused. The doctor assumes she and her husband are Lena's parents.

692:25 **Yes** Mrs. Hines's response to the doctor's remark that 'grandma and grandpa' are on hand.

692:30 **her attitude at once like a rock and like a crouching beast** Literally, her attitude makes her seem both immovable and ready to spring into action. The image suggests an Egyptian sphinx; see entry 693:20.

692:34 **I told him you would come in the back way this time** Before, Hines had not arranged for a doctor, had sat guard at the front door, and when Mrs. Hines tried to go for help out the 'back way,' he stopped her (see 679). This time, she says, the doctor came in the 'back way' so that her husband couldn't stop him.

692:36 **You can see to Milly now. I'll take care of Joey** Mrs. Hines confuses Lena and her child with her daughter Milly and the baby Joe.

692:37 **the life, the vividness fled suddenly** Throughout the first section of this chapter Mrs. Hines's mental state oscillates from confusion to joyous certainty that she has found Milly's baby to numb exhaustion.

693:7 **something terrible happened to him** We aren't told what this is right away. With the next words ('Mrs. Hines had called him from his tent'), we go back to a time earlier that morning and for four pages we follow the development of this 'terrible' thing in Byron's mind (see 693:24) until at 692:23 it 'overtook him from behind,' and at 695:30, 695:37, 695:40 we finally learn what the thing is.

693:20 **while somewhere in him the clawed thing lurked and waited . . . something terrible happened to him** This 'clawed thing,' as yet unidentified, is the 'something terrible' of 693:7. It is apparently both within him (as here) and outside him (at 695:23 it overtakes him 'from behind'). This 'terrible' and 'clawed thing' is Faulkner's image for the realization about Lena now beginning to dawn in Byron's mind.

Throughout this extended scene there are echoes of "The Second Coming," by William Butler Yeats, yet they do not work in a consistent way. The earlier description of Mrs. Hines as a sphinx (entry 692:30) recalls a similar passage in Yeats' poem:

somewhere in sands of the desert
A shape with lion body and the head of a man,
A gaze blank and pitiless as the sun.

Yet the poem's theme and subject also apply to Byron. The birth of the child brings an end to his "ceremony of innocence" concerning Lena's sexuality and changes his outlook on everything. The death of innocence, order, and the basic philosophic outlook of western culture is a major theme of the poem:

Things fall apart; the center cannot hold;
Mere anarchy is loosed upon the world,
The blood-dimmed tide is loosed, and everywhere
The ceremony of innocence is drowned.

Lena's child concludes one epoch of Byron's life and begins another. The birth is 'terrible' because it forces him to acknowledge the facts of Lena's sexual experience. Moreover, to Mrs. Hines, who confuses the infant with her own grandson, the birth is a literal second coming of the child she lost so many years earlier:

The darkness drops again; but now I know
That twenty centuries of stony sleep
Were vexed to nightmare by a rocking cradle,
And what rough beast, its hour come round at last,
Slouches towards Bethlehem to be born? (187).

The poem's evocation of a second coming applies equally well to Joe Christmas, for his entry into the lives of the other major characters changes them irrevocably.°

693:30 **his eyes had accepted her belly without his mind believing. 'Yet I did know, believe,'** Byron has known Lena is pregnant and that in principle she has slept with another man. But he does not 'know' or 'believe' in her pregnancy as an emotional reality: he has not fully comprehended it, until now: 'Then he heard the child cry. Then he knew' (695).

693:38 **put on, like a pair of hurried overalls** Byron recog-

nized the need for haste and immediately 'put on' the appropriate behavior—as a man would hurriedly don a pair of
overalls in an emergency.

694:7 **seemed to be speaking clearly to something in a
tongue which he knew was not his tongue nor that of any
man** the language of a woman in labor, which men, who
do not give birth, cannot speak or understand. Maybe the
'something' to which she seems to speak is God, or the baby,
or nothing at all.

694:9 **he saw her** 'her' = Lena. His continual thinking of
Lena as an abstract 'her' or 'she' suggests the shock of what
he is beginning to understand her condition actually means.

694:10 **He had never seen her in bed before and he believed
that when or if he ever did, she would be tense, alert,
maybe smiling** As we might have suspected, though Byron's tent is only fifty yards from Lena's cabin and he has
been looking after her for more than a week, his behavior
has been scrupulous. He has also imagined in some detail
and with anticipation the moment when he would first see
her in bed. As we learned at 434:10, 'Byron fell in love.'

694:19 **Her hair was loose and her eyes looked like two
holes and her mouth was as bloodless now as the pillow
behind her** The influence of "The Scream," by Norwegian
artist Edvard Munch, seems apparent in this description, as
it was once before in the face of Bobbie Allen after Simon
McEachern accosted her at the dance in chapter IX (see entry 550:14).

694:30 **He knew now that thinking went slow and smooth
with calculation** Though he is working fast, his mind, now
working logically and inexorably towards a conclusion,
moves with deliberate calculation: it has no need to rush.

694:31 **as oil is spread slowly upon a surface above a brew-
ing storm** This is old sailors' lore. The mind's ratiocinative
powers have a calming effect on the emotions stirred by the
conclusion Byron is about to reach.

694:33 **If I had known then. If it had got through then**

'then' = when he first saw her. If I had fully understood everything about her pregnancy when I first saw her.

694:37 **But he did not** He did not ride away then or now. Instead he rides for a doctor to assist in the birth of the baby.

694:39 **If I can just get past and out of hearing before she hollers again** then I won't have to think about her pregnancy or her pain and suffering

695:1 **That carried him for a while** 'that' = the belief that if he doesn't have to hear her holler again, he won't have to acknowledge what her pregnancy means

695:5 **the oil said** calculated thought said

695:7 **Then he had something else** to occupy his thoughts: convincing Hightower to come help Lena

695:10 **he could feel it, clawed with lurking** 'it' = the knowledge he has tried to avoid. See entry 693:20.

695:11 *Because I have never believed that I would need one.* Believing Lena to be a virgin, despite the evidence of her swelling belly, he never thought he would need to find a doctor to deliver her baby.

695:19 **Anyway it got him back to the cabin** 'it' = 'the need for haste' (695:13)

695:22 **the final hiatus of peace before the blow fell and the clawed thing overtook him from behind. Then he heard the child cry.** 'final hiatus of peace' = the last moments he can pretend not to understand the truth about Lena; 'the blow' = the cry of the child and what it means; 'the clawed thing' = the knowledge that Lena is not a virgin; 'overtook him from behind' = though he is headed for Lena's cabin, he in essence has been running away from the 'clawed thing' of truth, but now he cannot escape any longer. It catches up and overtakes him, and he must confront and accept it. See entry 693:20.

695:24 **Dawn was making fast** rapidly approaching; 'to make' = to come to fruition. The brightening dawn parallels Byron's quickly dawning knowledge about Lena.

695:29 **something all the while which had protected him**

against believing, with the believing protected him Byron's love, and his belief in Lena's innocence, protected him from accepting what her pregnancy signified.

695:36 *And this too is reserved for me, as Reverend Hightower says* Hightower says this on 687:3. There he spoke of the burden Byron would ask him to bear, the sacrifice he would have to make, and that Byron would have to make too, because of the events that began with Joanna Burden's murder and Lena Grove's arrival in town. Here Byron adapts that statement to his own situation, realizing that his sacrifice will be to hand over the woman he loves to another man.

695:40 *Why, I didn't even believe until now that he was so* that he existed

696:2 *words that never even stood for anything, were not even us, while all the time what was us was going on and going on without even missing the lack of words* All of this seems unreal, as if there are no words capable of describing us, and even in the absence of those words we continue to do what we do, unaware that there are no words adequate to describe us.

696:8 **'Luck,' Hightower says** Hightower remembers how the doctor congratulated him on 692:5 for successfully delivering Lena's baby.

696:14 **her dumb and furious terror** She fears her husband will somehow make off with this baby too.

696:14 **no less furious for being dumb** Her inability to express her terror did not lessen the intensity of her fury.

696:16 **she held it high aloft** as Hines did when his grandson Joe was born (679)

696:22 *She has already killed him* Having heard Mrs. Hines's story, Hightower assumes for a moment that she has killed Hines to prevent him from taking the baby.

696:28 **also in no known tongue** similar to the 'passionate and abject' tongue of Lena while in labor on 694:7

697:2 **while his hands are busy** Since the baby has already been born, the doctor is now probably severing and tying off the umbilical cord and seeing to the delivery of the placenta.

697:16 **the tail of a coarse cotton nightshirt thrust into his black trousers** Nightshirts typically extended down to the knees or shins. Hightower in his hurry did not put on a shirt but tucked his nightshirt into his pants before leaving his house.

697:20 **keeping time to his feet** As he walks he thinks repeatedly 'I am tired, and I shall not be able to sleep,' in time with, to the rhythm of, his walking.

697:31 **his thinking sounds querulous** His usual tendency to emphasize his own discomfort and inconvenience ('I know I shall not sleep') suddenly seems unjustified complaining, 'like the peaceful whining of a querulous woman.' By going out to the cabin to assist in the birth of Lena's baby, Hightower has broken his usual routine, and he is soon to convince himself that the experience has made a new man of him: 'Life comes to the old man yet.'

698:1 **leavings** leftovers

698:4 **fading glow disregards it** 'it' = the 'reprimand' of his conscience

698:10 **I'm not even going to wash them now** He's too busy feeling proud to ruin the moment by tending to dirty dishes. That is woman's work, and Hightower feels himself a man. In the next few lines he contrasts what a 'woman would do' with what he himself will do.

698:18 **the Tennyson** the collection of Tennyson's poetry, 'the fine galloping language, the gutless swooning full of sapless trees and dehydrated lusts' (634:12), the book he had chosen to read when he was envying Byron for being young ('To be young. There is nothing else like it'—633:32).

698:18 **this time also** He does something else that violates his usual pattern of behavior. Just as he did not wash the breakfast dishes, and as he did not go to his bedroom to make up the sleep he had missed, this time he chooses a different book to read, one more appropriate to his current euphoria.

698:19 **he chooses food for a man. It is Henry IV** Shakespeare's *Henry IV* is about the meaning of leadership and

the desired character of a ruler. In his present mood Hightower sees a link between himself and Prince Hal, who in
Henry IV, Part One takes on a character and personality befit-
ting the heir to the English throne. *Henry IV* is quite different from the hypnotic 'gutless swooning' and 'sapless trees'
of Tennyson.

698:25 **He goes to sleep soon, almost immediately** Faulkner must intend some irony in the fact that Hightower cele-
brates his reassertion of manhood by retreating to a book
and then to sleep. Hightower told himself three times (697:
18, 697:29, 698:22) that he would not be able to sleep.

698:36 **so I have surrendered too.** Hightower feared he
would lose in sleep the vitality he felt after delivering Lena's
child, but since on waking he still feels it, he surrenders to
what he takes to be its meaning: that he can reenter life.

698:39 **Perhaps this too is reserved for me** Earlier (687:3)
Hightower used this expression to refer to something un-
pleasant he thought he would have to endure; now he uses
it to mean that something good and pleasing might happen
to him. As we learn a few lines later, he is thinking that Lena
might name her baby for him, since he delivered it under
unusual circumstances.

699:3 *will take the* **pas** *of me* 'pas' = right of precedence.
Hightower believes Lena will feel that Byron has prior claim
to her gratitude and will name her child for him.

699:4 *She will have to have others, more* She will have to bear
other children, for that is her nature, and maybe one of the
others, fathered by Byron, can be named for me.

699:7 *the good stock peopling in tranquil obedience to it the
good earth* Romanticizing the mythic connotations of her
fertility, Hightower observes with some condescension that
Lena's destiny is to obey the Biblical mandate "Be fruitful
and multiply, and replenish the earth" (Genesis 1:28).

699:9 *But by Byron engendered next. Poor boy. Even though he
did let me walk back home* Even though he left me without
a mule to ride home, he doesn't deserve the fate of becoming
the father of Lena's children.

699:14   **lawn tie**   a necktie made of lawn, a fine linen or cotton fabric used in handkerchiefs, blouses, and curtains

699:19   **the loud silence**   the background noise of countless insects and small creatures of the woods

699:19   **I should never have lost this habit, too**   I should never have given up the habit of walking in the woods, just as I should not have given up the habit of prayer.

699:27   **To have not lived only a week longer, until luck returned to this place**   Hightower regrets that Joanna did not live long enough to share in the luck traditionally associated with a newborn child.

699:28   **these barren and ruined acres**   These words echo Shakespeare, Sonnet 73, "bare ruined choirs / Where late the sweet birds sang," but Hightower has borrowed the words without their context, for the happiness and vitality of the sonnet's "sweet birds" never blessed the Burden place.

699:31   **the quarters**   where the slaves who worked the farm lived in their cabins

699:33   **big house**   the main house, now burned down

700:2   **"I thought——" she says.**
"Who did you think?" he says   As he entered the cabin Hightower was hoping that Lena would be pleased to see him. But seeing her smile fade, he realizes she is waiting for someone else. He will ask again at 702:15 whom she was waiting for, fearing it was Byron (because he thinks it would be disastrous for Byron if Lena should choose him). At 703:35 he concludes Lena was expecting Lucas Burch, and is relieved ('*Thank God*' he thinks at 704:6). But in fact, as we learn on 704, she *was* waiting for Byron, or at least hoping for his return, and is heartbroken from her fear that she might never see him again. See entry 703:39.

700:5   **weazened**   wizened

700:5   **terracotta**   brownish red, the typical color of a newborn

700:21   **His face is grave now**   because he understands what Hines will try to do when he gets to town: incite the citizens to lynch Christmas. And he understands too that the Hines's disappearance from the cabin may oblige him to tell the lie that Byron has asked of him.

700:25 **gave out** ran out of energy

700:34 **squinching** contorting his face, squinting, as if to convey a secret message

701:2 **she wasn't winking and squinting, but I nigh wished she was** I almost wish she had been 'winking and squinting' at me, because the look she did give me—of anger (that her husband had run off) and fear (that he might incite the citizens of Jefferson to lynch her grandson)—was too much to bear. The change in Hightower's expression from 'gentle, beaming, and triumphant' (700:9) to 'grave' (700:22) to 'very grave' (701:9) suggests that he shares her fear.

702:8 **She says, too immediately, too easily** as if this explanation had been prepared beforehand. We learn on 703 that Byron has told her he is going to bring Lucas Burch to her. So clearly she is expecting him. But her reaction on 703–04 to Byron's absence suggests that she was hoping for his arrival in Burch's place, perhaps that she is waiting for his appearance to determine whose name the baby will bear.

702:17 **Her face is neither innocent nor dissimulating. Neither is it placid and serene** She does not try to pretend she does not understand Hightower's question or why he asks it, but for reasons not revealed until 703:39 it is a question she would rather not answer. And she does not answer it here.

702:20 **that ruthlessness which she has seen in the faces of a few good people, men usually** the ruthlessness of men (or people in general) who believe that right is on their side, and who thus feel justified in taking whatever steps are necessary to see that right is done

702:26 **And you are a good woman. Will be. I dont mean——** Hightower thinks carelessly aloud that when Lena eventually marries, she will become 'good.' But he immediately realizes that his words imply that this unmarried mother of a new-born infant is a bad or fallen woman. He is trying to show compassion.

702:29 **No. Not this. This does not matter. This is not anything yet** 'this' = Lena's current situation as the unmarried
mother of an illegitimate child

702:30 **It all depends on what you do with it, afterwards.
With yourself. With others . . . Let him go** 'it' = your present situation, and whether it will make you a 'good' woman
or a 'bad' one. Hightower means that she will be 'good' if she
decides not to attach herself to Byron. He is rationalizing,
trying to lure her towards a decision that will allow her to
feel she is a 'good' woman and that will, in his mind, 'save'
Byron.

702:33 **daughter** an affectionate, pastoral form of address

702:36 **And that too, his nothing, is as irremediable as your
all** Hightower tells Lena that Byron will no more be able to
overcome his inexperience and innocence than will she be
able to overcome her maturity and experience.

702:37 **He can no more ever cast back and do, than you can
cast back and undo** 'cast back' = 'backtrack'. Hightower
means that Byron can no more return to the past and make
up for his lack of experience than Lena can go back and
'undo' her relationship with Lucas Burch.

702:40 **You will be forcing into his life two men and only
the third part of a woman** The 'two men' with whom Byron would have to share Lena and his life are Lucas Burch
and the child. Byron would have only 'the third part' of a
woman because one-third of her would have already been
claimed by the baby and the other third by Burch.

703:1 **deserves at the least that the nothing with which he
has lived for thirtyfive years be violated . . . without two
witnesses** If the 'nothing' of Byron's life, the thirty-five
years of innocence and inexperience, must be violated, it
should not be by a woman who brings the memory of a Lucas
Burch and the presence of the child he fathered to witness it.

703:9 **"And you wont send him away? You wont say the
word?"**

 "I can say no more than I have said." Lena's response is honest but ultimately misleading—at least to Hightower. He learns at 703:19 that she will continue to say 'no' to Byron's marriage proposals at least until after she has seen Lucas. But she does *not* say that she has sent Byron away, or that she will do so, yet Hightower thinks her intention not to get involved with Byron is implicit in her words, for he 'sighs' and says 'I believe you.' See entry 703:39.

703:23 **suddenly her face is quite empty . . . Now there is nothing of dissimulation nor caution in it** Lena has been trying to speak openly, telling Hightower the truth yet also hiding her real feelings, which he has not explicitly asked her about. This effort keeps her alert and 'firm.' But now when Hightower asks her where Byron is, she cannot hide her feelings and must answer from the heart: 'I dont know.'

703:27 **about ten oclock he came back** 'he' = Byron

703:31 **'I come to find out when you want to see him' and I said 'See who? . . . Let who come?' and he said 'Lucas. Burch' and I said 'Yes'** Lena probably knows that Byron means Lucas Burch the first time he asks when she wants to see 'him.' But she pretends not to understand. Why? To let him know that she has lost interest in Burch, that now she wants to see *him*. But when Byron fails to get the hint, she allows him to play out his self-appointed mission of reuniting her with her 'husband.'

703:34 **Kennedy** Sheriff Watt Kennedy

703:39 **she begins to cry** Lena cries because Byron is gone and she thinks she will never see him again. She knows Byron is a good man, and a good man to serve as father and husband is what she came from Alabama to find. She has realized by now the sort of man Lucas Burch really is, and she no longer expects to marry him.

703:39 **She sits upright, the child at her breast, crying** an image of the Pietà, though like many other religious symbols in the novel its details and meaning are changed. The dead Christ is replaced by the infant child, and Lena grieves for the loss of Byron, not her son's death. The image is of purity, fertility, and life, melded with the sorrow of aloneness and lost love.

704:6 *Thank God, God help me. Thank God, God help me* Hightower understands why Lena is crying. He thanks God that Byron is 'safe.' But in 'God help me' perhaps he expresses remorse for having had a part in Byron's loss of the woman he loves.

704:19 **Saturday evenings too** Saturday afternoons too, when Byron also worked

704:35 **Grand Jury meets today. Special call** The Grand Jury has convened in a special session to consider the indictment of Christmas for the murder of Joanna Burden. The reason for the special session is not merely the seriousness of the crime but probably also the desire not to give townspeople time to organize a lynch mob.

705:3 **Poor man. Poor fellow** Now he is thinking about Christmas. Compare with 472:7: 'Poor man. Poor mankind.'

705:4 **No man is, can be, justified in taking human life . . .** Hightower's logic seems muddled in this apparent argument against representatives of the State carrying out the execution of criminals. The basis of his argument is the Sixth Commandment, "Thou shalt not kill" (Exodus 20:13): To paraphrase Hightower, "No one is justified in killing another person. This is especially true of an officer of the law, authorized by the state to protect human lives. When a law officer kills someone who has done him no wrong, then how can we expect an average citizen to refrain from violence against a person who has wronged him?"

705:5 **warranted officer** an officer authorized by the city or state to enforce the law

705:8 **call that victim by what name you will** i.e., regardless of the kind of man he might be

705:12 **So he departed without coming to tell me goodbye. After all he has done for me. Fetched to me. Ay; given, restored to me** Hightower begins by expressing irritation at Byron for not telling him goodbye but quickly goes on to express his gratitude for the newly restored sense of life he believes Byron has brought to him with his insistence that he involve himself in the affairs of Lena Grove.

705:15 **It would seem that this too was reserved for me. And this must be all** By 'this' Hightower means the Grand Jury hearing to indict Christmas, the ensuing trial, and whatever assaults on his sensibilities will result from the consequent uproar in the town, all of which he will have to face alone, without Byron Bunch; 'all' = the 'favor' Byron is asking of him.

705:17 **But it is not all. There is one thing more reserved for him.** Hightower fails to recall that Byron also got him involved with the Hineses (and therefore with the murderer Joe). He still has to play a role whose lines have already been written by Byron. See 742:12 for their delivery.

CHAPTER XVIII

706:1 **When Byron reached town** after leaving Lena's cabin just after her baby was born, after stopping at the planing mill to quit his job, but before Hightower's visit to her cabin reported near the end of the last chapter

706:5 **I know how** how to wait. Byron implies he has spent his entire life waiting, and that now he has lost Lena, he will just have to wait some more.

706:8 **flagged terrace** floor of the portico, covered with flagstones

706:14 **clerks and young lawyers and even merchants . . . not especially caring if the disguise hid the policeman or not** In contrast to the feigned 'grave purposelessness' of the farmers who have come to town on a weekday in case some excitement concerning Christmas erupts, the young men of the town make no attempt to disguise their willingness to join in vigilante action if it should develop.

706:17 **moved with almost the air of monks in a cloister** solemn and decorous, the opposite of what they are: willing participants in a possible lynch mob

706:19 **looking . . . upward at the ceiling** the ceiling of the portico. The Grand Jury must be meeting on the second floor of the courthouse.

706:20 **the Grand Jury was preparing . . . to take the life of a man** The Grand Jury can only indict Christmas and hand him over to a judge and jury for trial. This is Faulkner's way of saying that Christmas is as good as dead already: indicted, tried, and hanged in the minds of the townspeople.

706:36 *weeded another man's laidby crop, without any halv-*

ers 'weeded' = looked after, took care of; 'laidby crop' = a crop approaching time to be harvested; 'halvers' = half-shares. Byron believes the townspeople will ridicule him as a sucker who helped bring another man's child into the world and then stood by as the man appeared to claim the woman and child.

707:9 **And now I can go away** Conceding the truth of what he takes to be their conclusion, that he '*wasn't needed anymore,*' he feels free to 'go away.'

707:13 **something terrible would happen** as if the conflicting emotions within him were about to explode. Cf. Christmas twenty-four hours before he kills Joanna: '*Something is going to happen to me. I am going to do something*' (475:21).

707:16 **now Now NOW** These repetitions signify the explosive potential of dynamite, which Faulkner uses to convey the potential Byron feels within himself. See similar repetitions of 'now' on 670 and 763; both pertain to Hightower.

707:20 **who had believed that out there at the mill on a Saturday afternoon, alone, the chance to be hurt could not have found him** 'Saturday afternoon' = when Lena and Byron met. Byron thinks that, despite his best efforts to protect himself, events of the last ten days have involved him in the lives of other people, and he has been hurt as a result.

707:23 **I got to go somewhere** I've got to go somewhere or do something to escape from all of this before I explode.

707:24 **He could walk in time to that.** He could walk to the rhythm of that, to the notion of having to 'go somewhere.'

707:28 **I might see somebody reading or smoking in the window** Byron knows he's been gone long enough from Mrs. Beard's boarding house for her to conclude he's not coming back, and that she's probably rented his room to someone else. But he hasn't officially given her notice, so he can *pretend* that he still lives there (and that nothing has happened that would cause him to be evicted). If he looks up and sees someone in the window of his room, he'll *know* he's been moved out, and he wants to avoid that just now.

707:30 **He could smell wet linoleum, soap. 'It's still Monday.' he thought** Because Monday is wash day, the smell of the soap tells him it is Monday.

707:32 **Maybe it's next Monday. That's what it seems like it ought to be** So much has happened in the past week that it seems more than a week has passed.

708:1 **a fat lady that never had more trouble than a mopping pail could hold ought not to try to be . . .** Byron is searching for a word like "patronizing" or "condescending" or "judgmental." The apparent tone with which Mrs. Beard has just called him 'Mister Byron Bunch' (instead of her usual 'Mr Bunch') suggests she regards him as compromised, though as their ensuing conversation reveals she does feel sympathy for him.

708:3 **Again he could not think of the word that Hightower would know** 'Again' refers to 689:14: 'He could not think of the word midwife, which he knew that Hightower would use.'

708:12 **I reckon I owe you a little room rent** Byron's polite way of asking Mrs. Beard if he still has a room

708:14 **comfortable face** pleasant, relaxed face

708:15 **I thought you was settled. Decided to tent for the summer** Mrs. Beard's comments to Byron are sometimes sarcastic and disapproving but not bitter. Three times the text emphasizes that she was not unkind.

708:17 **She did it gently, delicately, considering** considering that he had been away for more than a week without letting her know whether he wanted to keep the room and that he had been involved in events of which she would disapprove

708:23 **I reckon I better——** get my things out of my room

708:25 **I put everything you left in your grip** That everything Byron owns can fit into a single suitcase suggests the spartan simplicity of his life in Jefferson.

708:32 **if it wasn't for getting some woman mixed up in it to help you, you'd ever one of you be drug hollering into**

heaven 'ever' = every. Mrs. Beard suggests that men are born innocent, but when they get involved with women they get corrupted.

708:37 **Dont no other woman need to that is going to** Other women may realize, as Mrs. Beard does, that they have no reason to criticize Lena, but they're going to do it anyway.

709:2 **it aint any woman but knows that she aint had any reason to have to be bad with you** Every woman would know that Lena did not need to be 'bad' with Byron to get him to do what she wanted.

709:9 **He was not looking at her now** Perhaps because he fears she may be right.

709:11 **She answered that too, before it was spoken. "I reckon you'll be leaving us soon"** Though Mrs. Beard assumes Brown and Lena will be reunited and married, she also assumes Byron will want to leave town, has his bags packed for him, and suggests his departure. She's assuming that he knows he has violated the town's standards (i.e., her standards), and that he will not want to remain.

709:12 **What have they done this morning? at the courthouse?** Has the Grand Jury indicted Christmas for murder?

709:15 **I bound that, too** I'm sure of that too. 'That' = the fact that the Grand Jury isn't finished deliberating, since they are being paid for their time.°

709:16 **county money** Members of the Grand Jury are paid for their services out of the county budget on a per diem basis.

709:21 **the other one** Brown

709:26 **they can get married** 'they' = Lena and Brown

709:33 **footloose** A week before neither she nor anyone else in the town would have described Byron as 'footloose.'

710:2 **squat on their heels** Byron and the sheriff do *not* 'squat on their heels,' as they would normally do, because both regard this as a formal occasion. Byron is also preparing to leave and does not have time or the desire to be sociable, and the Sheriff recognizes this.

710:6 **had been for seven days wellnigh a public outrage and affront** Byron lived in the tent near the cabin where Lena stayed for a week. Since they were unmarried, and she was pregnant with another man's child, the town found this scandalous.

710:31 **free agent** unmarried man

710:31 **his bond to appear as a witness** When the Grand Jury indicts Christmas, Brown can be released from jail and will be free except for his obligation ('bond') to appear as a witness at the murder trial. The sheriff may also mean that Brown's hope of getting the thousand dollar reward will guarantee his presence at the trial.

710:34 **believed that he would plead guilty to save his neck** In many states a person who pleads guilty to murder cannot be condemned to death and instead receives a life sentence.

710:36 **that durn fellow** Brown

711:18 **Take it out of Jefferson, though, anyway** 'it' = Christmas's neck: the sheriff believes Christmas will plead guilty to save himself and to have himself sent to the state prison, far from Jefferson and the scene of his crime.

711:24 **Percy Grimm'll get him with that army of his** 'him' = Hines. Grimm will play a significant role in the next chapter. See entry 731:35 for a full discussion of Grimm's name.

711:27 **Maybe Jefferson will treat you better next time** the sheriff's way of saying that he knows the town has made Byron pay a stiff price for his well intentioned involvement with Lena

711:35 **a sack of tobacco** for rolling cigarettes

711:36 **I can go now** I am free to go: there is nothing else here that I can or should do. He has kept Lena away from disapproving townspeople and prevented them from bothering her, he has assisted in the delivery of her baby, and now he has reunited her with her husband.

712:1 **battered yellow suitcase which is not leather** a heavy cardboard suitcase

712:3 **He does not look back** He refrains from doing so as an act of will. He is determined to leave Lena and his life in Jefferson behind.

712:5 **I can bear a hill** I've endured everything else: I can endure climbing a hill.

712:11 **He can even bear it to not look back, even when he knows that looking back or not looking back wont do him any good.** He can bear the remorse and regret he feels when he does not look back, even though he knows that nothing will change whether he looks back or not. This proves not to be true. In this progression of statements about what a man can 'bear,' Byron moves from contemplating the simple task of climbing a hill to the more profound and heart-wrenching grief of not being able to change the past or regain a lost love.

712:14 **The hill rises, cresting** Faulkner describes Byron's movement as if the ground is moving beneath him while he stands still, an effect similar to the chapter I description of how 'The red and unhurried miles unroll beneath the steady feet of the mules, beneath the creaking and clanking wheels' (420:2) of the wagon in which Lena is riding.

712:19 **And Byron Bunch he wouldn't even have to be or not be Byron Bunch** An allusion to the soliloquy from Shakespeare's *Hamlet*. Though Byron clearly thinks about the possibility of nonexistence here, he also thinks that in this "other world" he is about to ride into he would not have to bear the name of Byron Bunch, and could be called by another name, could *become* someone else entirely, without the memories and griefs of Byron Bunch.

712:22 **them rocks running so fast in space** meteors

712:25 **But then from beyond the hill crest there begins to rise that which he knows is there: the trees which are trees** But then, as he reaches the top of the hill, he sees on the down slope the trees that *are* called trees, and he knows he will not be riding off into the nothing but will remain in the world.

712:27   **distance which . . . he must compass forever and ever between two inescapable horizons of the implacable earth** 'compass' = enclose in his mind and memory; 'horizons' = the one behind him, the horizon of Jefferson, and the one he faces, of the pines ahead. They are 'inescapable' because he will always remember them: they enclose the town and the land where he found and lost his love. Faulkner regards the earth as 'implacable' because it is indifferent to human misery and need. He uses a similar phrase, the 'implacable and immemorial earth,' in Chapter I (420:20).

712:40   **the once broad domain of what was once seventy years ago a plantation house** A panoramic view of the ruined Old South, seen from the modern perspective of 1932, ironically embodied in the grounds and house of the Burden family.

713:5   **blackjack and sassafras and persimmon and brier** The first three are scrub trees, the fourth a prickly undergrowth. All spring up promptly in abandoned Southern fields.

713:20   **a cold, hard wind seems to blow through him. It is at once violent and peaceful. . . blowing hard away like chaff** This wind is similar to the one that blows through Joe Christmas in Chapter IX (558:34, 559:12, 559:19) as he begins to realize that Bobbie Allen isn't going to run away with him, and in Chapter XII ('the long wind of knowing'—603:34) when he realizes that Joanna Burden isn't pregnant. In each instance the wind accompanies a moment of enlightenment leading to a new course of action.

713:21   **blowing hard away . . . all the desire and despair and the hopelessness and the tragic and vain imagining** Byron's 'desire' (for Lena), 'despair' and 'hopelessness' (over that which cannot be undone), and 'imagining' (of falling off the edge of the earth and not being Byron Bunch) are part of the romantic self-image he has developed in the past two pages. The wind that blows through him as he sees Brown run from the cabin dispels this romanticism.

713:24 **rush back and empty again** 'rush back' = return to
that time two weeks ago before Lena had arrived; 'empty' =
a verb, to become empty of the emotions he has felt since
deciding to leave Lena to Brown.

713:26 **The desire of this moment is more than desire: it is
conviction quiet and assured** Byron's desire to beat Brown
up is more than a wish: it is something he *knows* he is going
to do, a 'conviction,' a 'quiet and assured' certainty he is going to *act*.

713:34 **Brown is fleeing again, as he himself had predicted**
as Byron predicted to Hightower on 473:5

714:2 **And now there is one more thing I can do for him**
whip him for getting Lena pregnant, lying to her, and abandoning her

714:8 **When the deputy called for him at the jail** The perspective changes here to Joe Brown. The change has an
especially comic effect on 715, when Brown finds himself
alone in the cabin with Lena.

714:28 **I reckon the bastard aint been whelped yet that can
beat you at anything** 'whelped' = born (usually, a reference to the birth of animals, especially dogs). Though Brown
doesn't know it, the deputy is talking here about Lena's child,
which the deputy thinks will indeed 'beat' Brown when he
sees it.

714:29 **They're waiting on us** As with almost everything
else he says to Brown, the deputy uses words that say what
he means, but which he knows Brown will take to mean
something else. Here the 'they' is Lena and her baby (which
is a bastard), but Brown thinks that the ones who are going
to give him the reward are waiting for him.

715:1 **Watt** the sheriff, Watt Kennedy

715:13 **I'm going to get the same as you, to a cent** nothing

715:18 **Brown jerked his head up and back with that movement of a free mule running in front of a car in a narrow
road.** He keeps looking to see who or what might be behind him. Faulkner employed this metaphor when Brown

first appeared in the novel: 'He had . . . a way of jerking his
head quickly and glancing over his shoulder like a mule does
in front of an automobile in the road' (425). See also 714:32.

716:25 **without pity, without anything at all, she watched
him with her grave, unwinking, unbearable gaze** Lena
knows that he is a liar and scoundrel whom she does not
want for a husband or a father to her child.

716:28 **of what sorry pride the desire for justification was**
The only vestige of pride remaining in Brown is his desire
to justify his failure to send for Lena as promised.

716:40 *He will have no more shame than to lie about being
afraid, just as he had no more shame than to be afraid because he lied* In this perceptive assessment, Lena realizes
that Burch is little more than a boy, a dishonest emotional
cripple: he's not ashamed that he lied about being afraid, just
as he's not ashamed that he's afraid now to be caught in the
lie he told her.

717:7 *Them bastards* Brown calls the sheriff and his deputy
'bastards' because they set him up, promising him the reward and instead taking him to the cabin where the woman
he made pregnant and the baby who is his son lie waiting.

717:14 **There is a preacher here** Throughout this scene
Lena is testing Brown, giving him a last chance to make good
on his promise to marry her. She most surely *doesn't* want
him to make good on that promise, and she probably feels
certain that he *won't*, but she gives him the chance. What she
engages in throughout this scene is comic torture. She goads
and eggs Lucas on, watching his panic grow, until he can't
stand it any longer and leaps running through the window
on 718.

717:30 **something on the string** something in the works,
plans in progress

717:33 **then you and me will . . . . . .** settle down, get
married

718:11 **I never worried. I knowed I could depend on you**
The irony and sarcasm are heavy. By assuring Lucas she

knew she could rely on him, she tightens the screws even further.

718:16 **as if . . . she released him of her own will, deliberately** She has enjoyed her victim's suffering but now drops the issue, relieving him of the need to tell more lies, freeing him to run, which he soon does.

718:23 **her grave face which had either nothing in it, or everything, all knowledge** Either it's the face of an idiot or a person of wisdom. Because Brown isn't sure which, he's even more afraid of Lena. But the description gives the reader a choice between viewing Lena as a mute, insensible earth mother, or a self-possessed and intelligent woman. This scene in which Lena with sly wit and psychological insight confronts the man who impregnated and abandoned her strongly suggests the latter choice.

718:28 **rods nor cords** A 'rod' is a fishing rod; a 'cord' is a rope with which a wild animal could be tied up and subdued. These terms are consistent with the suggestions on 718 that Lena is 'holding' Brown as if he is a wild animal struggling to escape.

718:29 **something** her total awareness of who and what he is

718:35 **tagend of shame** some last vestige of shame

718:35 **as a while ago it had been pride** 'it' = the reasons that compel him to continue his lies to her rather than simply running away without pause for explanation

718:38 **It's a man outside . . . waiting for me** There's a man outside I've got to avoid, run away from.

719:6 **railroad right-of-way** the narrow strip of land, cleared of trees and other obstructions, alongside the railroad tracks

719:13 **fellowaid** help from its fellow creatures

719:27 **last desperate cast in a game already lost** last toss of the dice in a lost game of craps

719:36 **Aunty** archaic, patronizing way to address an elderly black woman, the equivalent of calling an old black man "Uncle"

719:37 **Ise here** I is here.

720:8 **Some of the boys** 'boys' = black men. In the rural South of 1932, white speakers used 'boy' to refer to *any* black male, child or adult.

720:11 **a detachment almost godlike but not at all benign** The woman seems to understand from the first what sort of man Brown is and thus knows that she has nothing to fear. She takes him for a fool and is not going to help him unless he pays her.

720:29 **As though somehow the very fact that he should be so consistently supplied with them elevates him somehow above the petty human hopes and desires** 'them' = 'unpredictable frustrations.' Faulkner humorously suggests that the obstacles Brown must confront in his quest for the reward are so great that they elevate him to heroic status.

721:19 **the labored and hurried pencilling in which he had succeeded for an instant in snaring his whole soul and life** The note in style and substance expresses all the essential characteristics of Lucas Burch/Joe Brown: his false politeness, greed, self-centeredness, duplicity, and irresponsibility.

721:26 **if he is above ground** if he is alive

721:34 **He takes a coin from his pocket** Though the old woman has just told the boy to 'git your dollar,' the coin Brown takes from his pocket is surely not worth that much. He would probably consider a dollar too much to pay a black man for delivering a note.

721:39 **Then again caution, shame, all flee from him** Apparently this refers to the moment on 718 just before Brown's escape from Lena's cabin: 'perhaps it was some sorry tagend of shame, as a while ago it had been pride. Because he looked at her, stripped naked for the instant of verbiage and deceit.'

722:19 **gwine up ter de railroad grade** going up to the railroad tracks, where they climb the hill

722:27 **chessmen** Faulkner will use this metaphor again in the Chapter XIX account of Percy Grimm's pursuit of Christmas. The notion that the actions of individual human beings are controlled by some external, supernatural 'Player' is deterministic. A number of characters in *Light in August*—Christmas, Brown, and Gavin Stevens, for example, seem to believe that human actions, if not entirely predetermined, are influenced to a large degree by environment and heritage.

722:32 **even beyond despair** had forgotten for a moment the reward that he is beginning to realize now he will never receive

723:8 **All Lucas Burch wanted was justice. Just justice** Christmas makes similar statements at several points in the novel. In Chapter V: 'All I wanted was peace' (481) and 'That's all I wanted' (484); see also 644:5. Even Hightower, in Chapter XIII, says 'I just wanted peace' (628:22). All three men feel they have not received justice in life, though their own behavior and the faults they will not acknowledge are at least partially responsible for the miserable lives they have led.

723:10 **and where to find him** Brown is deluding himself. He did *not* tell the sheriff where Christmas was. But pretending that he did allows him to feel that much more cheated of the reward.

723:17 **bowlsheyvick** Bolshevik, a revolutionary Russian communist, a term often used by Americans of the 1920s and 30s as a synonym for communist.

723:18 **Thus he hears no sound at all** Because Brown is speaking aloud, 'almost crying,' he does not hear Byron's approach.

724:6 **time enough to reenter the world and time too** Andrew Marvell, "To His Coy Mistress":

> Had we but world enough, and time,
> This coyness, lady, were no crime.

The allusion is repeated at 724:17. Chapter XXI demonstrates the appropriateness of the reference. There Byron and Lena have the rest of their lives ahead of them and the whole of the world to travel through. She can afford to be coy for a while longer, and he can afford to let her be.

724:8 **He does not have to think about Brown now** Just as Lena played out her closet drama with Brown in the cabin, giving him the chance to make good on his promise to marry her, so here Byron plays out his role as the avenger of a woman wronged, a role he knew would end in his defeat. Now that it's done, he doesn't have to worry about Brown anymore.

724:12 **Brown. Lena Grove. Hightower. Byron Bunch—all like small objects which had never been alive, which he had played with in childhood and then broken and forgot** Byron is in the same state of mind—confused, disconnected, dissociated from life—as Christmas in Chapter X after he was beaten up by Max Confrey and the stranger.

724:19 **he aint broke anything that belongs to me** i.e., he didn't break any of my bones. Perhaps something else is intended as well: Lena's hymen, her maidenhead, which Brown did break, which thus never 'belonged' to Byron.

724:20 **it is time now, with distance, moving, in it** time to act. The phrase equates time with motion and travel, as if Byron in realizing that it is 'time' knows that he can sit still no longer, that he must get up and *do*.

724:24 **feel the grade** climb the grade. As the locomotive begins to climb the hill, its engine naturally slows and pulls harder against the force of gravity.

724:30 **almost headon to him** almost directly in front of him

724:35 **with the rapt and boylike absorption (and perhaps yearning) of his country raising** Faulkner may imply here that country boys are more fascinated with trains than city boys, who see trains fairly often. But what he specifically means through 'and perhaps yearning' is that the train evokes in the country imagination the prospect of adventure, of travel elsewhere in search of one's fortune.

724:38 **for the second time that afternoon he sees a man materialise apparently out of air, in the act of running** The first time was at 713:14 when he saw Brown appear 'as though by magic' from the rear of Lena's cabin

724:40 **He has progressed too far into peace and solitude to wonder** Byron is at rest now. Having vanquished Brown (even though Brown vanquished him), facing the prospect of return to Lena Grove, and still in a numbed state from the beating, he simply watches Brown without questioning his motives. His peaceful state of mind contrasts sharply with the complaints of Christmas and Hightower elsewhere in the novel that 'All I wanted was peace.' See entry 723:8.

725:14 **Great God in the mountain** an expression of wonder apparently derived from the Old Testament story of Moses' receiving the Ten Commandments from God on Mount Sinai (*Exodus* 19–20)

725:21 **the world rushes down on him like a flood, a tidal wave** With the wall of railroad cars (the 'dyke') no longer there to hold back the flood of 'the world, time, hope unbelievable and certainty incontrovertible' the flood suddenly engulfs him like a tidal wave. The phrase 'hope unbelievable and certainty incontrovertible' describes how Byron feels now that he has had restored to him the hope of Lena Grove. Though an hour before such a hope would have seemed 'unbelievable,' he feels no doubt now ('certainty incontrovertible') that he has another chance. See also 756: 'they were boys riding the sheer tremendous tidal wave of desperate living.'

Faulkner may have borrowed this metaphor comparing the sudden apprehension of reality to a 'tidal wave' from Bergson's *Creative Evolution*: "Life as a whole, from the initial impulsion that thrust it into the world, will appear as a wave which rises, and which is opposed by a descending movement of matter. . . . this rising wave is consciousness."°

725:22 **It is too huge and too fast for distance and time; hence no path to be retraced** 'it' = the tidal wave and the sudden realization it signifies, of a new life and a new future. Byron's new world is so unlike anything he has known

before that he cannot even remember at first the path back
to Lena's cabin. He is returning to her in wholly altered circumstances, as if he really did 'ride right off into nothing.
Where trees would look like and be called by something else
except trees . . . And Byron Bunch he wouldn't even have to
be or not be Byron Bunch' (712:16).

725:24 **It is as though he has already and long since out-
stripped himself, already waiting at the cabin until he can
catch up and enter** Byron thinks about what he will do
much faster than he can physically reach the cabin and present himself to Lena.

725:26 *And then I will stand there and I will . . .* Byron knows
he will present himself to Lena, but he does not know what
he will do or say when he arrives at the cabin and opens the
door.

726:4 **I fell down** the kind of flip answer Byron would not
have given before this afternoon—like Joe's telling Mrs.
McEachern that her husband was 'at a dance' (552:11) or
the deputy's telling Brown he was going to the cabin to 'get
your reward' (715:21).

CHAPTER XIX

727:5 **run to earth** tracked down. A term from fox hunting, 'run to earth' means to chase the fox to its burrow.

727:6 **It was as though he had set out and made his plans to passively commit suicide** This may in fact be the explanation for Christmas's behavior at the end of Chapter XIV, where he feels peaceful after deciding to accept his blackness and to head for Mottstown where, in Chapter XV, he allows himself to be captured, knowing that his prospects for survival as a man believed to be the black murderer of a white woman are slim.

727:9 **Like to like** i.e., the 'easy ones' who say this recall the 'old tales' implying that Hightower was a homosexual with a taste for black men. They believe it is only logical that Christmas, whom they regard as black, would be drawn to Hightower's house. 'Like to like' is a traditional proverb meaning that similar people are inevitably attracted to one another. One of the saw mill workers applies it to Christmas and Brown in Chapter II (430:14).

727:9 **the easy, the immediate, ones** those quickest to state an opinion, jump to a conclusion

727:10 **the old tales about the minister** Chapter III, 450–51, tells how Hightower was taken out and beaten after having a Negro man live in his house as a cook.

727:13 **if someone had not seen him run across the back yard and into the kitchen** 'someone' = Percy Grimm. See 741:24.

727:16 **Gavin Stevens** a principal character in *Intruder in the Dust*, *Knight's Gambit*, *Requiem for a Nun*, *The Town*, and *The*

Mansion, as well as in the title episode of *Go Down, Moses* (1942). *Light in August* marks his first appearance in a Faulkner novel. His first story appearance was in "Smoke," published some six months before the novel.

727:16 **District Attorney** in Mississippi, an elected county official (usually a lawyer) elected to prosecute criminal cases for the state

727:17 **Phi Beta Kappa** a national college and university honorary organization whose members are elected in recognition of their academic distinction

727:18 **cob pipe** a corn cob pipe with a bowl fashioned from the end of a hollowed-out corncob

727:22 **Colonel Sartoris** the man who shot Joanna's grandfather and brother 'over a question of negro voting' (582:6) and a major figure in *The Unvanquished* and Yoknapatawpha County history

727:29 **southbound train . . . from the neighboring State University** Faulkner's Jefferson is largely based on his hometown of Oxford, Mississippi, where the University of Mississippi is located. Jefferson has no state university, however. Faulkner places it some forty miles away, though he never says precisely where.

727:36 **goat's beard** A goat's beard is narrow, scraggly, uneven, and sometimes fairly long.

727:37 **catalepsy** a condition wherein the victim occasionally lapses into a comatose or sleeplike state for anywhere from a few seconds to several hours

728:8 **flagman** "a man who signals with flags, lanterns, etc., on a train in a railroad yard. He has more responsibility and status than a brakeman."°

728:13 **I'll see that the boy is on the train in the morning** He will see that Christmas's body is shipped to Mottstown on the next day's morning train. To say 'the boy' is less unfeeling than "the body." Stevens is not using the word here in its derogatory racial sense.

728:18 **I think I know why it was, why he ran into High-**

tower's house for refuge at the last. I think it was his grandmother On 730:18 Stevens explains this theory: visiting Christmas in his jail cell, Mrs. Hines 'told him about Hightower, that Hightower would save him, was going to save him.'

728:26 **Decently hung by a Force, a principle; not burned or hacked or dragged dead by a Thing** executed by the force of an organized system of legal justice, the Law, not murdered and mutilated by a lynch mob

728:29 **the straw that started the hurricane** a confused improvisation on "the straw that broke the camel's back"

729:9 **too much reality . . . and too much that must be taken for granted . . . ; too much of the inexplicable** These clauses gloss the last four sentences of the previous paragraph, which explains what confronted Mrs. Hines after the birth of Lena's baby. They characterize her confusion over her long lost grandson's sudden appearance in Mottstown, his pending murder indictment, and the birth of Lena's baby, which she confuses with the infant grandson lost to her some thirty years before.

729:25 **Doctor Hightower** Many Southern preachers had a "D.D." degree, which allowed them to be addressed as Doctor, to the irritation of preachers with a genuine doctorate in theology, which had to be earned.

730:4 **what she was telling Christmas in the jail today** Thus we learn that Mrs. Hines did get to see and talk to Christmas before he tried to escape.

730:7 **mad as a hatter** Insanity was once an occupational hazard of hatters, poisoned by ingesting mercuric nitrates in the felt from which hats were made. The most famous Mad Hatter is in Lewis Carroll's *Alice in Wonderland*.

730:9 **kept it in trust** 'it' = 'devil's spawn,' Joe. To save or protect it until a predetermined day. Trust funds accrue interest, which is why the 'devil's spawn' had to grow and mature until its term came due.

730:10 **Or perhaps she was on her way to see him in the jail**

when she left the cabin 'him' = Christmas. Stevens suggests that either Mrs. Hines left the cabin to follow her husband to town to prevent him from inciting a mob, or that she went straight to the jail to see Christmas.

730:17 **planning a jailbreak** Stevens theorizes that Mrs. Hines suggested to Christmas that he should try to escape to Hightower's house, where he could hide.

730:18 **I believe she told him about Hightower, that Hightower would save him** This is the only explanation Faulkner gives for why Christmas went to Hightower's house. Although it is speculation, it seems likely, considering what *did* happen. Mrs. Hines visited Christmas in his jail cell.

730:24 **it had already been written and worded for her in the night when she bore his mother** 'it' = what she told the sheriff; more generally, her desire to protect her grandson

730:26 **she had learned it beyond all forgetting and then forgot the words** typical Gavin Stevens rhetoric: the compulsion to protect her offspring is so deeply ingrained that she acts on it blindly even though she lacks the language to articulate or even to be aware of what she is doing.

730:31 **a sanctuary which would be inviolable not only to officers and mobs, but to the very irrevocable past** a safe place of refuge from the intrusion of civil authorities and mobs, a sanctuary from physical danger and from the 'very irrevocable past'—the murder of Joanna Burden, Christmas's entire life.

731:6 **all those successions of thirty years** all those generations before him that, in Stevens's view, bred either into his white blood or his black blood the sense of doom and fatality to which he surrenders. Stevens is unaware of the ambiguous origins of Christmas's supposed black blood.

731:6 **that which had put the stain either on his white blood or his black blood** Stevens uses 'blood' as a metaphor for Christmas's conflicting white and black identities. To him 'white' means rational and good, while 'black' means irrational and bad. He is not the only character to suggest such a theory: the people of Mottstown, surprised at how easily Christmas was captured, thought 'it must have been the nigger blood in him.' (657:27). Asked about Stevens's theory about black and white blood battling for control of Christmas, Faulkner commented: "that [Christmas's black blood] is an assumption, a rationalization that Stevens made. That is, the people that destroyed him made rationalizations about what he was. They decided what he was. But Christmas himself didn't know and he evicted himself from mankind."°

731:9 **run with believing** run with the belief that he might escape

731:18 **chimaera** a fantastic illusion that can never be attained or realized—Mrs. Hines's religious faith

731:18 **a blind faith in something read in a printed Book** 'Book' = the Bible. See 730:2, about 'the voluntary slaves and the sworn bondsmen of prayer.' Mrs. Hines's enslavement is apparent in her advice that Christmas should seek help from the exminister Hightower.

731:35 **Percy Grimm** 'Percy' was at one time a dashing and romantic name. It is the diminutive of Percival, the hero of Arthurian romance, notable for his virtue and and his dedication to his faith. Percy's last name—Grimm—describes the fate he brings to Christmas and the humorless intensity of his devotion to what he regards as duty.

In a September 1945 letter to Malcolm Cowley, Faulkner recalled Grimm as "the Fascist galahad who saved the white race by murdering Christmas. I invented him in 1931. I didn't realise until after Hitler got into the newspapers that I had created a Nazi before he did." At the University of Virginia, he elaborated: "I wrote that book in 1932 before I'd ever heard of Hitler's Storm Troopers, what he was was a Nazi Storm Trooper . . . I wouldn't say that there are more of him in the South, but I would say that there are probably more of him in the White Citizens Councils than anywhere else in the South, but I think you find him everywhere, in all countries, in all people."°

731:36 **captain in the State national guard** The national
guard is a state militia, at least partially funded by the
national government. Although its chain of command resembles the U. S. Army's, it is a military organization that
operates under the command of the governor of the state. It
has little significant function except in times of national crisis, when it becomes part of the Army.

731:38 **the summer encampments** summer camp where national guard units meet for drill and training

732:1 **the European War** World War I, 1914–1918.

732:5 **in a fair way** likely, well on his way

732:6 **the terrible tragedy of having been born not alone too
late but not late enough** To Grimm, his tragedy is not only
that he was too young to serve in World War I (like Faulkner), but also that he was old enough to hear and know about
the war while it was occurring.

732:20 **The result was foregone; even Grimm doubtless
knew that** Byron Bunch has similar thoughts before his
fight with Lucas Burch: 'It does not last long. Byron knew
that it was not going to' (723).

732:26 **civilian-military act** "the National Defense Act of
1920, which reorganized the National Guard and made it
essentially a branch of the regular army"°

732:34 **corridor** See entry 481:4.

732:35 **freed now of ever again having to think or decide**
He surrenders completely to the concept of Authority embodied in the military. This more than anything else makes
him the crypto-Nazi Faulkner described (see entry 731:35).

732:37 **insignatory brass** his brass National Guard insignia

733:1 **all that would ever be required of him in payment for
this belief, this privilege, would be his own life** Giving
up his life seems to him a small price for being able to believe
in the superiority of America and the white race. The mock-
ing tone of this sentence suggests how dangerous Faulkner
thought a man like Grimm to be.

733:8 **his bars** two bars denoting his rank of captain

733:11   **American Legion**   an association for retired members of any one of the American military services

733:11   **that was his parents' fault and not his**   He blames his parents for his having been born too late to serve in World War I.

733:14   **Post**   the local American Legion unit

733:17   **it is the right of no civilian to sentence a man to death**   He means that no mob should be allowed to lynch Joe. But what he says suggests that he rejects the legitimacy of civil courts of justice, that the only court he believes in is a military court.

733:32   **vide**   Faulkner employs this word loosely. 'Vide' literally means "see" or "refer to," and is used to direct a reader's attention from one item in a text to another. Here it means "because of."

734:10   **a shot on his own account**   The post commander withheld the flippant remark he had been about to make (733:37), but that doesn't stop Grimm from voicing his own parting insult.

735:34   **That evening after supper the sheriff went back downtown**   to make sure Grimm's platoon was not stirring up trouble

735:39   **cotton office**   main office for the cotton gin and/or warehouse to which farmers bring freshly picked cotton to be weighed, ginned, and shipped to market.

736:1   **orderly room**   working headquarters of a military unit

736:1   **P.C.**   post of command—command post

736:2   **Come here, boy**   The sheriff addresses Grimm in this way to let him know that he does not take him seriously and that he feels he is serving no legitimate purpose.

736:7   **I reckon I'll have to make you a special deputy**   Kennedy does this to avoid conflict with Grimm, but it is a big mistake.

736:14   **That's what we both said**   The sheriff, agent of constitutional justice, has just tried to tell Grimm, agent of vigilante justice, not to draw his pistol unless ordered to do so. By seeming to agree with Kennedy, Grimm effectively prevents him from asserting his authority. When Grimm says, 'Dont you worry. I'll be there,' he seems to be stating his support for the sheriff but in fact maintains his independence.

736:20 **trump card** winning card

736:30 **night marshal** the town's official night watchman

736:35 **summer colors** bright colors

736:38 **hidden and unsleeping and omnipotent eye watching the doings of men** perhaps an image borrowed from the Freemasons, who regard the "all-seeing eye" as an "important symbol of the Supreme Being"°

737:8 **the suttee of volition's surrender, they were almost at the pitch where they might die for him** suttee = the act of a Hindu woman who allows herself to be cremated with her husband's body as proof of her devotion. The 'suttee of volition's surrender' refers to the men who, influenced by the town's respect for Grimm and 'his vision and patriotism and pride in the town,' are willing to sacrifice their lives to prove their devotion to him and to what they believe he stands for.

737:11 **reflected light** whose source is the radiance of Grimm

737:12 **khaki** the color of military uniforms

737:20 **Ware M.P.'s** Beware, Military Police. Playing soldier, Grimm's men refer to the town marshall in military fashion.

737:23 **the immemorial sound** a raspberry, the sound of flatulence

737:26 **they now wore uniforms. It was their faces** Their faces are their uniforms. They all wear the same stern and devoted expression as their leader.

737:37 **Special officer sent by the governor** He is not such an officer. That the crowd doesn't even recognize Grimm as a local resident says something about his usual insignificance. It also says something about the crowd's willingness to believe any rumor that adds to the excitement. See the similar crowd descriptions in Chapter XIII, 612 and 613–14.

738:4 **that damned Buford** the sheriff's deputy

738:7 **Stevens had done told me he would plead guilty and take a life sentence** In Mississippi, a man accused of first-degree murder can by pleading guilty escape the death penalty and be sentenced instead to life in prison. Apparently, by attempting to escape, Joe changed his mind. Perhaps Mrs. Hines's promise that Hightower could save him (if that is what she told him), together with his own dread of losing his freedom and spending the rest of his life in prison, convinced him to try to escape.

738:12 **Fair Day** the opening day (perhaps the only day) of the county fair, when everyone would be in town to attend

738:24 **overtaking and passing them, since he had an objective and they did not; they were just running** He has a reason to run fast, his desire to capture the escaped Christmas, while the townspeople are merely running from excitement.

738:28 **faces blanched and gaped, with round toothed orifices** an impressionist description of the excited crowd, their faces drained of blood ('blanched') and openmouthed, revealing their upper and bottom teeth ('round toothed orifices')

738:34 **the inevitable hulking youth in the uniform of the Western Union, leading his bicycle** Western Union delivery boys typically used bicycles. The 'youth' is 'inevitable' because he provides the bicycle that is a necessary part of Grimm's chase. Had the boy not been there, Grimm might not have caught Christmas. A few pages later Grimm moves 'with that lean, swift, blind obedience to whatever Player moved him on the Board' (741:7). The boy *had* to be there, and the 'Player' insured he was.

739:1 **served by certitude, the blind and untroubled faith in the rightness and infallibility of his actions** like McEachern, Hines, and Lena Grove, who at crucial moments in their lives have been driven by forces beyond their rational understanding. Grimm's instinct takes over. He does not *think* about what he is doing: he simply acts.

739:20 **deep ditch which was a town landmark** Calvin Brown believes the original of "this ditch was in Oxford, exactly as it is described . . . and Joe Christmas could have gotten into it, by the route indicated, within less than two hundred yards from the courthouse. . . . This gully ran along the back edge of the boys' playground of the old Oxford High School. It was indeed a town landmark, and was known to generations of schoolboys simply as The Ditch. It was off limits but was regularly used for crap games and serious fights."°

739:36 **the implacable undeviation of Juggernaut or Fate** 'juggernaut' = an irresistible, undeviating force. The term comes from a onetime Hindu practice in which a "large statue of Jagganatha, an incarnation of Vishnu, was drawn through the streets on an enormous cart whose wheels crushed the faithful seeking immolation."° Much the same language describes Simon McEachern's pursuit of his stepson on the night of the school house dance: see entry 548:17.

740:15 **the man who even now was not free** Even now, despite his decision to be black at the end of Chapter XIV, his capture in Chapter XV, and this attempt to escape, Christmas is still not free, is still running as he has been doing all of his life, is still following the 'street which ran for thirty years' (649:40).

740:19 **There was nothing vengeful about him either, no fury, no outrage. Christmas saw that himself** Grimm is caught up in the game of the chase. But Christmas may be tricked by Grimm's expression into miscalculating how dangerous his opponent is, which may be one reason why instead of continuing to run for his life he seeks refuge in Hightower's house.

740:29 **Christmas now carried a heavy nickelplated pistol** acquired in the Negro cabin; see 731:14. In Chapter XIV, Sheriff Kennedy assumes that *all* Negro cabins have guns (642:16).

740:35 **until one of us gets a shot** Clearly, Grimm doesn't mean to wait for the Sheriff to order him to use his gun. Christmas has a gun now, and Grimm has drawn his own

pistol and is ready to use it. If Grimm shoots an armed escaped black man accused of murdering a white women, he
can claim self-defense.

741:4 **blunt, cold rake of the automatic** Grimm is apparently pointing the gun down towards the ditch, panning it
back and forth as he looks for a shot.

741:5 **that serene, unearthly luminousness of angels in
church windows** Throughout this scene Grimm seems
overwhelmed with intense, almost religious ardor. We have
already learned that the civilian-military act 'saved him' (732:
26) by letting him dedicate his life to the National Guard,
and to the cause of American patriotism and white supremacy. On 742:15 he shouts with a 'voice clear and outraged
like that of a young priest.' Here his 'serene' and blissful exaltation is like that of a martyr dying for his faith—a look
similar to McEachern's when his foster-son brains him with
the chair (549) and on Christmas's face as he dies (742).

741:7 **whatever Player moved him on the Board** The motif of a Player moving pieces on a chess board continues
throughout this passage. See 741:17, 741:31, 742:19, 742:
28, for instance. The 'Player' is not to be seen so much as
God as simply an external force: Fate, the natural and envi-
ronmental forces that govern many characters in this novel.
The metaphor suggests that Grimm and Christmas have no
real control over their actions: they are merely doing what
circumstances and years of living have conditioned them to
do. But they still *believe*, especially Grimm, that they are making their own decisions. See entry 722:27.

741:11 **the cabin sat some two feet above the earth** It sits on
brick- or stone-and-mortar pillars, so that Christmas can
peer beneath it and watch Grimm's legs on the other side.

741:37 **It was upon them, of them: its shameless savageness**
'It' = 'the savage summer sunlight' of the previous sentence.
In a larger sense, 'It' is the moment of horror and murder,
of retributive communal violence for which Grimm has prepared himself, and which Christmas's behavior throughout

the book has made almost inevitable. The 'ritual' the men now witness overcomes them. They act not according to individual will but to the role that ritual dictates for them.

742:11 **he too . . . was terrible** 'too' = like Joe, who 'resembled a vengeful and furious God'; 'terrible' = awe-inspiring. This is the moment Byron Bunch has compelled Hightower towards. Struck down by Christmas, then telling the lie and entering into life, he undergoes suffering that effects a transfiguration. To see him at this moment is to see something 'terrible,' something that experiences as well as inspires terror.

742:13 **He was with me the night of the murder** Hightower's lie. See entry 687:39. The lie is one that once might have succeeded, but now it merely serves to reveal that Grimm means to carry out a punishment against Christmas that he regards as appropriate for a black man who slept with and killed a white woman and who, he thinks, has had sex with this preacher as well.

742:16 **Has every preacher and old maid in Jefferson taken their pants down to the yellowbellied son of a bitch?** Grimm's incredulous comment on what he supposes to have been Christmas's sexual relationship with Hightower as well as Joanna Burden

742:25 **automatic's magazine** small compartment containing the pistol's supply of bullets

742:28 **But the Player was not done yet** By its references to the Player's moving pawns on a Board, this section seems to endorse the notion that human beings have no control over their actions, that they are pawns of a process rather than independent agents. For Joe Christmas, at least, Chapter XIX provides the final evidence that his actions are predetermined, that he has no free will, is trapped on the 'street which ran for thirty years' (649:40) and must travel it until it runs out. Chapter XXI, however, suggests that not everyone travels such a narrow, undeviating path.

742:32 **when they saw what Grimm was doing** i.e., cutting

off Christmas's genitals. This act is not simply Grimm's sadistic idea nor Faulkner's sensationalistic plot device. The lynchings of black men accused of offenses against white women often did end with the victims' castration. Technically, Grimm's castration and murder of Christmas is not a lynching—an act of vigilante 'justice' carried out by community members on behalf of the community. The men following Grimm did not intend for him to do what he did. The mutilation is his act alone. But the community would not necessarily have disapproved.

742:38 **with something, a shadow, about his mouth** The nature of the shadow is unclear. Christmas may be moving his mouth, trying to speak. Or the shadow may be his blood. See entry 487:14.

742:39 **looked up at them with peaceful and unbearable eyes** Why in this moment of pain and approaching death are Joe's eyes peaceful? Perhaps his eyes are 'unbearable' because instead of pain they reflect bliss over the impending escape from the torment of his life or masochistic pleasure at the pain he is experiencing. Moreover, the men in the room probably cannot bear to look into the eyes of the man whose mutilation and murder they have been accessories to.

743:1 **Then his face, body, all, seemed to collapse, to fall in upon itself** i.e., he dies and his body begins bleeding profusely, as if emptying itself of everything.

Christmas's murder resembles in some details the September 1908 lynching of Nelse Patton in Faulkner's hometown of Oxford, Mississippi. According to two different accounts, Patton, a Negro trustee in the county jail, was taking a message to a white woman named Mattie McMillan, whose husband was imprisoned in the jail. When he walked into her house without knocking, she asked him to leave. Angry words ensued, and Patton cut her throat with a razor, nearly decapitating her. He was captured shortly afterwards and taken to jail. Later that evening a lynch mob stormed the jail, spent three to four hours hacking its way into Patton's cell, and

shot him to death. He was castrated and his face disfigured.
His body was taken outside, dragged around the town square
by a car, and left hanging by rope from a tree outside the
jail. Faulkner, a boy of almost eleven at the time, was not
present, but he learned about it from the town paper and his
friends, especially John Cullen, who assisted in Patton's capture, and whose father was a local deputy sheriff. Faulkner
makes use of his memories of this episode here. Yet the dif-
ferences between Patton and Christmas are more numerous
than the similarities—Christmas is not lynched (in the com-
monly understood sense of the word): his murder is committed by one man, Percy Grimm, rather than by a mob.°

743:3   **pent black blood**   'pent' = confined, previously held
in. The blood's 'black' color may simply convey the scene's
horror and Christmas's suffering. Doreen Fowler suggests an
additional reading: "All his life Joe Christmas has been running in terror from a 'black pit' [483], a 'black abyss' [643], a
'black tide' [650] .... running from himself, from those mild
qualities in his own nature that ally him with women and
blacks. Thus, he could never outrun the black tide because,
as he always suspected, it ran in his veins, and, after a lifetime of suppression and denial, as Joe dies, it finally 'rush[es]
out of his pale body' in a 'black blast' of 'pent black blood'
expelled like a long 'released breath' [743]."°

743:4   **like the rush of sparks from a rising rocket. Upon that
black blast**   He bleeds so suddenly and profusely that the
rush of blood is like the 'sparks from a rising rocket.' The
emotional intensity of this passage also accounts for the metaphor, which describes the effect of his death on those who
witness it, and the translation of this event into the town's
communal memory.

743:5   **the man seemed to rise soaring into their memories
forever and ever**   Christmas is resurrected through the
immortality he achieves in the memory of the men in the
room and of the town. This is the culmination of the Christ
parallelism in the novel. Christmas was born the son of a

young woman and an uncertain father, a mysterious Mexican. He received his name on Christmas night, the anniversary of Christ's birth, in a drunken ritual which parodies the biblical genealogy at the beginning of the book of Matthew. His initials are 'J.C.,' those of Christ, which is the first syllable of his last name. He resists temptation, as when in chapter XII the lure of domestic bliss and financial security tempt him to remain with Joanna Burden. Joe Brown, his disciple (431:20), betrays him in hopes of receiving the reward money. The Chapter XIV episode wherein he terrorizes the black church parallels the biblical account (Mark 11:15–19) of Christ driving the moneychangers from the temple. According to some chronologies, he is thirty-three years old when he dies, the age of Christ at the crucifixion. Finally, certain details of Christmas's death parallel literally and symbolically the death of Christ, and for both men death is followed by a resurrection that has a lasting impact on the people who learn about it.

743:7   **They are not to lose it**   'it' = the 'black blast' of Christmas's blood that 'rises soaring into their memories forever and ever'

CHAPTER XX

744:1 **Now the final copper light of afternoon fades . . .**
Chapter XX begins on the Monday evening after Christmas's
murder in Hightower's kitchen. Asked about the placement
of this chapter, Faulkner explained: "It seemed to me that
was the most effective place to put that, to underline the
tragedy of Christmas's story by the tragedy of his anti-
thesis. . . . Hightower was a man who wanted to be better
than he was afraid he would. He had failed his wife. Here
was another chance he had, and he failed his Christian oath
as a man of God, and he escaped into his past where some
member of his family was brave enough to match the moment. But it was put at that point in the book, I think, because I thought that was the most effective place for it."°

744:1 **the final copper light of afternoon** one form of 'light
in August'

744:2 **the street . . . prepared and empty** ready for the start
of Hightower's reverie: empty in the late afternoon sun light

744:3 **framed by the study window** François Pitavy observes
that 'Hightower is above all the man at the window, through
which he communicates with the past and is held prisoner by
his ghosts; moreover, his wife, whom he had refused to love
by remaining locked in his dead past, throws herself through
the window of a Memphis hotel. Lena escapes through a
window to go in search of Lucas Burch, whose child she
bears, and Burch himself flees through a window, leaving
her with the child. Lastly, Joe leaves by the window when he
goes to meet Bobbie, the prostitute. Later he climbs through
the kitchen window of Joanna, who prostitutes herself for

him.' According to the concordance, there are 115 references to windows in this novel.° Often in Faulkner's work windows serve as a means of escape from an oppressive life as well as a barrier, a symbol of isolation dividing the observer from the world. Hightower's window serves both these functions: as an escape, through which he can dream his reverie of the past, and as a sign of his separation from human society and the world.

744:7 **dying yellow fall of trumpets** dying fall = a sound fading away in the distance. It is yellow because the text says the copper light seemed to Hightower 'almost audible.' Michel Gresset locates the source of Faulkner's use of this phrase in the opening lines of Shakespeare's *The Tempest* and in Eliot's "Lovesong of J. Alfred Prufrock." Gresset associates the phrase with "wistfulness, in the sense of 'longing with little hope,' which . . . is common to all dying falls in modern literature, and most certainly, in Faulkner's case, to the ending of all of his early novels except two: *Mosquitoes* and *As I Lay Dying*."°

744:13 **But he had never told anyone that. Not even her** Though his wife knew the story of his grandfather's death in the chicken raid, knew too that he daydreams by the window about that raid, he had never told her or anyone of the intensity of his vision.

744:14 **when they were still the night's lovers** when they were lovers who felt passion for one another. This passage suggests that Hightower's obsession with his hallucination replaced or even destroyed his passion for his wife.

744:15 **shame and division had not come** the shame she felt when their marriage began to fail, when Hightower began to withdraw, thus causing the 'division' between them. His performance as a minister in Jefferson later shames her, worsening the 'division.'

744:15 **she knew and had not forgot with division and regret and then despair** 'She knew' the kind of dreamy, romantic man he was, and the nature of the reverie that obsessed him. 'Division' came when she realized how wrapped up in his reverie he was; she felt 'regret' for having failed to recognize his character, for having married him at all; she felt 'despair' not only for these past mistakes, but for her inability to find an escape from the life that had entrapped her.

744:18 **Not even to her, to woman. *The* woman. . . . the recipient and receptacle of the seed of his body but of his spirit too** '*The* woman' = his wife. He once believed the seminary, which trains ministers to preach God's word, to be the receptacle of the 'seed' (the root of 'seminary' is the Latin *semen*, meaning seed) of God's body and spirit in the world. He believes his wife was to have been that receptacle: God created her to receive his seed and spirit. But Hightower felt that he could not tell his wife the truth about his vision of his grandfather and the cavalry charge, the sound of which is 'almost audible' in the Mississippi sunset.

744:24 **his father** Hightower's father, not named. His role in the Civil War as a military chaplain, along with his own father's brash, pugnacious personality, may have mingled to influence Faulkner's depiction of a minor character some thirty years after *Light in August*. In *The Reivers* (1962), Faulkner mentions Hiram Hightower, a Baptist minister who "on Sunday from 1861 to 1865 had been one of Forrest's company chaplains and on the other six days one of his hardest and most outrageous troopers" (75), a man who tames a wild river house and saloon "with a Bible and his bare hands."

744:31 **an age and land where to own slaves was less expensive than to not own them** one reason Southerners gave for resisting slavery's abolition

744:32 **he would neither eat food grown and cooked by, nor sleep in a bed prepared by, a negro slave** an attitude similar to that of Joanna Burden's grandfather, Calvin, who denies the Catholic church because some of its members are slave holders. See 576–78.

745:1 **God will provide** a common religious saying, possibly derived from Psalms 68:10, "in thy goodness, O God, thou didst provide for the needy," or from 2 Corinthians 9:8.

745:5 **He was a minister** 'He' = Hightower's father

745:6 **before his father** Hightower's grandfather, his father's father

745:7 **a member in good standing** His name appears on the church rolls, but he is apparently not active in church affairs.

745:10 **riding sixteen miles each Sunday to preach in a small Presbyterian chapel in the hills** exhibiting the same devotion as two other characters: Byron Bunch who every Saturday evening rode thirty miles to lead the choir in a country church; and Doc Hines, who went 'about the county, usually on foot' preaching in black churches about the superiority of the white race.

745:19 **somber frock coat** a black, knee-length dress coat worn by many chaplains in place of a uniform°

745:21 **he returned home in '65** when the Civil War ended

745:31 **The copper light has completely gone now; the world hangs in a green suspension in color and texture like light through colored glass** This realistic description of the Mississippi sky after sunset vividly conveys the strained, hallucinatory state of Hightower's mind. A similar description occurs at 749:10. Here it may be another evocation of the light in the novel's title.

746:14 **a kind of hushed and triumphant terror which left him a little sick** 'hushed' in awe ('terror') of the death that the blue patch signifies, 'triumphant' that the death came at the hands of a Confederate soldier (though he later apparently learns that his father never fired a weapon during the war). He feels 'terror' because this image of the past enthralls and repels him, leaving 'him a little sick' with fear and excitement.

746:18 **and with something else** with another feeling that at first he cannot define but which he finally recognizes 'was not even triumph: it was pride' (747:3).

746:21 **the Pit itself** Hell

746:25 **between whom and himself there was so much of distance in time** The distance of fifty years in age between Hightower and his father is one measure of their dissimilarity. But they are separated by more 'distance' than 'years

could measure.' On 749 we learn that Hightower's father returned from the war looking 'forward,' ready to make a life
out of the experience and skills he gained in the war. But his
son never looks forward, never has any experience from
which to acquire practical skills, is enthralled by the story of
his heroic grandfather so that, in effect, he lives in the past.

746:29 **he would not tell what it was** 'it' = the cause of his
sickness, his excitement

746:30 **who was his mother too** Since his mother is by now
a bedridden invalid soon to die, the only mothering he receives is from the black woman Cinthy.

746:36 **wondering with still more horror yet at the depth
and strength of his desire and dread to know** As much as
the blue patch on his father's uniform horrifies him, he is
even more horrified at his own curiosity to know exactly
what it means.

747:2 **when he listened now it was without terror. It was not
even triumph: it was pride** because now Cinthy is telling
him not about his father but his *grand*father, who *did* kill
Yankees

747:4 **The grandfather was the single thorn in his son's
side** The narrative shifts focus here from Hightower as a
boy to the relationship of his father and grandfather.

747:11 **humor which lacked less of purport than wit** humor more intent on evoking laughter than in making a
point; forced and crude: e.g., his toasts with whiskey to his
abstemious son (747:17) or his greeting comment to his son's
new wife (747:39)

747:26 **his 'boy'** his personal servant

747:30 **by main strength** by sheer determination

747:32 **surrey** a four-wheeled carriage with front and back
seats. This one has a fringe around its top, for at 748:3 it is
referred to as a 'tasselled surrey,' used more for courting
than for family transportation.

747:32 **matched team** pair of horses matched in size and
color°

748:4 **demijohn** large whiskey jug

748:6   **She was not offered, and so not refused**   Because the old man did not offer his abolitionist son the use of his cook, the son did not have to refuse her. The father probably does not make the offer because he knows it will be refused.

748:15   **he invaded a protracted al fresco church revival**   a church revival, held out of doors, lasting at least several days. Carl Ficken notes that 'The grandfather interrupted country church services in much the same fashion as Joe Christmas and his grandfather [Doc Hines], although the elder Hightower's aim was to turn revivals into horse races.'°

748:24   **But that was not the reason . . . that there was delicacy of behavior and thought in the old man**   The son understands that his father would be insulted by the 'aspersion' that he had 'delicacy of behavior and thought.' The old man would have taken such a suggestion as an insult to his manliness. The son knew that his father did not fear being corrupted, and would have argued with anyone who made the suggestion, for he knew that his father was a considerate man who moved out of the house in deference to his son's abolitionist sympathies.

748:30   **the Republicans did have a name for it**   for opposition to slavery—abolitionism. The Republicans were the dominant political party of the North and of anti-slavery Southerners.

748:30   **he completely changed the name of his convictions**   He refused to call himself an abolitionist, which meant a Republican enemy of the South and of slavery. He remained opposed to slavery but showed his Southern loyalty by serving as a chaplain and doctor in the Confederate army.

748:34   **servant of Chance and the bottle**   gambler and drinker

748:37   **'deodorised' . . . of sanctity somewhat**   cleansed of sanctity; a verb the old man would use in his unreformed and ironic sense. War made a realist of the son, relieving him of his piety though not his desire to serve humankind.

749:9   **But sanctity is not the word for him**   Hightower is remembering that his grandfather had previously referred to his son as a 'sanctimonious cuss' (747:39)—his eyes 'kind' as he said it. The passage soon following explains ('It was some throwback to the austere and not dim times not so long passed . . .') that the son is governed not by sanctity but by the austerity his forebears found necessary for survival on the frontier.

749:9 **the son's son** Hightower—identified in this way to show his place as the inheritor of the traditions and experience just described; he is not only a minister but the son of a minister.

749:10 **the world hangs in that green suspension beyond the faded trumpets** With Hightower lost in his reverie, reality and the world simply cease to exist, or at least come to a stop 'beyond the faded trumpets' that announce his vision. See entry 745:31.

749:13 **It was some throwback** 'It' = the word or quality that 'sanctity' is not the right word for

749:13 **to the austere and not dim times not so long passed** when the land was first being settled by whites, when unremitting hard work and self-denial were necessary

749:19 **That was where his disapproval of slavery lay, and of his lusty and sacrilegious father** Hightower's father lived under the influence of a tradition that emphasized careful and austere maintenance of one's resources. The ownership of slaves required time and energy he did not feel he had to give. Moreover, slavery allowed the owner to require others to do work that he ought to do himself, to enjoy 'physical ease' (749:18) at the expense of others. Slaves were thus an unnecessary luxury, a squandering of resources, as was his father's wanton lifestyle.

749:37 **with their eyes stubbornly reverted toward what they refused to believe was dead** They continued to believe in the Old South, whose defeat they would not concede, locking themselves (like others in this novel) into the past and an unchanging paralysis, much like Hightower himself.

750:4 **grew to manhood among phantoms, and side by side with a ghost** The phantoms, as the next sentence says, were his father, his mother, and the old black woman Cinthy, who looked after him as a child. The ghost was his grandfather. The distinction between 'phantom' and 'ghost' is explained at 752:22. See entry 752:13.

750:11 **between puritan and cavalier** the conflicting forces of the father's heritage—the New England tradition of his Puritan-derived religion and the Southern Cavalier tradition. 'Cavalier' was often used by nineteenth- and early twentieth-century Southerners to denote what they regarded (without much accuracy) as their genealogical heritage—that of the English and Scot nobles who fled to the Virginia colony after the execution of Charles I by the Puritan government of Oliver Cromwell in 1649. In his 1888 speech "The New South," Henry Grady used this phrase to characterize conflicting Northern and Southern traditions: "from the union of these colonists, Puritans and Cavaliers, from the straightening of their purposes and the crossing of their blood, slow perfecting through a century, came he who stands as the first typical American, the first who comprehended within himself all the strength and gentleness, all the majesty and grace of this republic—Abraham Lincoln. He was the sum of Puritan and Cavalier."°

750:14 **layingon of hands** a supposed method of healing wherein the preacher places his hand on a sick person, thereby transmitting the healing powers of the Holy Spirit. Jesus practiced this method of healing in the New Testament, and many Christian ministers after him also claimed to use it. The text suggests that Hightower's father became a doctor because he interpreted this ritual literally, as a means of ministering to the body as well as the soul.° Alternative reading: the phrase refers to a protestant church ritual in which deacons "lay hands on" a new deacon as a form of initiation.

750:26 **the two eyes which daily seemed to grow bigger and**

bigger a symptom of emaciation, often seen among the dying

750:28 **with one last terrible glare of frustration and suffering and foreknowledge** Hightower imagined that his mother's eyes signified her growing awareness of what death would be: she knew what it would be because her life as an invalid had become a living death; she had 'foreknowledge' of the hereafter.

750:29 **when that finally happened, he would hear it: it would be a sound like a cry** 'that' = the moment when her eyes finally 'embrace all seeing, all life, with one last terrible glare of frustration and suffering and foreknowledge,' the moment of her death

750:31 **he could feel them through all walls** 'them' = her eyes

750:31 **They were the house: he dwelled within them** He felt as if he were living inside her eyes—as if he saw through them. Her vision of life and the world shaped his.

750:37 **so quickly does the body's wellbeing alter and change the spirit. He was more than a stranger: he was an enemy** That is, physical health directly affects one's spirit. The vitality of Hightower's father struck the dying wife and sickly son as foreign and dangerous.

751:3 **he too as helpless and frustrated as they** He could understand them no better than they could understand him, nor could he very well tolerate their physical weakness, for which he felt 'unconscious contempt.'

751:7 **returned in '66 still a slave** The Emancipation Proclamation of 1863 in principle freed the slaves in states at war with the Union, and when the war ended in 1865 slavery was no more. Cinthy, who doesn't think much of freedom (see 752:8), returns 'still a slave' voluntarily, out of loyalty to her dead master and her husband, and also because she knows no other life.

751:9 **the mask of a black tragedy between scenes** She assumes the face and demeanor, the 'mask,' of a tragedy.

'Mask' refers to the masks that actors in classical Greek drama wore on stage to make clear to the audience emotions they were portraying. The tragedy is a 'black' one because Cinthy herself is black, also because its outcome is black: bleak and pessimistic. The mask of tragedy is always marked by grief and suffering. It may be passionless and relaxed between scenes, but it remains permanently tragic and composed, 'irascible and calm.' Cinthy plays out this tragic role as a way of confronting her grief.

751:22 **Van Dorn's cavalry** See entry 443:6.

751:33 **Mistis coffee pot and de gole waiter** The coffee pot is likely a silver tea service—a heavy, probably sterling coffee server with cream pitcher and sugar bowl. The gold waiter is probably gold-plated. Even in the 1860s the cost of a karat gold serving tray would have been too high for most wealthy families.

752:5 **de box** the box where wood for the cook stove is stored

752:9 **Marse Gail** Thus we learn that Hightower bears his grandfather's name. Many slaves addressed their owner as 'Marse' followed by his first name. The 'r' in Marse is not pronounced: Mahss (rhymes with first syllable of hacienda).

752:10 **Pawmp** Pomp, diminutive of Pompey, a common name among Southern slaves. Slaves were customarily named by their masters, who frequently gave them classical names: Caesar, Thucydides, Missy Lena (for Messalina), etc.

752:13 **he was little better than a phantom too** As we learn at 752:22, 'ghosts' are creatures of the past and of imagination, 'never seen in the flesh' and thus not real. A phantom, on the other hand, is a flesh-and-blood creature of the present day who seems *not* to be real. Though in Chapter III Hightower waited for the 'phantoms' of his reverie at nightfall, as if phantoms and ghosts were indistinguishable, here Faulkner distinguishes between a phantom as the *memory* of someone Hightower had actually known (father, mother, ex-slave, even his eight-year old self) and the ghost of his grandfather, whom he knows only through impressions received from the 'phantoms' and his imagination.

752:14 **talked about the ghost** about the grandfather

752:19 **on the contrary** i.e., violently, not peacefully, in contrast to the boy's 'peaceful shuddering'

752:21 **No horror here** The fact that his grandfather and the men he presumably killed, along with Pomp and the man he tried to kill, 'are just ghosts, never seen in the flesh, heroic, simple, warm,' and not alive, prevents the boy from being terrified.

752:25 **So it's no wonder . . . that I skipped a generation** Hightower means that, because of the old black woman's talking, he is not surprised that he feels tied to his grandfather, whom he thinks of as 'heroic, simple, warm,' rather than to his father, whom he 'feared' and who was 'more than a stranger: he was an enemy' (750).

752:27 **my only salvation must be to return to the place to die where my life had already ceased before it began** Hightower's words must be understood first on the literal level, and then with the premise that their logic is muddled. He knows that he is so obsessed with his grandfather's death twenty years before his birth that life in the present has no meaning for him. He ceased to live, in effect, when his grandfather died, i.e., before he was born. The only remedy that will give his life meaning, allow him to *live*, is to return to the scene of that death, thus bringing the past into the present. He has never actually been to Jefferson, but because he has imagined it so often, and because he so passionately identifies with his dead grandfather, he can think of his arrival there as a 'return.'

752:31 **the high and sanctified men who were the destiny of the church** They controlled church affairs and thus its future. Perhaps also it was the 'destiny of the church' to produce men such as these, 'high and sanctified.'

752:35 **shot from the saddle of a galloping horse in a Jefferson street** The details of this incident are told inconsis-

tently. On 443:15 'his grandfather was shot from the galloping horse' but on 757 he was 'killed in somebody else's hen
house wid a han'full of feathers. Stealin chickens.' Hightower seems to prefer the shot-in-the-hen house version: 'I
like to think so. It's fine so. Any soldier can be killed by the
enemy in the heat of battle . . . But not with a shotgun, a
fowling piece, in a hen house' (758:9).

752:36 **one night twenty years before it was ever born** This
chapter refers consistently to the twenty years between the
death of the grandfather and Hightower's birth, but on 443:
28 the figure is given as 'about thirty years,' the product of
the town's careless memory.

752:38 **He went there, chose that as his vocation, with that
as his purpose** 'that' = the story 'too fine not to be believed' and which Hightower feels summoned to tell. By devoting himself to that story rather than to the orthodox duty
of a minister—the preaching of God's word—he substitutes
the Calvary of redemption for the calvary of his private
obsession.

752:40 **He had believed in the church too** Clearly he did
understand that his 'vocation' and 'purpose' were not the
normal ones of a Christian minister. Perhaps he even intended to fulfill these goals at the same time he intended to
pursue his private ones.

752:40 **ramified and evoked** confirmed and suggested

753:4 **the call** God's summons to preach

753:5 **his future, his life, intact on all sides complete and
inviolable like a classic and serene vase** He felt that the
privilege of serving God and the church would make his life
complete, that there was no better goal. Even so, he continues to confuse his private vocation with that of the Church.
Once more the novel employs the image of an urn to connote an intact and inviolable ideal. See entry 538:18.

753:7 **where the spirit could be born anew** Since his 'life
had already ceased before it began' (752:28) his spirit would
have to be born anew before it could die 'peacefully.'

753:7 **sheltered from the harsh gale of living** a phrase reminiscent of the "vale of tears" of Shelley's "Hymn to Intellectual Beauty," or in Keats's famous letter,° both of which Hightower is likely to have read. Presumably Faulkner intends to draw an ironic link between Gail Hightower's first name and the 'harsh gale of living' from which he seeks shelter in the seminary, and in the back street house to which he retreated after his wife's death and his dismissal from the pulpit.

753:8 **the far sound of the circumvented wind** Literally, the 'wind' Hightower would like to avoid or 'circumvent' is the wind of life, the 'harsh gale of living' whose sound he would barely be able to hear. By retreating to the seminary, then to the pulpit, Hightower has circumvented life and time, vaguely suggested here in the wind's 'far sound.'

753:9 **with scarce even a handful of rotting dust to be disposed of** Genesis 3:19: "Dust thou art, and unto dust shalt thou return"; T. S. Eliot, *The Waste Land*: "I will show you fear in a handful of dust." Both Eliot and Genesis use the image of dust to signify human mortality.°

753:11 **the hampered and garmentworried spirit could learn anew serenity to contemplate without horror or alarm its own nakedness** The clothing/no clothing metaphor follows from 753:2: 'if ever truth could walk naked and without shame or fear, it would be in the seminary.' Clothing symbolizes the false values and beliefs of the world with which the spirit can shroud itself, while in the seminary the spirit ought to be able to shed this false clothing and contemplate truth and 'without horror or alarm its own nakedness.' By 'learn anew' Faulkner apparently means to suggest that when Hightower died his 'first death' with his grandfather, he forgot how to contemplate truth. Now in the seminary, and in the position he hopes to be called to in Jefferson, he can 'learn anew' this ability.

753:14 **'But there are more things in heaven and earth too than truth' he thinks, paraphrases** Shakespeare, *Hamlet*: "There are more things in heaven and earth, Horatio, /

Than are dreamt of in your philosophy" (I.v.166–67). Four lines later, Hightower modifies this notion by 'thinking how ingenuity was apparently given man in order that he may supply himself in crises with shapes and sounds with which to guard himself from truth.' It was 'truth,' at 753:3, which Hightower originally thought he would find at the seminary. Hightower has just begun an extended comparison of the qualities of the seminary and of woman, starting with the hypothesis 'that if ever truth could walk naked and without shame or fear, it would be in the seminary' (753:2). As soon as he concludes that the seminary is a shelter for the spirit, he moves towards a further, contrastive consideration, beginning with 'But.' He has just concluded that in the seminary truth could walk naked. 'Nakedness,' the last word in the preceding paragraph, arouses a new, as yet unspoken association with woman, the 'She' that opens the following paragraph.

753:15 **not quizzical, not humorous; not unquizzical and not humorless too** Hightower's thinking is as yet tentative. He has no idea where it may lead him.

753:17 **his head in its white bandage looming bigger and more ghostly than ever** When Christmas ran into Hightower's house, he struck the old man with his manacled hands, injuring him; hence the 'white' and 'ghostly' bandage he wears over the wound.

753:18 **more things indeed** 'things' other than truth, 'things' that might conflict with or negate truth. Obviously he has one of these 'things' already in mind, 'ingenuity,' which provides 'shapes and sounds with which to guard himself from truth.'

753:23 **He had not needed to live in the seminary a year before he had learned better than that** He had not lived a year in the place where he believed that truth walked naked before he learned better than to reveal himself fully to others; before he learned the necessity of deception.

753:25 **And more, worse: that with the learning of it, in-**

stead of losing something he had gained, had escaped from something. And that that gain had colored the very face and shape of love 'it' = the possibility of deception. The second sentence must be read with an invisible comma after 'something.' In addition to having learned that it was better not to have told the elders what he had been planning to say, he learned ('gained') something far worse: the knowledge that truth could be circumvented, a cynical understanding of the necessity of deception, and a means of denying that truth is a thing of value. This new knowledge affected his belief in love, and his attitude towards the woman he would marry.

753:27 **And that gain had colored the very face and shape of love . . . when he did see her he did not see her at all because of the face which he had already created in his mind** Hightower's discovery of the convenient art of deception affected even his idealistic conceptions of love. When he learns that truth is not always something to be valued, he simultaneously realizes that love was something less than he had thought. The 'face and shape of love' refers as well to his fiancée, whose true face he could not see 'because of the face he had already created in his mind.' When she speaks to him for the first time of marriage ('suddenly and savagely'), he 'sees her face for the first time as a living face.' This disillusioning discovery parallels the similar discovery by Joe Christmas about women, menstruation, and sexuality in chapter VIII.

753:37 **a hollow tree in which they left notes for one another** like the notes left by Joanna Burden for Joe Christmas

754:2 **He did not see a small oval narrowing too sharply to chin and passionate with discontent** Hightower did not see that she was rife with dissatisfaction, implied in the angularity of her chin, which Faulkner takes as the sign of an anxious disposition.

754:6 **eyes . . . like those of a harassed gambler** eyes like those of a gambler who has only one wager left to make, and who, losing it, will lose all. The woman sees Hightower as her last chance for marriage. She waits three years for him to broach the idea of marriage, and then she brings it up herself.

754:16 **He was used to that; he had grown up with a ghost** 'that' = his belief in marriage as a 'dead state.' 'Ghost' = his parents and their marriage, 'a dead state.'

754:18 **When he found out at last what she meant by escape from her present life, he felt no surprise** Throughout this passage marriage and escape are rhetorically linked. At 754: 8 she spoke 'suddenly and savagely' of marriage. Then, at 754:17, 'she talked suddenly and savagely' of 'escape.' Thus instead of thinking of marriage as a relationship in which two people bear responsibility for one another, he thinks of it as 'escape' from responsibility.

754:25 **He was not surprised** He is beginning to see that there are many things he misunderstands, and he is not surprised to find that his fiancée's face is among them.

755:7 **I was wrong about it too** 'too' refers to two earlier occasions when Hightower discovered that he was wrong: at 754:28 where he realized that his beliefs about the seminary were 'false, incorrect,' and at 755:4, when his fiancée informed him that the elders would not accept his explanation for why he wants to be assigned to Jefferson.

755:16 **The desperation was still in them, but now that there were definite plans, a day set, it was quieter, mostly calculation** The 'desperation' of the 'harassed gambler' (754) is relieved by her certainty that she will marry. Since she knows she can escape both seminary and spinsterhood, she can channel her 'desperation' into her plans for their marriage and their life.

755:19 **call** assignment to a church. See entry 448:31.

755:31 **demagoguery** Hightower and his wife manipulate the church hierarchy by gossip and small deceptions, playing people off against one another, to get the call to Jefferson.

755:37 **the train of the journey's last stage** the train they take on the last leg of their journey to Jefferson; figuratively, the last step in their plan to secure the call to Jefferson

755:37 **the consummation of his life** his supreme goal: to live in Jefferson until he died. Compare with 752:27: 'my only salvation must be to return to the place to die where my life had already ceased before it began.'

755:40 **the difference lay not outside but inside the car window** The difference lay not in the land but in himself.

756:6 **neither had he seen passion again** Hightower's fiancée is described on three occasions as passionate: on 754:3 her face is 'passionate with discontent'; on 754:23 she is 'headlong with passion'; and on 755:22 she again discusses their plans for 'escape' with 'that passionate and leashed humorlessness.' The passion that Hightower has not seen since their marriage is linked with the 'desperation naked in her face,' also no longer there. Both emotions are linked with escape. Marriage relieves her discontent for a time.

756:13 **There is a difference, you know, between civilian and military casualness** As the lines following this sentence suggest, military casualness is a product of last-stand desperation that would prompt an unexpected raid for supplies behind enemy lines. Civilian casualness is the opposite: it results in trivial actions of trivial consequence.

756:17 **Cinthy** diminutive of Cynthia

756:18 **grandfather wore no sword** In general during the Civil War swords were worn only by officers. Cavalry troops, however, officers or not, used sabers, formidable weapons similar to swords in appearance. The grandfather's lack of a sword emphasizes the desperate recklessness of the chicken-house raid.

756:20 **the troops who had opposed them for four years** Since the Civil War lasted from 1861 to 1865, this sentence would place the raid on Grant's stores in Jefferson sometime near the end of the war—1864 or 1865. Other evidence, however, suggests 1862 as the date. See the Chronology for further discussion. General Van Dorn's actual raid on Grant's stores was in December, 1862, and occurred at Holly Springs, Mississippi, not Oxford (the prototype for Jefferson). In *Light in August*, as in other novels, he occasionally (and cautiously) molds the facts of history to meet the needs of his fictional story.

756:37 **sheer tremendous tidal wave of desperate living** See entry 725:21.

756:40 **That makes the doings of heroes border so close on the unbelievable . . . that their very physical passing becomes rumor** The events and characters in the story must emerge only briefly now and then, so that they do not seem so incredible that reason and truth refuse to believe them. 'Their very physical passing' = their passing by in the street, normally a mundane occurrence, but in the context of the heroism with which Hightower invests them, a marvel; 'rumor' = myth, legend; 'with a thousand faces' = with a thousand different versions; 'before breath is out of them' = They become legend even before they die.

757:4 **lest paradoxical truth outrage itself** the truth about these heroes is so fantastic that it might seem impossible. The 'truth' of their heroic exploits would seem a paradox, something so impossible and self-contradictory that it would 'outrage itself.'

757:23 **the sharp gables of houses like the jagged edge of the exploding and ultimate earth** an apocalyptic image produced by the imagination of a seminarian trained in the metaphors of Revelations. Like the trees, the sharp gables of the houses were also backlighted by the fires of the burning warehouses and thus appeared as pieces of the exploding earth.

757:25 **Now it is a close place** where the raiders, hemmed in by town buildings and threatened by the fire of the Northern troops, are in greatest danger of being captured

757:36 **the crash of the shotgun comes: then blackness again** Hightower imagines this scene as if *he* is his grandfather, to whom the 'crash of the shotgun' brings blackness and death. This is the point of greatest excitement for him.

757:39 **A man growed, wid a married son, gone to a war whar his business was killin Yankees, killed in somebody else's hen house** the moment Hightower thinks so glorious: his grandfather's death while stealing chickens. He is not wholly unaware of the absurdity of it (as his use of Cinthy's scornful comment suggests), but the absurdity is not what fascinates him. It is the vision of foolhardy heroism and glory that obsesses him. On one level he takes seriously his fixation on his grandfather, but another part of him lives in the real world and recognizes the disastrous consequences of his fantasy for himself and others (consequences that the image of the turning wheel later in this chapter makes explicit).

758:9 **It's fine so** The story is fine told that way. Hightower's notion that his grandfather was killed by a 'fowling piece' held by 'the wife of a Confederate soldier' is his own fabrication. It provides the irony and absurdity that give the story the right tone and meaning. The suggestion here is, then, that over the years Hightower has altered the story's details, though probably not the essential facts, to suit his needs.

758:12 **a fowling piece, in a hen house** A 'fowling piece' is a shotgun intended for shooting birds. Hightower seems fascinated by the irony in the pun: a fowling piece used to shoot a chicken thief in a hen house

758:14 **when God looks about at their successors, He cannot be loath to share His own with us** 'their successors' = the living descendants of the dead. 'His own' = God's successors, Christ, the saints and apostles, the men of the church who carry on God's work. Hightower thinks it no wonder that God, seeing the poor quality of those now living, would not hesitate to give the living the redemptive solace of 'His own,' whose help he considers they need.

758:23 **heaven must have something of the color and shape of whatever village or hill or cottage of which the believer says, This is my own** Hightower muses that heaven always appears in the 'color and shape' of the believer's native soil, his or her *patria*. He regards the land out his window as *his* heaven because it is the land he considers 'my own.'

758:26 **the slow aisle, still interrupted with outlooking**
They make their way slowly down the train's aisle, towards
the door, pausing now and then to look out the windows at
the town.

758:26 **then the descent among faces grave, decorous, and
judicial** They descend into the crowd of elders and others
from the church, the first reference to the 'faces' that figure prominently in Hightower's reverie at the end of the
chapter.

758:30 **he thinks** From this point on the chapter is narrated
in the present tense; the story which began on 753 about his
meeting his future wife at the seminary and their coming to
Jefferson is over, and we are now being told what he is thinking on this Monday in the August of the novel's present time.

758:30 **But perhaps that was all I did do, God forgive me**
Hightower realizes that although he admitted his parishion-
ers had been fair to him, he had not been honest with
them—'I was the one who failed, who infringed' (759:12).
This is the first of his confessions of guilt and responsibility.
See also entries 759:11, 760:8.

758:36 **he can feel the two instants about to touch** like
Christmas waiting for the instant when the 'wireends knit
and made connection' (562:12)

758:38 **the suspended instant out of which the *soon* will
promptly begin** that moment just before dark, when time
stops and his reverie begins; 'the *soon*' = his anticipation of
the approaching hooves

758:40 **when his net was still too fine for waiting** This
hunting term characterizes a young man's impatience. A 'net'
is a hunting dog's sense of smell. A young, inexperienced
dog will go after any scent (its net is so fine that it senses
every scent without discrimination), while an experienced
dog will wait until it recognizes a scent worth pursuing.

759:3 **Perhaps that is all I ever did, have ever done** This
refers back to 758:30, 'But perhaps that was all I did do:
God forgive me,' where he realizes his failure of responsi-

bility to his parishioners. See also 759:34: 'And I accepted that.'

759:5 **the church which they were putting into his hands almost as a father surrenders the bride** This metaphor reflects the traditional identification of the Church as the bride of Christ. It emphasizes the serious trust the elders are extending to Hightower—a trust he will violate. It extends to Hightower's bride as well, for he will also violate his vows to her. The book of Revelation contains examples of this metaphor: "And I John saw the holy city, new Jerusalem, coming down from God out of heaven, prepared as a bride adorned for her husband" (21:2); the Holy City is the "bride, the wife of the Lamb" (21:9). See also Revelation 22:17.°

759:9 **the side, by the way, which the subject and proprietor of the picture has to look at, cannot help but look at** Because he *is* the picture, its owner and its subject, he cannot escape the doubt and frustration that often occupy his mind. The Hightower who manipulated his way into the Jefferson pulpit may have seen only what he expected to see; the Hightower who recalls that experience now sees it from the other side.

759:11 **'They did their part; they played by the rules,' he thinks. 'I was the one who failed, who infringed. Perhaps that is the greatest social sin of all; ay, perhaps moral sin** In his second confession of guilt and blame, Hightower admits that the elders treated him fairly. It was he who failed to honor his obligation to them (the antecedent of 'that'). That failure 'is the greatest sin of all.' To fail to honor his charge as a minister responsible for the spiritual welfare of his congregation is a *moral* sin, practically a *mortal* sin as well. See also entries 758:30, 760:8.

759:14 **Thinking goes quietly, tranquilly, flowing on, falling into shapes quiet, not assertive, not reproachful, not particularly regretful** See the opening lines of chapter VI (487:1). Note similar uses of this expression on 404, 475, 495, 562, 694, 694, 695, 760, 760, 761, 762. The frequency of the verbal form 'thinking' reflects the importance of the novel's focus on the link (or its absence) between thought and action. Thinking that goes 'quietly, tranquilly,' is linked to the oil metaphor that describes Byron's thinking on 694–95. In this passage, 'Thinking' is a reverie, unrolling smoothly under its own power. This is thought without moral comprehension; i.e., Hightower reflects on his thoughts without really comprehending them. He accepts blame for 'the greatest sin of all' in principle but not in fact.

759:21 **the Church's cloistered apotheosis** the seminary

759:31 **like one of those barricades of the middle ages planted with dead and sharpened stakes** chevaux-de-frise, used in the Middle Ages (and as late as World War II). They are crisscrossing stakes (made of wood that, being cut, is 'dead') set in the ground at an angle with 'sharpened' tips pointing in the direction of the attack they are meant to oppose; 'dead' may also mean 'the dead'—bodies impaled on the sharpened stakes.

759:32 **against truth and against that peace in which to sin and be forgiven which is the life of man** Hightower 'seems to see' that the church is fiercely armed against the very functions it is supposed to serve: truth, forgiveness, redemption.

759:39 **brought with me one trust, perhaps the first trust of man** his obligation to his wife, whom he had sworn to love and cherish in marriage. This 'trust' can also refer to the mission the church has entrusted to him: the preaching of the gospel and saving of souls.

760:8 **perhaps at that moment I became her seducer and her murderer** her 'seducer' because he married her for a dishonorable motive: to improve his chances of being sent to Jefferson; 'murderer' because his subsequent failure to respond to her needs led to her death. This is the third of his confessions. Carl Ficken suggests that "Once he understands that the galloping hooves had led him to sin against the church, then he knows as well that they cause a larger sin

against his wife . . . . He made that revelation to her of the
'depth' of his 'hunger,' of course, when he told her his
grandfather's story. Now, finally, he grasps what he did to
the woman, using her as a 'means toward his own selfish-
ness,' 'an instrument to be called to Jefferson.'"° See also entries 758:30, 759:11.

760:12 **Thinking begins to slow now. It slows like a wheel
beginning to run in sand** This 'wheel' is the controlling
metaphor for the remainder of the chapter. When his reverie is going smoothly, 'quietly, tranquilly, flowing on, falling
into shapes quiet, not assertive, not reproachful, not particularly regretful' (759:14), the wheel runs easily, but when his
thinking begins to trouble him, the wheel begins to slow, as
if bogging down in sand. Hightower's mind now begins to
accuse him of responsibility for his wife's shame and death.

Martin Bidney suggests that Faulkner borrowed an image
for this passage from Alfred Lord Tennyson's *In Memoriam*:

> Be near me when the light is low,
>   When the blood creeps, and the nerves prick
>   And tingle; and the heart is sick,
> And all the wheels of being slow. [Ll. 1–4].

Carl Ficken comments more generally: "Faulkner is working
with an ancient and universal symbol and is thereby moving
the novel away from a narrow and limited situation into that
association with an older civilization, with all time. Carl G.
Jung has analyzed in some detail the frequency with which
the mandala, or ritual circle, has been found in ancient symbolism and in the dream-level consciousness of modern man:
he sees the mandala as a universal symbol of wholeness, or
the desire for wholeness, which men have used for centuries
in order to come to terms with or to escape an inner self.
'The true mandala [Jung writes] is always an inner image,
which is gradually built up through (active) imagination, at
such times when psychic equilibrium is disturbed or when a
thought cannot be found and must be sought for, because it

is not contained in holy doctrine.'"° See also entry 588:28.

760:14　**the axle, the vehicle, the power which propels it**
Hightower's mind and imagination

760:16　**He seems to watch himself among faces**　At first
these are the faces already mentioned—of his Jefferson parishioners—but as his thinking becomes more troubled, the
faces come to include Lena, Byron, Christmas, Grimm, and
even God.

760:19　**the faces seem to be mirrors in which he watches
himself . . . he can read his own doings in them**　He can
see in the expressions on the faces what must have been the
significance of his actions.

760:23　**a charlatan preaching worse than heresy, in utter disregard of that whose very stage he preempted**　'that' = the
purpose of the church; 'stage' = the pulpit and the sermon.
His sermons were worse than heresy because they were delivered from the church pulpit and were about his grandfather and were of no relevance to his mission as a minister.

760:33　**in his turn unaware**　The faces before him mirror 'astonishment,' then 'puzzlement,' then 'outrage,' finally 'fear'
as they look 'beyond his wild antics' and see that which they
were unaware of before, 'the supreme Face itself.' The fear
on their faces reflects how they are aware, and he is not
aware, that the 'Face Itself' of God is looking down on him.

760:33　**the final and supreme Face Itself**　On the one hand
this is the Face of God. Yet it also is the Face of Truth, about
to discover to Hightower the failures of his life. Taken with
the chapter's discussions of Hightower's phantoms, the 'Face'
also suggests the previously noted section 108 of Tennyson's
In Memoriam: see entry 634:15. Carl Ficken: "That Hightower is thinking of God here is clear from what the Face
says to him about the call to Jefferson: 'not for My ends but
for your own.'"° God here 'speaks' to Hightower in much
the same way He 'spoke' to Doc Hines in Chapter XV.

760:35　**the trust of which he proved himself unworthy, be-**

ing used now for his chastisement He thinks he is now being judged (and chastised) by God for his failure to his wife, and perhaps also for his failure to the church.

760:39 **Shall I be held responsible for that which was beyond my power?** 'that' = preaching the gospel to his congregation, which he apparently feels did not lie within his power to do effectively. He makes a dishonest argument, for only a page earlier (760:11), he has admitted that 'there must be some things for which God cannot . . . be held responsible.' He begins here a series of rationalizations: 1) Perhaps I accepted more than I could perform. But is that criminal? Shall I be held responsible for that which was beyond my power? 2) But I was young then (761:30). 3) I have already paid for what I did (761:33). 4) Any man should be free to destroy himself—so long as he doesn't injure anyone else. But none of these rationalizations works for him. See 762:16, 762:19, and 762:21 for his final rationalization.

761:1 **It was not to accomplish that that you accepted her** the first 'that' = the role of a minister, which Hightower has just protested he should not be blamed for not performing satisfactorily. The second 'that' introduces a noun clause in which God says that he knows Hightower did not marry his wife in order to become a good minister: he married her to improve his chances at being assigned to Jefferson.

761:5 **He sees himself again as when the shame came** thinks back to the time of his wife's death

761:6 **He remembers that which he had sensed before it was born, hiding it from his own thinking.** He remembers the shame and guilt that he has begun to suspect he should feel even before he knew there was actual reason to feel it, and he remembers how he had tried to keep from acknowledging it.

761:10 **there was within him a leaping and triumphant surge of denial** a denial of the sop of 'fortitude and forbearance and dignity' with which he has just tried to convince himself that he resigned the pulpit for 'a martyr's reasons.' This is the denial of a delusion, and a step towards truth.

761:12 **a face which had betrayed him, believing itself safe behind the lifted hymnbook, when the photographer pressed the bulb** his own face that, in the scene on 448, appeared to be 'smiling . . . like the face of Satan in the old prints.' This is not the face of a martyr, nor of a man grieving over his dead wife or the desertion of his parishioners. It is, thus, a face that betrays him, especially since it may have been published in a newspaper.

761:19 **casting his sops** still offering paltry evidence of his martyred life: dividing his income with the Memphis institution, allowing himself to be persecuted.

761:19 **flinging rotten fruit before a drove of hogs** An ironic play on Matthew 7:6, "Give not that which is holy unto the dogs, neither cast ye your pearls before swine, lest they trample them under their feet, and turn again and rend you."

761:25 **that patient and voluptuous ego of the martyr** like McEachern's 'dreamlike exaltation of a martyr' (549:38) as he walked toward the descending chair Joe swung at his head

761:26 *How long, O Lord* Revelation 6:10: "And they cried with a loud voice, saying, How Long, O Lord, holy and true, dost thou not judge and avenge our blood on them that dwell on the earth?" What Hightower means is: 'How long, O Lord, must I put up with this?'°

761:27 **he lifted the mask** and presumably revealed the 'face of Satan' he had tried to hide behind the hymn book at 448:22

761:29 *That's bought and paid for now* 'that' = the martyrdom. I've suffered martyrdom for my dead grandfather; I've paid the price I owed him (and the town for coming here under false pretenses) and now can proceed with my life unmolested.

761:30 **But I was young then** another rationalization ex-
empting him from responsibility. See entry 760:39.

761:34 **I have bought my ghost** the ghost of his dead grandfather, which has haunted and shaped his life. He 'bought' it
by paying for it with his own life; thus, he has taken 'a single
instant of darkness' as his own life: 'I am my dead grandfather on the instant of his death' (762:21).

761:36 **'so long as he does not injure anyone else, so long as
he lives to and of himself—' He stops suddenly** He stops
because, as the long dash indicates, he realizes that what he
is thinking is not true. He has injured not just himself but
also his wife and parishioners, and therefore has not lived
just 'to and of himself.' He has made others pay part of the
price of his ghost—and this realization brings upon him 'a
consternation which is about to be actual horror.'

761:39 **He is aware of the sand now** For the first time he is
fully and consciously aware that his reverie has led him
where he did not want to go. His soothing nightly ritual has
gone off its usual unruffled path and the wheel of the 'vehicle,' now sand-clutched, no longer rolls effortlessly.

761:40 **with the realization of it he feels within himself a
gathering as though for some tremendous effort** Hightower becomes aware that something has slowed and blocked
his thinking. He does not want to go where his undirected
thinking has taken him, so he is preparing by an effort of the
will to think his way out of the difficulty.

762:2 **Progress now is still progress, yet it is now indistinguishable from the recent past** The wheel moves so slowly
that its progress is barely evident from one moment to the
next. He has progressed almost to the conclusion he has resisted all along: that he is the instrument of his wife's 'despair
and shame,' that as his 'dead grandfather on the instant of
his death,' he is 'the debaucher and murderer of his grandson's wife' (762).

762:3 **like the already traversed inches of sand which cling
to the turning wheel, raining back with a dry hiss** As

the wheel turns slowly, some of the sand clinging to it is
cast backward, raining down in a dry hiss that should have
warned him before now.

762:8 **a sentence seems to stand fullsprung . . . *I dont want
to think this. I must not think this. I dare not think this*** The
unstated sentence is his admission of responsibility for his
wife's death. He never utters it, retreating instead to his rationalization at the end of the paragraph, which blames all
on his dead grandfather.

762:12 **sweat begins to pour from him, springing out like
blood, and pouring** He sweats as if he is being tortured.
This is the moment of his crucifixion, parallel to the dying
moments of Joe Christmas in the previous chapter.

762:13 **the instant** the arrested moment of realization.

762:13 **the sandclutched wheel of thinking turns on** The
nature of the wheel shifts throughout the chapter. Here it is
the 'wheel of thinking.' Earlier it was a reverie—undirected,
smooth, not troubling. In a few more lines it will be a wheel
of torture. Later a wheel of faces will surround him like a
halo.

762:14 **with the slow implacability of a mediaeval torture instrument, beneath the wrenched and broken sockets of his
life** The medieval wheel of torture caused pain by stretching, bending, and otherwise mutilating the victim's body.
The 'broken sockets' refer metaphorically to the limbs of torture victims being pulled from their sockets. By bringing
him to this final realization, the 'wheel of thinking' thus becomes a wheel of torture.

762:16 **if this is so, if I am the instrument of her despair and
death, then I am in turn instrument of someone outside
myself** If I am the cause of my wife's despair and death,
then in turn someone or something else must have been acting on me—i.e., he continues to try to evade responsibility.

762:18 **for fifty years I have not even been clay** In Genesis
God fashioned Adam's body from clay. Hightower means
that in the fifty years of his life he has not even been a crea-

ture of substance but has instead been 'a single instant of
darkness in which a horse galloped and a gun crashed'—an
illusion, a ghost.

762:21 **if I am my dead grandfather on the instant of his
death, then my wife, his grandson's wife . . . the debaucher
and murderer of my grandson's wife** Hightower reasons
that because he has lived his life only through his imagined
vision of his grandfather's death, he has not lived at all,
that his grandfather is responsible more than he for his
wife's death. This is the last and greatest of Hightower's
rationalizations.

762:29 **the lambent suspension of August into which night
is about to fully come** This passage comes closer than any
other to standing as the source of the novel's title. At the
University of Virginia, Faulkner used similar language to explain the title's meaning: "Oh that was—in August in Mississippi there's a few days somewhere about the middle of the
month when suddenly there's a foretaste of fall, it's cool,
there's a lambence, a luminous quality to the light, as though
it came not from just today but from back in the old classic
times"°; see "Title."

762:30 **it seems to engender** 'it' = the whirling wheel

762:31 **The halo is full of faces** Within the halo, Hightower
sees all the faces he has known in his life, the faces of his
wife, the parishioners and townspeople, Lena Grove, Joe
Christmas, Byron Bunch, even his own face.

762:34 **They are peaceful, as though they have escaped into
an apotheosis** 'apotheosis' = transcendence from the mortal to a divine state.

763:2 **as though in the now peaceful throes of a more recent,
a more inextricable, compositeness** The meaning is unclear. Perhaps Hightower's close encounter with Christmas,
and the latter's death in his kitchen, is referred to. Christmas, having just died, has only recently become part of the
'apotheosis.'

763:4 **it is two faces** Hightower has just realized his responsibility for his wife's death. He has accepted his metaphoric identity as executioner, an identity that fits Grimm, who murdered Christmas, as well as Christmas, who murdered Joanna Burden. Hightower recognizes that he is as guilty as they, and with the enormity of this realization 'some ultimate dammed flood within him breaks and rushes away.'

763:6 **the desire of the wheel** the need and desire of Hightower's thinking. The two faces 'seem to strive to free themselves one from the other' because that is what Hightower wants them to do. He needs to keep them separate so he can recognize them and know who they are rather than be forced to understand the single face they compose.

763:11 **that. . . . . . boy** Percy Grimm

763:14 **some ultimate dammed flood within him breaks and rushes away** On 725:21, Faulkner used a similar metaphor ('the world rushes down on him like a flood, a tidal wave') to describe Byron Bunch's sudden recognition that he may still win Lena Grove. More significant, at the moment of Joe Christmas's death a flood of 'pent black blood seemed to rush like a released breath' from his body. There the flood signifies not only death for Christmas, his release from life's suffering, and also a recognition among the people of the surrounding countryside that a tragic and brutal event has occurred implicating them all. For Hightower the flood of recognition brings only a return to the sterile existence that has been his for more then twenty years.

763:15 **feeling himself losing contact with earth, lighter and lighter, emptying, floating** These feelings convince Hightower he is dying. Whether he is or not, he is losing contact with the world he so briefly entered when he assisted Lena with her child's birth and attempted to help Joe.

763:16 **I am dying** In 1957 Faulkner said that Hightower "didn't die" and explained the minister's statement by pointing to the failure of his life. Yet evidence does exist for Hightower's frail physical condition. In Chapter XIII, he seems on the verge of collapse (627–28), and in Chapter XVI he

appears to faint (688). Faulkner revised Hightower's statement in the manuscript from 'Maybe I am dying' to the published 'I am dying' to emphasize the minister's conviction.°
Whatever the case, Hightower has realized the sterile existence he has lived since coming to Jefferson.

763:18 **With all air, all heaven, filled with the lost and unheeded crying of all the living who ever lived** This image of heaven filled with unanswered prayers is an absolute rejection of Christian faith.

763:21 **I wanted so little. I asked so little** Compare with Christmas, at the end of Chapter V, 'That's all I wanted . . . That don't seem like a whole lot to ask' (484:4). Compare also with 644:5: 'That was all I wanted . . . That was all, for thirty years. That didn't seem to be a whole lot to ask in thirty years', and with Hightower's thought at 628:22: 'I just wanted peace.' Both men blame their failure to get what they 'wanted' more on the injustice of the world than on their own actions. In Christmas such an attitude is part of his fatalism. In Hightower it reflects his failure in this last scene to learn anything or to be changed for the better by his experiences with Byron, Lena, and Christmas.

763:22 **The wheel turns on. It spins now, fading, without progress** The wheel of Hightower's thinking is now stuck permanently in the sand, spinning uselessly, without traction.

763:27 **so that it can be now Now** 'it' = the vision of the charging cavalry. The conjunction *so* is crucial. It suggests that what immediately preceded this clause—the fading away of the wheel of thought that had carried Hightower towards his revelation—was a necessary preliminary to his return to his vision. In essence, he has to escape from reality back to his world of reverie. When the wheel has faded completely, the vision can begin: 'now Now.' Hightower can confront only so much truth at one time and must return to his reverie because the truth that he has just realized was more than he could absorb. Thus we see demonstrated what we learned at 753:19: that one can 'supply himself in crises with shapes

and sounds with which to guard him from truth,' from having to acknowledge that which can sometimes be more than
he can bear.

763:29 **It is as though they had merely waited until he could
find something to pant with, to be reaffirmed in triumph
and desire with, with this last left of honor and pride and
life** 'they' = the ghostly cavalry. It is as though the cavalry
waited to appear until Hightower found something he could
still believe in, something that would make him feel 'reaffirmed in triumph and desire,' which would permit him to
cling to a last remnant of 'honor and pride and life.' That
'something' is his envisioned image of the charging cavalry.
Faulkner observed that this image was all Hightower had
left: "that was one thing that was pure and fine that he
had . . . the memory of his grandfather, who had been
brave."°

764:4 **it seems to him that he still hears them: the wild
bugles and the clashing sabres and the dying thunder of
hooves** Confronted with the harsh truth of his failures, he
grasps the only image that has ever held meaning for him,
the image of his grandfather's charging cavalry, an image of
bravery and heroism, yet wholly disconnected from reality.
This chapter concludes by leaving Hightower lost and unre-
deemed. The previous chapter presented an equally bleak
end to the story of Joe Christmas. In the next chapter Byron
Bunch's story will end as well, though in a considerably less
pessimistic manner.

CHAPTER XXI

765:1 **the state** Mississippi

765:1 **furniture repairer and dealer** buyer, repairer, and seller of used furniture. The story he tells his wife is colored with a warm and healthy humor that contrasts markedly to the general tone of much of the rest of the novel.

765:5 **the truck (it had a housedin body with a door at the rear)** not a pick-up truck but the equivalent of a van, the 'housed-in' portion built either of metal, wood, or a combination. In *The Town* and *The Mansion* V. K. Ratliff drives such a truck, with the housed-in portion built of wood.

765:12 **he and his wife are not old either, besides his having been away from home . . . for more than a week** The salesman and his wife are about the same age as the couple about whom he tells the story. He and his wife have just finished making love when he begins his story, a fact he alludes to several times, establishing not only an ironic parallel between himself and Byron Bunch, but also jokingly trying to titillate his wife. His account of Byron's valiant, desperate pursuit of Lena is the account of one lover's pursuit of his beloved told by another lover to his own wife.

765:26 **the kind of fellow you wouldn't see the first glance if he was alone by himself in the bottom of a empty concrete swimming pool** a remarkable metaphor that testifies to the salesman's narrative abilities and that shows he reacted to Byron as did most of the people in Jefferson before him

765:30 **Jackson, Tennessee** a town in western Tennessee, about thirty-five miles north of the border, and due north of Oxford, Mississippi°

765:32 **a accommodation** a help, a favor.

766:7 **Whyn't** Why don't

766:10 **leatherlooking paper suit cases** cheap suitcases made of imitation-leather cardboard°

766:24 **anything to show folks to prove it** that is, a baby

766:28 *Anyway, I cant see you blushing any* The narrator jokingly implies that because his wife isn't blushing, she isn't a lady. He also probably implies that her recent behavior with him in their dark bedroom, where he couldn't see her blush to begin with, wasn't very ladylike either.

766:36 **Not if I know color** The baby's reddish skin-color shows it to be much younger than eight weeks.

766:39 **Like he had done told her not to talk about it** If Byron did tell Lena not to talk about recent events in Jefferson, he must have done so out of a desire to protect their privacy and to keep their identities hidden.

767:12 **tourist camp** Tourist camps were for travelers of limited means.° They provided tents or small houses, water, and food for a small fee.

767:18 **I knowed what he wanted me to say** to invite them to sleep in the truck

767:32 **something that he would die before he would even think about doing it** What Byron wants to do, as the furniture dealer learns later, is to make love to Lena, but he doesn't yet know how to try to make that happen.

767:40 *Maybe I'll show you, too* Maybe I'll do to you what he wanted to do to her.

768:3 **his face all shined up** radiating (feigned) happiness and enthusiasm

768:23 *How come it took him all that time and trouble, anyway?* The furniture dealer's wife, who understands very well what her husband's story is about, wonders why Byron took so long to try to get in bed with Lena. Her husband has not yet made clear that Lena would probably be Byron's first lover.

768:30 *he was just giving her one more chance* one more chance to respond to his proposals, either to marry him or to sleep with him or both. In fact, it is himself he is giving the chance to.

769:5 **she began to tell him** to remove their belongings from the truck so as not to impose on the furniture dealer, who was planning to sleep there

769:7 **those two fellows that used to be in the funny papers, those two Frenchmen that were always bowing and scraping** Alphonse and Gaston, "a super-polite team of comic Frenchmen created by Fred Opper for the Hearst Sunday pages in the early 1900's."° While Byron argues that the furniture dealer should sleep in the truck, the furniture dealer argues that Byron and Lena should have the truck, and neither gives any ground.

769:14 **I reckon you might say that I won. Or that me and him won** 'won' in the sense that neither ended up sleeping in the truck. Lena slept there, 'like we all might have known all the time it would be.'

769:20 **I reckon that was why he brought in all that firewood** enough to keep the two men warm while they slept on the ground. The furniture dealer thinks that Byron also had known what the outcome of their argument would be and that he is bringing the extra firewood to make amends for the inconvenience the furniture dealer will suffer.

769:25 *I reckon she had a little more patience than you* a sexual double entendre. The furniture dealer jokingly suggests to his wife that she is less willing than Lena to put off sex with the man she loved.

769:33 **hunting for somebody, following him** The pretense for Lena's trip is that she is hunting Lucas Burch. The furniture dealer may even have heard Lena and Byron discussing Burch. But the reality of her travel is something quite different: she has probably already decided to accept Byron. She is simply enjoying the freedom of travel before settling down to marriage.

769:36 **another gal that thought she could learn on Saturday night what her mammy waited until Sunday to ask the**

minister Lena decided to learn about the sexual part of marriage before the marriage vows.

770:8 **it aint only since she has been riding on the seat of my truck that she has travelled out in front** The dealer realizes that Lena is directing her journey with Byron, who, whether he knows so or not, is doing exactly what she wants.

770:14 **she knew that she never even had to bother to say either yes or no to him** She knew she had him hooked and that whether she did what he wanted or not he would follow her as long as it took for her to agree to their getting married.

770:27 **what she might have been advising him to do all the time** that is, be more aggressive

771:3 **fetched a snore** produced a snore, pretending to be asleep so as not to scare off Byron

771:4 **walking like he had eggs under his feet** walking carefully, on tiptoes, quietly

771:6 **if you'd a just done this last night, you'd a been sixty miles further south than you are now** If Byron had tried the previous night to climb into the truck with Lena, she would have accepted him then, and they could have stopped traveling north and started looking for the place where they would spend their lives together. If Byron had tried to make his move on Lena two nights before, then they would have stopped traveling before the dealer ever got a chance to meet them. 'Sixty miles further south' may also be the furniture dealer's sexual joke about where Byron would be on Lena's body if he had behaved differently.

771:20 *I reckon the reason you knew you never had to worry was that you had already found out just what she would do* The wife teasingly implies that her husband had already made an advance on Lena himself and thus had discovered how she would react.

771:27 *durn little cuss* Byron

771:36 **Why, Mr Bunch. Aint you ashamed. You might have woke the baby, too** In a 1955 interview, Faulkner called this passage "one of the calmest, sanest speeches I ever

heard. . . . She was never for one moment confused, frightened, alarmed. She did not even know that she didn't need
pity."°

772:19 **face or no face** that is, however embarrassed the
look on his face might be

772:27 **And that if my wife was to hear about me traveling
the country with a goodlooking country gal and a three
weeks' old baby** In another of his characteristic fragmentary sentences, the furniture dealer says that if his wife
learned he had been traveling with a young girl, he would
have hell to pay.

772:30 **Or both husbands now** the father of the baby (Lucas
Burch) as well as the man who wants to marry her (Byron
Bunch)

772:37 **gum branch** branch of a gum tree, used as a broom

773:1 **I reckon I'll ride back here** so that when they catch
up with Byron he will not find her riding in the front of the
truck with the furniture dealer and become jealous or angry

773:8 **fellow being caught in the depot with a strange baby
on his hands** The furniture dealer refers to a generally
known joke or story of his day about a man caught in such a
situation.

773:11 **full of husbands and wives too, let alone sheriffs** all
of them out tracking down this illicitly eloping couple

773:13 **burn that new truck up** by driving too fast and ig-
noring the need to break it in by driving slowly (the chapter's
first paragraph explains that the furniture dealer means to
drive slowly so as to break in the truck properly)

773:19 **You cant beat them.** You can't beat women; you can't
outsmart them.

773:29 *face and no face* a variation on the 'face or no face'
expression at 772:19. Byron's face showed embarrassment
(that hangdog look) and something else that counterbal-
anced the embarrassment—determination.

773:31 *now he knew he wouldn't ever have to desperate himself
again* Together with Lena's comment to Byron that 'Aint
nobody never said for you to quit' (774), this is the novel's

best and only evidence that Byron will ultimately get what he wants. The furniture dealer believes Byron has finally mustered the resolve he needed before, and that this time he will succeed with Lena.

773:40 **whatever he done, he wasn't going to mean it** that is, even if he did run off, he would be back before too long. She knows he won't give up so easily.

774:21 **Saulsbury, Tennessee** small village five miles north of the Mississippi line

774:26 **My, my. A body does get around. Here we aint been coming from Alabama but two months, and now it's already Tennessee.** At the end of chapter I a month earlier, Lena made practically the same observation on first seeing Jefferson (420).

APPENDIX

A Chronology for *Light in August*

The present-time events of *Light in August* occur in August of 1932. The narrative provides sufficient information to allow the birth dates of both Joanna Burden and Gail Hightower (as well as a number of other characters) to be determined. These dates, combined with other chronological information in the narrative, establish the year of the novel's present time as 1932. Stephen Meats, in his chronology of the novel, explains: "A convenient cross-check of this date [1932] can be calculated using 1865, the year in which Gail Hightower's father returns from the Civil War. Twenty-five years later, Hightower discovers the Yankee coat his father wore home from the war [745]; the year is 1890. Gail Hightower is eight at this time [745]; his birth year, therefore, is 1882. In the present time of the novel, Hightower is fifty years old [434, 669]. His age, added to 1882, also establishes the year of the present time as 1932."° Similar information about Joanna Burden, almost as clear, also points to 1932 as the present-time year of the novel.

Cleanth Brooks has gone so far as to pinpoint the precise days in 1932 which the novel concerns. Carefully analyzing and comparing the important chronological references, he concludes that Joanna Burden was murdered on August 6, 1932, and Christmas on August 15.° Brooks's argument succeeds if every chronological reference in the novel is taken literally, that is, if *two months* means precisely two months, no more or less. Unfortunately, many characters in the novel habitually refer to time in a careless, offhand way: even when they are being careful, *two months* to them might mean anywhere from six weeks to ten weeks. As a result a number of inconsistent references to time occur. Even Faulkner can be inconsistent: on 651 the narrative states that Christmas was captured in Mottstown on Friday, while all other references clearly point to Saturday. It thus seems safe not to date precisely the events of the novel. Meats suggests that Faulk-

ner deliberately withheld the information which would have allowed specific dates to be determined: "he apparently had reasons for not wanting
the reader to know the exact dates. Determining the dates of the present
time, as tempting as it might appear, would therefore seem to be beside
the point."°

This chronology attempts to date, within reason, the linear sequence of
important events, past and present, in *Light in August*. A few dates are
actually given in the text. Most are interpolated from evidence in the narrative: in either case the page numbers indicate where the evidence is to
be found.

1812 Calvin Burrington born [576]

1824 Calvin runs away, age 12; spends a year in a monastery. [576]

1832 Gail Hightower's father is born. [744]

1835 Calvin reaches Missouri. [576]

1835 "Three weeks after he arrived" in Missouri Calvin marries. [576]

1836 "a year later [Calvin Burrington] was a father." [576]

1836 Nathaniel Burden born [577]

1850 Nathaniel Burden runs away at age 14, does not return for 16
years. [578]

1852 Hightower's father begins preaching "in a small Presbyterian church
back in the hills." [745]

1854 Calvin II born to Nathaniel and Juana. [580]

1861 Calvin loses arm in Kansas fighting, "two years ago." [578]

1862 December 20: Gail Hightower's grandfather killed during General
Van Dorn's raid on Jefferson. The date is that of General Van Dorn's
raid on Holly Springs, which Faulkner probably used as the model for
the raid on Jefferson. See entry 443:6. [751]

1863 Nathaniel Burden's second message from Old Mexico arrives by
messenger. [578]

1865 Gail Hightower's father returns from the Civil War and begins
practicing medicine. [745]

1866 Nathaniel Burden returns with Juana and Calvin.

1866 Old Calvin Burden is in his "late fifties." [579]

1866 Nathaniel Burden and Juana marry. [584]

1866 Calvin II is "twelve." [584]

1874 Calvin "had just turned twenty when he was killed." [582]

1874 Miss Atkins, orphanage dietician, is born. [489]

1882 Doc Hines and wife marry: "For fifty years I have suffered it," Mrs. Hines says in 1932. [674]

1882 Gail Hightower is born. [434]

1885 Juana, "Calvin's mother," dies. [583]

1886 "Nathaniel said, 'I am fifty years old.'" [583]

1886 Nathaniel Burden marries his second wife, Joanna's mother. [583]

1888 Joanna Burden "was not born until fourteen years after Calvin was killed." [582]

1888 "two years later [after the second wedding] Joanna was born" [584].

1890 For the first time Hightower examines his father's crudely patched Civil War uniform. [745]

1892 Nathaniel Burden shows his daughter Joanna the cedar grove where the two Calvins are buried. [584]

1895 December: Milly Hines ("about 18") becomes pregnant by circus "Mexican." [675]

1896 September: Christmas is born. Milly dies. Hines leaves. Sends first moneypaper from Memphis. This birthdate, which makes Christmas thirty-six at the time of his death, is the result of a literal reading of chronological clues in the text. A looser reading of those clues could allow for a birthdate that makes him thirty-three at his death.

1896 November: Hines sends second moneypaper from Memphis. [680]

1896 December 23: Hines steals the infant from Mrs. Hines and takes him to Memphis. [680]

1896 December 25, evening: Christmas is found on orphanage steps and named by the staff. [682]

1901 late October: Christmas, 5, is caught in the dietician's closet, kidnapped by the janitor (Hines). We know it is "late" in 1901 because of references to the cold, and because soon after this event Christmas is adopted "two weeks before Christmas" (503). Joe was discovered in the dietician's closet "two months" before McEachern adopted him (505).

1901 (late in the year) Hines loses job at orphanage, returns to Mottstown.

1901 Wednesday, December 11: McEachern arrives "two weeks before Christmas" to adopt the boy. [503]

1902 Doc Hines and wife arrive in Mottstown. See 681. [651]

1904 A Sunday morning: the catechism episode. Christmas is "a boy of eight." [507]

1907 Percy Grimm is born. In 1932 he is "about twentyfive." [731]

1907 (first six months) Hightower graduates from seminary and marries the daughter of "one of the . . . teachers in the college" (753). [755]

1907 (second six months) Hightower arrives to serve as "minister of one of the principal churches of Jefferson," twenty-five years before present-time action. Hightower is 25 (in 1932 he is 50 [434]). Shortly after his arrival his wife begins slipping off to Memphis. She dies on a Saturday night (441). He loses his position in the church. See 670. [433]

1910 A Saturday: the "womanshenegro" episode. Christmas is "fourteen" (514). Around this time he learns about menstruation (535) and kills the sheep to wash his hands in its blood. [535]

1912 Lena Grove born [401]

1913 A fall weekday, at noon, McEachern takes Joe to the back-street cafe where he first sees Bobbie Allen. "It began in the fall when he was seventeen." [526]

1914 Saturday in the spring: Joe returns to the cafe "six months" (528) after the initial visit and buys coconut pie. [529]

1914 Saturday, one month later: Christmas returns to cafe to repay Bobbie but she's not there. As he leaves he meets and makes a date with her for the following Monday evening. [533]

1914 The following Monday evening: Joe's first date with Bobbie. [535]

1914 Monday, a week later: Joe drags Bobbie into trees. [539]

1914 one month later, early summer: Joe sleeps with Bobbie in her room for the first time. [542]

1914 summer: McEachern misses the heifer; Christmas is 18 (520). That same night (524), Christmas goes to the school house dance which ends with his attack on McEachern (549). Joe is then beaten up at Max and Mame's house and enters the "street which was to run for fifteen years" (563), a length of time suggesting that when it stops running—when he arrives and settles down in Jefferson—he is 33 years old, and the year is 1929. [517]

1924 Lena is 12. Her mother and father die and she goes to live with brother McKinley. [401]

1929 August: Christmas arrives in Jefferson. "He was thirtythree years old" (565). The context clearly suggests this was his age when he arrives at Joanna Burden's cabin. [421]

1930 spring: Christmas goes to work at sawmill. [575]

1930 September: Joanna appears in the cabin and tells her family story to Christmas. She tells Christmas she is 41, which means she was born in 1889. Other evidence (582, 584), however, clearly suggests she was born in 1888. This may be an inconsistency; on the other hand, Joanna could easily have been born late in 1888 and still be 41 in September 1930. [575]

1931 September: Joanna tells Christmas she wants a child. [594]

1931 "Just after Christmas": Joanna tells Christmas she is pregnant. [594]

1 9 3 2

January: Lena discovers she is pregnant. She is 20 now; McKinley is 40 (403). Lucas runs away shortly after her discovery; it probably takes him about a month to reach Jefferson, the same amount of time it takes Lena. [403]

February: Joanna's note summons Christmas to her bedroom, where he learns she wants to reform him. "This was how the third phase began" (596). [403]

mid-February: Joe Brown/Lucas Burch arrives in Jefferson, takes a job at the sawmill [425].

sometime between Feb and May: a second note summons Christmas to Joanna's bedroom, where she suggests he get an education and oversee her affairs. He realizes she isn't pregnant (603). Precise date not given. [599]

May evening: A third note summons Christmas to Joanna's bedroom, where she implores him to pray with her. [604]

mid-July: Lena leaves her brother's home and sets out to find Lucas Burch. [403]

Wednesday, mid-August: A fourth note summons Christmas to Joanna's bedroom, where she again begs him to "Kneel with me" (606). He realizes he will have to kill her. [605]

early Friday morning, next day: Christmas lies awake in cot, beats Brown, leaves cabin, walks naked and confronts car, goes to sleep in barn. [474]

Friday dawn: Christmas wakes, shaves, sleeps in "small valley in which a spring rose." [479–80]

Friday mid-morning: Christmas wakes again, eats breakfast, reads magazines, drains whiskey tins by which time it is afternoon. [480, 482].

Friday: Lena has been on the road for one month. [401]

Friday: Lena spends night with Armstids. [408]

Friday 7:00 pm: Christmas eats supper in town. [482]

Friday 9:00 pm: Christmas stands outside barbershop watching Brown, begins walk which leads to Niggertown. [482]

Friday 10:00 pm: In middle of road near Joanna Burden's house Christmas hears the town clock strike "two miles away." [485]

Friday 11:00 pm: Christmas sits "with back against tree" outside Joanna Burden's house [486]

Friday midnight: Christmas hears the town clock strike "two miles away" as he still sits against the tree outside Joanna Burden's house. [486]

Saturday morning, just after midnight: Joe Christmas kills Joanna Burden. He gets up to enter her house as the "last stroke of the far clock" dies away. [486, 606]

Saturday, around noon: Lena arrives in Jefferson

Sunday morning: The bloodhounds arrive by train in Jefferson and the posse begins tracking Christmas. [617]

Sunday night: Byron Bunch visits Hightower to tell him of his meeting with Lena Grove and of events surrounding Joanna Burden's death. [454]

Tuesday morning: Christmas asks farm woman what day it is; she says Tuesday. [644]

Tuesday evening: Byron visits Hightower and tells him of his plans to move Lena out to the cabin at the Burden place. [619]

Tuesday evening: Christmas invades and terrorizes a Negro revival service. [637]

Wednesday 3 am: Negro man arrives in town to report Christmas's terrorism at the church. [637]

Wednesday 8 am: Sheriff and bloodhounds arrive at church to track Christmas. [640]

Wednesday evening: Byron visits Hightower and explains that he is staying in a tent out near the cabin where he has established Lena. [628]

Friday morning: Christmas shaves, begins wondering what day it is. [647]

Friday noon: Christmas has walked 8 miles and catches a ride to Mottstown. [649]

Saturday morning: Christmas captured in Mottstown. Page 651 says he was captured on a Friday. Page 657 says on a Saturday morning. The presence of large crowds downtown for the weekend suggests that Saturday is the more likely day. In his chronology of the novel's present-time events, Stephen Meats agrees that Saturday was the day of Christmas's capture.°

Saturday afternoon: Doc and Mrs. Hines wander around Mottstown. [653]

Saturday afternoon: Percy Grimm organizes his platoon to protect the streets of Jefferson. [734]

Sunday 2 am: Doc and Mrs. Hines leave on train for Jefferson. [665]

Sunday 3 am: Doc and Mrs. Hines arrive in Jefferson. [728]

Sunday afternoon: Byron visits Hightower and tells him about Christmas's capture. [667]

Sunday evening: Byron brings the Hineses to tell their story to Hightower. See first sentence on 689. [671]

early Monday morning: Lena's child born. Byron wakes up Hightower to help. He returns to town and quits his job at the planing mill. [689, 704]

Monday morning: Grand Jury meets to indict Christmas for the murder of Joanna Burden. [706]

Monday 1 pm (approx.): Byron visits Sheriff Kennedy at his house and arranges for Lucas Burch to visit Lena at the Burden cabin. He announces his intentions to leave Jefferson. [709] Mrs. Hines gets Sheriff Kennedy's permission to visit Joe Christmas in his jail cell, where she suggests, according to Gavin Stevens, that Hightower might protect or save him. Kennedy had "just got back from dinner."

Monday afternoon: Hightower pays his second visit to Lena. [699]

Monday 4 pm: Byron watches as a deputy drives Lucas Burch up to the Burden cabin. A few minutes later he sees Burch jump through the cabin window and run away. [711]

Monday 5 pm: Christmas escapes from deputy Buford as he is being taken across the town square, probably to the court house to hear the reading of his indictment. After a pursuit which lasts only a few minutes, Percy Grimm chases him into the house of Gail Hightower. There Grimm shoots Christmas five times and castrates him. [726]

Monday 6 pm: After losing his fight with Burch, Byron heads back towards the Burden cabin and Lena. He learns of Christmas's death from a man he meets on the way. [726]

Tuesday morning: Gavin Stevens ships the body of Joe Christmas back to Mrs. Hines in Mottstown on Tuesday morning (at least he promised to do so). [728]

September, three weeks after the birth of Lena's child: a furniture dealer gives a ride to Lena Grove and Byron Bunch and later relates the story to his wife. [766]

NOTES

The annotations cite the following editions of works by Faulkner. Original publication dates appear in brackets when they differ from the date of the text used.

Absalom, Absalom! [1936], *Faulkner: Novels 1936–1940*. New York: Library of America, 1990.
Collected Stories of William Faulkner. New York: Random House, 1950.
Flags in the Dust, ed. Douglas Day. New York: Random House, 1973. Published in shortened form as *Sartoris* in 1929.
Light in August [1932]. *Faulkner: Novels 1930–1935*. New York: Library of America, 1985.
The Mansion. New York: Random House, 1959.
The Reivers. New York: Random House, 1962.
Requiem for a Nun. New York: Random House, 1951.
Sanctuary [1931]. *Faulkner: Novels 1930–1935*. New York: Library of America, 1985.
Sartoris. [1929] New York: Random House, 1961.
The Sound and the Fury. [1929] New York: Vintage, 1987.
The Town. New York: Random House, 1957.
Uncollected Stories of William Faulkner, ed. Joseph Blotner. New York: Random House, 1979.

Title

1. Joseph Blotner and Frederick L. Gwynn, ed. *Faulkner in the University: Class Conferences at the University of Virginia, 1957–1958* (Charlottesville: Univ. of Virginia Press, 1961), 199.

2. Joseph Blotner, *Faulkner: A Biography*, 2 v. (New York: Random House, 1974), 702.

3. Blotner, *Faulkner: A Biography*, 702.

4. Alfred Lord Tennyson, *In Memoriam*, eds. Susan Shatto and Marion Shaw (Oxford: Clarendon Press, 1982), 43.

Chapter 1

401:2   Blotner, *Faulkner: A Biography*, 703; *Faulkner in the University*, 74; James B. Meriwether and Michael Millgate, ed. *Lion in the Garden: Interviews with William Faulkner, 1926–1962* (New York: Random House, 1968), 253.

402:17   *Encyclopedia of Southern History*, eds. David C. Roller and Robert W. Twyman (Baton Rouge: Louisiana State Univ. Press, 1979), 603.

402:21   Brown, *A Glossary of Faulkner's South* (New Haven: Yale Univ. Press, 1976), 130.

402:25   Henri Bergson, *Creative Evolution*, tr. Arthur Mitchell (1944), (rpt. Westport, Connecticut: Greenwood Press, 1975), 6; Beverley Bateman, "Time and Memory: Faulkner's Use of Bergson in *Light in August*" (MA Thesis: Georgia State Univ., 1977).

402:25   Blotner, *Faulkner: A Biography*, 1302; *Lion in the Garden*, 70.

403:15   R. G. Collins, "The Game of Names: Characterization Device in 'Light in August'," *English Record*, 21 (October 1970), 84; Beach Langston, "The Meaning of Lena Grove and Gail Hightower in *Light in August*," *Boston University Studies in English*, 5 (Spring 1961), 49.

403:23   Brown, 144.

404:27   Henri Bergson, *An Introduction to Metaphysics*, tr. T. E. Hulme (New York: G. P. Putnam's Sons, 1912), 21; see also Thomas McHaney, "The Elmer Papers: Faulkner's Comic Portrait of the Artist," *A Faulkner Miscellany*, ed. James B. Meriwether (Jackson: Univ. Press of Mississippi, 1974), 55–57.

405:2   Carl Ficken, "A Critical and Textual Study of William Faulkner's *Light in August*" (Univ. of South Carolina, 1972), 40–41n.

405:26   Gertrude Grace Sill. *Handbook of Symbols in Christian Art* (London: Cassell & Co., 1975), 29, 115.

406:5   Brown, 65.

406:36   Brown, 35, 193.

407:27   Nollie Hickman, *Mississippi Harvest: Lumbering in the Longleaf Pine Belt: 1840–1915* (University, Mississippi: Univ. of Mississippi Press, 1962), 162; Brown, 149–50.

410:31   Brown, 83.

411:37   Langston, 48; Blotner, *Faulkner: A Biography*, 396, 660–1; Sir

James Frazer, *The Golden Bough*, one v., abridged ed. (New York: Mac-Millan, 1922), 9. See also Langston, p. 50; Ficken, p. 29; Norman Holmes Pearson, "Lena Grove," *Shenandoah*, 3 (Spring 1952), 6–7.

Chapter 2

421:1 Mario D'Avanzo, "Love's Labors: Byron Bunch and Shakespeare," *Notes on Mississippi Writers*, 10 (Winter 1977), 81; Ficken 73–74; Bidney, "Faulkner's Variations on Romantic Themes: Blake, Wordsworth, Byron, and Shelley in *Light in August*," *Mississippi Quarterly*, 38 (Summer 1985), 282.

422:19 *Faulkner in the University*, 117

422:27 *Faulkner in the University*, 97

425:16 Tad Burness, *Cars of the Early Thirties* (Philadelphia: Chilton Book Co., 1970), 256–64.

430:28 Brown, 116.

431:4 Brown, 214.

437:39 Brown, 185.

Chapter 3

440:5 Joan Serafin, *Faulkner's Uses of the Classics* (Ann Arbor, Michigan: UMI Research Press, 1983), 13–14; Robert E. Bell, *Dictionary of Classical Mythology* (Santa Barbara, CA: ABC-Clio, Inc., 1982), 170.

440:33 Blotner, *Faulkner: A Biography*, 102n; David L. James, "Hightower's Name: A Possible Source," *American Notes & Queries*, 13 (September 1974), 4–5; Regina K. Fadiman, *Faulkner's Light in August: A Description and Interpretation of the Revisions* (Charlottesville: Univ. of Virginia Press, 1975), 31.

441:15 *Census of Religious Bodies: 1926*. 2 v. (Washington: U. S. Government Printing Office, 1930); *Census of Religious Bodies: 1936*. 3 v. (Washington: U. S. Government Printing Office, 1941).

443:6 Shelby Foote, *The Civil War: A Narrative*, v. 2 (New York: Random House, 1963), 61, 70–71. See also Hubert McAlexander, "General Earl Van Dorn and Faulkner's Use of History," *The Journal of Mississippi History*, 40 (Fall 1977), 360.

448:31 *The Westminster Dictionary of Church History*, ed. Jerald C. Braver (Philadelphia: Westminster Press, 1971), 672–73; Ernest Trice Thompson, *Presbyterians in the South* (Richmond, Va.: John Knox Press, 1973),

v. III, 303; Lefferts A. Loetscher, *A Brief History of the Presbyterians*, third ed. (Philadelphia: Westminster Press, 1978), 169.

450:25   Jesse M. Coffee, *Faulkner's Un-Christlike Christians* (Ann Arbor: Michigan: UMI Research Press, 1983), 109.

451:14   Part II, chapter IX of *The Proverbs* (1546), in *The Proverbs, Epigrams, and Miscellanies of John Heywood*, ed. John S. Farmer (London: Early English Drama Society, 1906), 93.

Chapter 4

464:18   Joseph Conrad. *Heart of Darkness*, ed. Robert Kimbrough (New York: Norton, 1971), 3, 6.

465:30   Blotner, *Faulkner: A Biography*, 762–63.

466:9   Juan E. Cirlot, *A Dictionary of Symbols*, tr. Jack Sage (New York: Philosophical Library, 1962), 154.

Chapter 5

475:23   Brown, 160.

476:9   Thomas Wolfe, *Look Homeward, Angel* (New York: Scribner's, 1929), 253.

479:37   Tony Goodstone, *The Pulps* (New York: Chelsea House, 1970).

481:4   *"Light in August": A Concordance to the Novel*, ed. Jack L. Capps (Faulkner Concordance Advisory Board, 1979), 2 vol.

481:6   "The Love Song of J. Alfred Prufrock," T. S. Eliot, *Collected Poems: 1909–1962* (New York: Harcourt, Brace & World, 1963), 3.

482:26   Brown, 86, 139.

484:2   "The Love Song of J. Alfred Prufrock," Eliot, *Collected Poems*, 5.

486:5   Frazer, 162, 127–8; Cirlot, 205, 78; Frazer, 9.

Chapter 6

487:1   Pitavy, 50. Correspondence of André Bleikasten, Noel Polk, and Karl Zender with James Hinkle about this passage provided useful insights.

487:3   Zender and Polk, correspondence with James Hinkle.

487:14   Cirlot, 277.

494:12   Sill, 29.

494:17   T. S. Eliot, *Collected Poems* 54.

496:21   James Orr, ed. *International Standard Bible Encyclopedia*, v. III (Grand Rapids: Eerdmans, 1939), 1675–76.

504:34   James Hinkle provided this pronunciation.

504:37   Coffee, 95.

Chapter 7

507:9   Brown, 139.

507:15   Virgilius Ferm, *A Protestant Dictionary* (New York: Philosophical Library, 1951), 274–75.

508:33   Brown, 99.

514:23   See Doreen Fowler, "Joe Christmas and 'Womanshenegro,'" in *Faulkner and Women: Faulkner and Yoknapatawpha, 1985*, ed. Doreen Fowler and Ann J. Abadie (Jackson: Univ. Press of Mississippi, 1986), 156.

523:32   Cirlot, 206.

Chapter 8

526:1   Sill, 122.

526:27   Brown, 71; *Mississippi: A Guide to the Magnolia State*, Federal Writers Project of the Works Progress Administration American Guide Series (New York: Viking Press, 1938). Thomas McHaney suggested the similarities between Water Valley, Mottstown, and the town in which Joe Christmas meets Bobbie Allen.

528:30   Robert M. Slabey, "Myth and Ritual in *Light in August*," *Texas Studies in Language and Literature*, 2 (Autumn 1960), 331–32.

534:21   J. M. Dickinson, *Monastic Life in Medieval England* (New York: Barnes & Noble, 1961), 104–05.

537:2   Francis J. McConnell, *International Standard Bible Encyclopedia*, ed. James Orr (Grand Rapids, Michigan: Eerdsmans, 1939), vol. IV, 2541–44.

540:13   John E. Harkins, *Metropolis of the American Nile* (Woodland Hills, Ca.: Windsor Publications, 1982), 127.

540:32   *Union List of Serials*, v. 5, 3rd. ed., ed. Edna Titus Brown (New York: H. W. Wilson Co., 1965), 4584–85.

Chapter 9

548:9   Brown, 46.

550:14   Edvard Munch, *The Scream* (1896, National Museum, Oslo).

550:24   Brown, 141–2.

559:5   Munch, *The Scream.*

559:32   *Light in August: Holograph Manuscript,* v. 1 of *William Faulkner Manuscripts 10* (New York: Garland Publishing, Inc., 1987), 87; *Light in August: Typescript Setting Copy,* v. 2 of *William Faulkner Manuscripts 10.* New York: Garland, 1987), 226.

Chapter 10

563:16   Eliot, *Collected Poems* 3.

564:23   Brown, 175.

565:20   *Holograph Manuscript,* 89; *Typescript Setting Copy,* 234; Blotner, *Faulkner: A Biography,* 763.

566:32   Brown, 156, 219.

Chapter 11

576:33   *The Westminster Dictionary of Church History,* 414–15.

577:5   C. Williams, "Slavery and the Church," v. xiii, *New Catholic Encyclopedia* (New York: McGraw-Hill, 1967), 282; Michael V. Gannon, "Catholic Church," *The Encyclopedia of Southern History,* ed. David C, Roller and Robert W. Twyman (Baton Rouge: Louisiana State University Press, 1979), 189–90; Eric Partridge, *Macmillan Dictionary of Historical Slang* (New York: MacMillan, 1974), 347.

577:11   *The Westminster Dictionary of Church History,* 835–36.

577:20   Coffee, 104.

578:15   Brown, 86.

580:30   "Evangeline" was finally published in 1979 in *Esquire* and *Uncollected Stories of William Faulkner,* ed. Joseph Blotner (New York: Random House, 1979), 583–609.

581:12   Julian Samora, Joe Bernal, and Albert Pena, *Gunpowder Justice: A Reassessment of the Texas Rangers* (Notre Dame: Univ. of Notre Dame Press, 1979), 1–14, 157–68.

581:19   C. Vann Woodward, "The Northern Crusade Against Slavery," *American Counterpoint: Slavery and Racism in the North-South Dialogue* (Boston: Little-Brown, 1971), 140–62.

584:23   George R. Bentley, *A History of the Freedman's Bureau* (Philadelphia: Univ of Pennsylvania Press, 1955), 72–73.

585:26   Ronald Wesley Hoag, "Expanding the Influence: Faulkner and

Four Melville Tales," *South Atlantic Review*, 50 (November 1985), 84–5.

586:3   *Selected Letters of William Faulkner*, ed. Joseph Blotner (New York: Random House, 1978), 374; *Holograph Manuscript*, 99; *Typescript Setting Copy*, 263.

586:20   *Holograph Manuscript*, 99; *Typescript Setting Copy*, 264; Blotner, *Faulkner: A Biography*, 763.

Chapter 12

588:33   Brown, 100.

590:23   Mery, 44.

590:31   Slabey, 331.

591:35   Ilse Dusoir Lind, "Faulkner's Women," in *The Maker and the Myth: Faulkner and Yoknapatawpha, 1977*, ed. Evans Harrington and Ann J. Abadie (Jackson: Univ. Press of Mississippi, 1978), 95–96.

594:2   Martin Bidney, "Victorian Vision in Mississippi: Tennysonian Resonances in Faulkner's *Dark House in August*," *Victorian Poetry*, 23 (Spring 1985), 49–50.

594:4   *The Confessions*, Book VIII, Chapter VII, in *Basic Writings of Saint Augustine*, ed. Whitney J. Oates (New York: Random House, 1948), I, 120; Ficken, 144–45n.

594:29   *Holograph Manuscript* 103.

601:22   Brown, 200.

603:5   Frederick Asals, "Faulkner's *Light in August*," *Explicator*, 26 (May 1968), Item 74.

606:27   See Doreen Fowler, "'In Another Country': Faulkner's *A Fable*," *Studies in American Fiction*, 15 (Spring 1987), 43–54, for a discussion of Faulkner's use of the phrase in other works, specifically *A Fable*.

606:31   *Lion in the Garden*, 255.

607:23   Francis A. Lord, *Civil War Collectors' Encyclopedia* (Harrisburg, Pa.: Stackpole, 1963), 206.

Chapter 13

617:28   *Rail Talk: A Lexicon of Railroad Language*, ed. James H. Beck (Nebraska: James Publications, 1978), NP.

619:32   Henry David Thoreau, *Walden and Civil Disobedience*, ed. Owen Thomas (New York: W. W. Norton & Co., 1966), 50.

625:33   *The Book of Common Prayer* (New York: Church Pension Fund, 1945), 303.

628:34   Coffee, 115.

634:15   Tennyson, *In Memoriam*, 126; *Faulkner in the University* 93.

Chapter 14

638:23   Brown, 164.

641:38   Brown, 60.

642:39   Brown, 77.

644:33   *Holograph Manuscript*, 129; *Typescript Setting Copy*, 345.

646:32   C. Hugh Holman, "The Unity of Faulkner's *Light in August*," *PMLA*, 73 (March 1958), 157–58.

649:25   Brown, 220.

Chapter 15

661:3   Maurice Horn, *The World Encyclopedia of Comics*, v. 2 (New York: Chelsea House, 1976), 421.

665:10   James H. Beck, ed., *Rail Talk: A Lexicon of Railroad Language* (Nebraska: James Publications, 1978), No. 5.

Chapter 16

675:39   T. G. Pinches, "Ham," in *The International Standard Bible Encyclopedia*, v. II (Grand Rapids: Eerdmans Publishing Co., 1937), 1323–24); Coffee, 89–90.

677:26   Brown, 115–16.

682:34   Coffee, 107.

683:4   *Faulkner in the University* 72; see also 97, 118.

686:20   Tennyson, *In Memoriam*, 59.

Chapter 17

693:20   "The Second Coming," in *The Poems of W. B. Yeats*, ed. Richard J. Finneran (New York: MacMillan, 1983), 187.

Chapter 18

709:15   Brown, 108.

725:21   Bergson, *Creative Evolution*, 6; Bateman, 39.

Chapter 19

728:8   Brown, 83.

731:6   *Faulkner in the University*, 72.

731:35   *Selected Letters*, 202; *Faulkner in the University*, 41.

732:26   Brown, 55.

731:35   *Selected Letters*, 202; *Faulkner in the University*, 41.

736:38   Albert G. Mackey, *An Encyclopedia of Freemasonry* (New York: Masonic History Co., 1921), v. 1, 47–48. Cf. *Pylon*, in *Faulkner: Novels 1936–1940* (New York: Library of America, 1990), 939, 948, 950.

739:20   Brown, 227.

739:36   Benjamin Walker, *The Hindu World* (New York: Frederick A. Praeger, 1968), Vol. 1, 491–92.

743:1   See Blotner, *Faulkner: A Biography* (113–14) and John B. Cullen's *Old Times in the Faulkner Country*, in collaboration with Floyd C. Watkins (Chapel Hill: Univ. of North Carolina Press, 1961), 89–98.

743:3   Doreen Fowler, "Joe Christmas and 'Womanshenegro,'" in *Faulkner and Women: Faulkner and Yoknapatawpha, 1985*, ed. Doreen Fowler and Ann J. Abadie (Jackson: Univ. Press of Mississippi, 1986), 158.

Chapter 20

744:1   *Faulkner in the University* 45.

744:3   Pitavy, 41; *"Light in August": A Concordance to the Novel*.

744:7   Michel Gresset, "Of Sailboats and Kites: The 'Dying Fall' in Faulkner's *Sanctuary* and Beckett's *Murphy*," in *Intertextuality in Faulkner*, ed. Michel Gresset and Noel Polk (Jackson: Mississippi, 1985), 59–60.

745:19   Brown, 86.

747:32   Brown, 126.

748:15   Ficken, 230.

750:11   "The New South," *Writings and Speeches of Henry Grady* (Savannah, Ga.: The Beehive Press, 1971), 3–13.

750:14   *International Standard Bible Encyclopedia*, v. 2, 333–34.

753:7   *The Letters of John Keats: 1814–1821*, Ed. Hyder E. Rollins, v. II (Cambridge: Harvard Univ. Press, 1958), 159–60.

753:9   Eliot, *Collected Poems*, 54.

759:5   *The Interpreter's One-Volume Commentary on the Bible*, ed. Charles M. Layton (Nashville, TN: Abingdon Press, 1971), 324.

760:8   Ficken, 234

760:12   Bidney, "Victorian Vision, 52–53; Ficken, 236–37; Carl G. Jung, "The Symbolism of the Mandala," in *Individual Dream Symbolism in Relation to Alchemy*, Collected Works, XII, trans. R. F. C. Hull (Princeton: Princeton Univ. Press, 1968), 96.

760:33   Ficken, 238.

761:26   Coffee, 104.

762:29   *Faulkner in the University*, 199.

763:16   *Faulkner in the University*, 75; *Holograph Manuscript*, 183.

763:29   *Faulkner in the University*, 75.

Chapter 21

765:30   *Tennessee State Planning Commission Preliminary Population Report* (Nashville, Tn., June 14, 1935, section III, 12); Ficken, 25n.

766:10   Brown, 145.

767:12   *A Dictionary of Americanisms*, ed. Mitford M. Matthews (Chicago: Univ. of Chicago Press, 1951), v. 2, 1752.

769:7   Bill Blackbeard, "Alphonse and Gaston (U. S.)," in *The World Encyclopedia of Comics*, ed. Maurice Horn, 77–78.

771:36   *Lion in the Garden*, 253.

Chronology

1. Stephen Meats, "The Chronology of *Light in August*," *William Faulkner's Light in August*, ed. François Pitavy (New York: Garland, 1982), 235.

2. Cleanth Brooks, "Chronology of *Light in August*," *William Faulkner: Toward Yoknapatawpha and Beyond* (New Haven: Yale Univ. Press, 1978), 426–9.

3. Meats, 235.

4. Meats, 231.

INDEX

This index lists the most substantive notes on important names, terms, and concepts in the novel.